iGuzzini

BARCELONA CORPORATE BUILDING

JOSEP MIÀS

4 FOREWORD
Foreword– Adolfo Guzzini
Photographic foreword– Jordi Bernadó

24 INTRODUCTION
Contemporary brutalism– Marco Atzori
Beyond the lightness– Sebastiano d'Urso
Between the lines– Josep Miàs

46 iGUZZINI BCN HEADQUARTERS
Metropolitan lighthouse– Vicente Guallart
A project draft– Josep Miàs
Togetherness– Josep Miàs

100 BEGINNING A PROJECT
Competition abstract– Josep Miàs

122 GOING UNDERGROUND
Preparing the landscape– Jorge García de la Cámara

142 SUSPENDING A STRUCTURE
Structural systems– Agustí Obiol
Axile development– Josep Ramon Solé
A glossary of wildlife– Silvia Brandi

218 LOOKING THROUGH
The invisible shell– Jaume Avellaneda

240 CASTING A SHADOW
Selective membrane– Josep Maria González

268 BUILDING IN SUSTAINABILITY
Systems & mechanics– Josep Juliol

284 MANAGING THE PROCESS
Work in progress– Carles Bou

302 LIGHTING LIGHTNESS
iGuzzini lighting iGuzzini– Josep Masbernat

334 CREDITS

FOREWORD

Light and architecture lie at the base of the iGuzzini Illuminazione strategy.

If Le Corbusier defined architecture as "the masterly, correct, and magnificient play of masses brought together in light", today the relationship between volume and light has been enriched with new elements, primarily the search for a sustainable architecture able to reduce energy consumption.

In Josep Miàs's project we immediately sensed the possibility of combining these values through a volume embodied in light. During the day a "natural", organic form, premised on the goal of harnessing sunlight to create high-quality, highly-ergonomic workplaces. At night, the building is transformed by artificial light into a glowing landmark in the landscape, a gigantic lantern. The project is the result of profound technological research, which, however, is not the protagonist: the goal is not the ostentation of technology but the quality of the spaces.

Once again we find a great similarity with the iGuzzini strategy, in which technological research and the constant drive towards innovation are primarily aimed at the quality of light to improve the quality of life: the rational use of artificial light, far beyond the necessary respect of its functions, promotes new relationships between people and the environment. A strategy that places design in the role of catalyst and leader in product definition.

When in the early 1990s, in a pioneering attitude for a lighting manufacturer, we suggested to international public opinion the need to reduce light pollution, we were adhering to a clear ethical principle which demanded that companies address and resolve the question of environmental impact, a commitment we followed up on with the our "$-CO_2$, Re-lighting" project to reduce emissions through the widespread introduction of LED systems and lighting management.

Concern for the environment and the quality of work are two of the objectives that the company has stipulated in its own buildings, all of which are the result of the most advanced architectural design criteria for sustainability. Even in our buildings, we seek to realise Adriano Olivetti's idea of a company as an open system, destined to exchange with the outside world, responsible for the economic and social fabric in which it moves, and in which goods and services as well as knowledge and culture are produced.
This building by Josep Miàs is a work of architecture that fills with pride all who work at iGuzzini round the world, because it expresses masterfully the industrial culture that is the foundation of their work.

Adolfo Guzzini,
president of iGuzzini Illuminazione

14

17

FOREWORD

INTRODUCTION

Contemporary brutalism

Marco Atzori

The work of the Catalan architect Josep Miàs lies within a domain of architecture in which the construction and the physicality of space constitute a field of continuous research and experimentation. If some architects intend a project as a materialisation of theoretical speculations, in the work of MiAS Architects lie the possibilities inherent in a construction process that defines an approach that is projected into the dimension of the avant-garde.

Discussing the work of Josep Miàs calls to mind, in addition to the architect Enric Miralles, Miàs's true spiritual father, such figures as the first James Stirling or Louis Kahn, architects who built a unique plan within which existed a theory and materialisation of architectural work which expressed its completeness in the complexity of its realisation.

As extrapolated from these premises, the evolution of the work of Miàs has two phases, which in the structure of this article are also premise and epilogue. In the first instance as one focuses on his work one sees the materiality of his works, with their explosive force. In the second instance is highlighted the opening of a new phase, in which the character of his work is redefined to more readily evince the personality of the architect, thereby revealing in him more depth and originality.

The early works of Josep Miàs, in fact, define a strong and irrepressible personality that manifests itself through rich and generous design. Each of his buildings seems to be an expression of a childlike vitality that works constantly and volcanically on the relationships among the building, its structural components, and the landscape and topography of the site, all of which interact with the building's spatial organisation. The buildings are inserted as elements of an ecosystem, whether camouflaging themselves in the topography, as does the Pyrenees Golf Club in Fontanals, or reinventing places, as does Barceloneta Market. That is, Miàs uses materials and construction techniques to integrate his projects into the existing landscape, like animals able to camouflage themselves in order to disappear, and which must then be discovered by their users, as in the

Top: Pyrenees Golf Club, Fontanals de Cerdanya (Girona, Spain). Bottom: Promenade House, Caselles d'Avall (Girona, Spain).

Golf Club—or to provide evidence of a latent dimension of a place that materialises through its invention, as in Barceloneta Market.

In both these works the spiritual presence of Enric Miralles remains evident, but even as Miàs recognises this closeness with his foster father, he gives signs of distancing. Seen in this light, the market project develops as a version of Miralles's toughest and most dissonant works, like, for example, the pergolas in Avinguda Icària, Barcelona.

Josep Maria Montaner, one of the most important Spanish critics, asserts that the study of the work of Miàs leads one away from the traditional idea of beauty through an ability to incorporate a strategic error, and makes the case that "the imperfection" and the chaos evoke a similarity not only to Miralles, but also to Gehry, more as a builder than a theoretical architect, as well as to Coop Himmelb(l)au.

This praise for imbalance and imperfect beauty provides the key to how Josep Miàs brings his architecture to approach the human condition, always hovering between the affirmation of its powerful nature and the awareness of its limitations, occupying a dimension far from perfection, imprisoned from what it craves by its own frailty.

The construction of the projects will evolve over time, if the house in Caselles may be seen as a passage in which the topographical concept takes for itself a language close to tradition. Thus in the work for the Rubí town market and the house in Llavaneres important changes are defined. The formal complexity of the Rubí market is hardened by an industrial sheet metal used to define the façade. In the house in Llavaneres, the topographical structuring of the residence is coupled with a more brutal material.

If the Pyrenees Golf Club was developed in continuity with the ground, the house in Llavaneres has a harder volumetric development, with its materials matched in a more direct way. The result is an object in which the compositional balance is altered, almost mixed. The zinc roofs and cement façades vie for domination over one another; the covering occasionally seems to take the upper hand, but then retracts in some places. Similarly, there

Top: Rubí Central Market, Rubí (Barcelona, Spain).
Bottom: Topographic House, Llavaneres (Barcelona, Spain).

27

Tibidabo
Funicular
Station
refurbishment,
(Barcelona,
Spain).

is a break between the ground and cover that did not exist in the Fontanals Golf Club. If the Golf Club seemed to emerge from the place, the Llavaneres house instead becomes an element that behaves in a more ambiguous way, with a front providing an open view onto the landscape and another face that evinces a rather hard radicalism in the choice of materials and composition. Somehow, the Llavaneres house is a project of passage. Miàs seems to experience here a change which will come to maturity in the later buildings.

From this point on, the works of Josep Miàs become drier in terms of their geometry, and more mature and personal. The materials, the construction technologies, and structural concept are defined by their subtractions rather than by their additions, thereby striking a pose that is even more radical and "brutal". In this way Miàs completes his separation from his teachers, entering his own dimension, one that indicates lines of thought more representative of our age. If we observe all the work of Josep Miàs through a larger perspective in which we introduce the issue of the relationship with the contemporary global condition, we can push the reasoning about his work onto a more general and theoretical plane. If the first stage of Miàs's work expressed the charming imperfections of the human condition, the evolution of his more recent work seems to assume the value of a profound criticism of the current structure of society and the ways in which architecture has become an instrument of these values.

The radicalism in his latest design choices shows a relationship between the architectural object and its elements of construction that seems to have been overshadowed in the architecture of the last few years. Over the last twenty years we have witnessed the growth of a trend that has favoured the adoption of complex forms in architecture, marked by extraordinary objects, the value of which seems to be embodied solely in their originality. This line of thought, which often referred exclusively to formal research, was identified by the primacy in the space of the building's skin. The constructive aspect of the buildings was hidden for the sake of the prevalence of a certain scenographic effect. This represents a way of consolidating architecture by means of a "numbing", in which the constant abuse of the senses wrought by the wonder of absent technological solutions inhibited any critical perception. The seductive appeal of such architecture exalted the wealth of a society in continuous expansion and emerged from a state of optimistic confidence in the future and the technological possibilities it offered.

But current conditions—the economic crisis, the awareness of the limits of global development, and the social and political instabilities that occur as consequences of economic imbalances—have rendered anachronistic such architectural research.

It seems clear that complexity, a distinctive feature of modernity, cannot be interpreted merely as a didactic materialisation of non-linear forms, nor as a spectacular materialisation of skins and their decoration. The rise of increasingly sophisticated alternatives in building materials and technologies represents a range of other aspects that determine the relationship between architecture and the present cultural construction of reality.

In addition, such complicated projects as were formerly dominant cannot currently be sustainable. The difficulties in such design, which it was naively thought could be revolutionised through digital technology, and the excessive cost of post-construction management, when the building ceases to be a virtual object and becomes a complex system of materials, technologies and construction techniques which must now be managed through the structural elements and systems that must make the building work, have brought about the progressive decline of this simplistic interpretation of the relationship between complexity and architecture.

The architecture of Josep Miàs may be placed in direct contrast such work. As may be seen, his work does not give up on experimentation with geometry, shape and materials, but at the same time, it reintroduces consistency in the relationship between building and architecture. The works of Miàs are not accommodating, do not look for consensus, but like a knife, they affect reality. The Annexa-Joan Puigbert School in Girona and the Plug-In building in Barcelona's district 22@ render the skin fleshless to show its underlying layers and the systems it contains, violently baring the constructive system of the buildings, revealing tissue and nerves. The structure, made of steel, is much in evidence, while the cladding, whether made of corrugated sheet metal or glass, is resolved brutally and without affectation, almost as if to stir the conscience and persuade the observer to take a stand.

In the iGuzzini headquarters, the work on the structure acquires even greater importance, as it unbinds from its envelope and becomes an exoskeleton. Miàs herein makes explicit reference to Russian Constructivism and Golosov's Lenin Institute, but the geometric configuration of the skeleton brings to mind the work of Buckminster Fuller and Louis Kahn with Anne Tyng for the Philadelphia City Hall. With this project Miàs definitely opens a further perspective on the work of these figures, concentrating on the search without compromising the relationship between the structural components of the building.

If, especially in the iGuzzini headquarters, this direction could represent a sort of renewed interest in hi-tech, the Catalan's choices realise an interesting historical parallel with theories articulated by Reyner Banham in his essay "The New Brutalism," published in December 1955 in the *Architectural Review*, at a time when the character of the movement called "New Brutalism" was taking shape in England, especially thanks to Alison and Peter Smithson. Commenting on the house in Soho built by the Smithson's, Banham, in codifying the New Brutalism, summarised its aspects in this way: "1, formal legibility of plan; 2, clear exhibition of structure, and 3, valuation of materials for their inherent qualities 'as found.'" In the projects considered above we can establish an explicit connection with Banham's theories, but the work of Miàs goes beyond this historical continuity, because through it he lays out a basis for a reflection which is not merely formal. The appro-

Annexa-Joan
Puigbert School,
(Girona, Spain).

priation of brutalist language in this contemporary rein-
terpretation defines a new critical position which calls into
play the fundamental elements of architectural thought
in relation to its construction, and rebuilds a "constructive sincerity" in which architecture ceases to mask itself,
whilst continuing to be an experimental material for the
construction of reality.

The works of Josep Miàs thus identify a line of action in
which the readability of the systems, their constructive coherence and their control build a conscious and effective
response to the problems that our society is experienc-
ing, and address an emerging need for sincerity, concrete-
ness and a new critical spirit. A reading of all the works
of Josep Miàs leads us to theorise upon the emergence of
a "Contemporary Brutalism"–an expression, through the
tool of investigative architecture, of the paradigm shift
introduced by the global economic crisis–and a phenomenon that finds in the work of Josep Miàs one of its first
and most important actors.

Marco Atzori,
Ph.D. in Civil Engineering, researcher at UNISS Alghero
and member of the Editorial Board of C3 Magazine

Plug-in
Building,
22@ District
(Barcelona,
Spain).

Beyond the lightness
Sebastiano d'Urso

Beyond the lightness is the light. Lightness is the continuous challenge to the force of gravity, which irreparably forces us to down to earth. Light, on the other hand, projects us toward the images it illuminates, which arouse gentle and coloured thoughts. The world as it is would not exist without the force of gravity and the light. Architecture would not exist without these fundamental components. All life, and architecture with it, containing it on the earth, takes place by the force of gravity and in light.

Together with the lightness is the light. In English language, lightness and light are associated and they are expressed by the same word: light. As a noun, the term is in fact defined as "the natural agent that stimulates sight and makes things visible". As an adjective, on the other hand, it is what weighs little, what is lightweight, "of little weight". The same holds for the German words *Licht* (light as a noun) and *leicht* (light as an adjective), which are associated in the same way as the English words are, by epitomising lightness and light in just one concept.

Lightness and light are then conditions which are in mutual correspondence even in language. In architecture, they represent the immaterial constants every building must deal with. Moreover they represent the chimeras chased by every architect in building his work: architectural spatiality, the plasticity of forms, the composition of volumes, and the appearance of materials correspond to light; tectonics and the consistency of the work conform with gravity.

How is a project which, from its inception, seems to be able to satisfy these features, born? What are the conditions for such a project to be as it is? Two other fundamental components are certainly necessary: an enlightened (the term could not be more appropriate) client and an architect equipped with great passion and courage. Passion in order to face, together with lightness (in the meaning adopted by Calvino[1] but not only him), the problems the project invariably holds for its architect; courage in order to take up the challenges inherent in architecture.

The Miàs-iGuzzini relationship perfectly embodies the figures defined by these traits. iGuzzini is an Italian firm, world

1   Italo Calvino, *Lezioni americane. Sei proposte per il prossimo millennio*, Mondadori, Milano 2009, pp. 5-37.

leader in lighting system design, which, for more than fifty years, has looked to the top designers and architects in creating its products and buildings. Josep Miàs is an architect who relies on formal research and on constructive experimentation in his work. With the lightness associated with youthful intellect, he takes on the project and develops it according to an infinite process which, coiling round yet firmly centred on the starting point of his work, makes and remakes the architectural project, not just any project. Values and rigour in the planning process shape the continuity of his work: each successive step is built upon those which have preceded it, and he often retraces his steps in order to re-examine the path.

Calvino's definition lightness describes exactly Miàs's attitude to planning: "Lightness for me goes with precision and determination, not with vagueness and the haphazard."[2]

If lightness as defined by Calvino is the mental attitude with which Miàs approaches the project, it becomes at the same time, together with light, in the new iGuzzini Building in Barcelona, the rationale of his peculiar formal-architectural experimentation: subtraction of weight from the language, freeing of the architectural form from heaviness; definitive consigning of architecture to light and sky.

The rationale of lightness, of the lightness-heaviness dichotomy, runs through the entire history of mankind. In architecture, the light-heavy dualism represents two extreme and opposing ways of inflecting a project, as Renzo Piano also said: you can choose to be heavy, seconding the action of the force of gravity, by feeling the attraction from the earth and hooking yourself up it; or you can try to challenge gravity, through the search for lightness, through the utopia of lightness, through the forms of harmony, through the structures of grace and the ideal of suppleness.

This untiring search for lightness as a state of the human being, however, leads Milan Kundera[3] to wonder: "But is heaviness truly deplorable and lightness splendid? The heaviest of burdens crushes us, we sink beneath it, it pins us to the ground. But in the love poetry of every age, the woman longs to be weighed down by the man's body. The heaviest of bur-

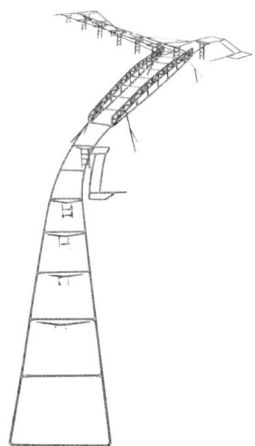

Wire model of Miàs's footbridge project in Palafolls (Barcelona, Spain).

2   I. Calvino, op. cit., p. 20.

3   Milan Kundera, *The Unbearable Lightness of Being*, Adelphi, Milano 1985.

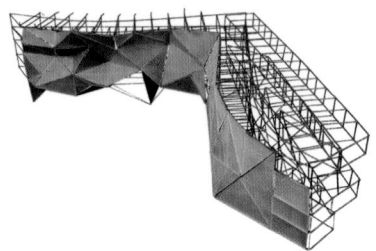

Wire and Japanese paper model of Miàs's Thalassotherapy Centre project in Gijón (Spain).

4   Siegfried Giedion, *Lo spazio in architettura*, Dario Flaccovio Editore, Palermo 2001, p. 57.

dens is therefore simultaneously an image of life's most intense fulfilment. The heavier the burden, the closer our lives come to the earth, the more real and truthful they become. Conversely, the absolute absence of a burden causes man to be lighter than air, to soar into the heights, take leave of the earth and his earthly being, and become only half real, his movements as free as they are insignificant. What then shall we choose? Weight or lightness?"

The answer is at all not easy, because if, on the one hand, we experience daily heaviness, on the other, it is just as human to pursue lightness, Icarus's dream, the rush towards unexplored and uncommon horizons, release from the burden of the body. An upwards motion, towards the sky and immensity. The poet Samuel Taylor Coleridge writes: "To the eye [the sky] is an inverted goblet, the inside of a sapphire basin, perfect beauty in shape and colour. To the mind, it is immensity."

This mental immensity, lyricised by the poet, would seem to lend iGuzzini's Spanish headquarters its name: the Sky. iGuzzini Sky would represent that "inverted goblet", but in this case it is seen by Miàs as antithetic to solid immobility; in opposition to the latter, the architect created a light sphere of light and transparency, going beyond the image of the goblet and defining a different symbolic apparatus, contrary to the world turned to stone by Medusa's gaze.

The architecture of iGuzzini Sky and the strength of the symbol played by its geometry are allied to the hermeneutic role according to which, in Giedion's words, "it is a trait of architecture to confer expression upon the symbol":[4] if the square indeed represents the earth, the sphere symbolises the sky, then the name of the building is not accidental. The choice of the spherical form, universal in value, is however particular because it changes its shape under the action of an impulse urging it upwards. A tenuous wrapping of a common substance—light—swells with air and seeks to detach itself from the earth. An experience of the form rising to the cosmic scale and availing itself with absolute geometries. Air dynamics corrupts geometric perfection and evokes motion within the pure form.

The upwards push suggested by this spheroid—this balloon of air and light, all taut and tight—can be traced back to that experience of vertical travel in the ether described by Bachelard on the basis of that "upward psychology"[5] he contrasts to the fall, to the attraction of the force of gravity. The symbolism of the building is not exhaustive at the thin border dividing the air—the sky—between an inside and an outside. It is overt even in its interior, where a mighty central metallic structure reaches out upwards, like the trunk and branches of an "aerial tree" (to cite Bachelard again), to house the experience of uprightness and the upward line within the building too.

The identity of the spherical form and the recognition of its symbolic value are accomplished even with respect to the inclusion within the context of the landscape.

The building, indeed, seems to distance itself from its context only apparently: it wants to detach itself from that metropolitan territory only to house itself and so to belong—like the sky—to all places at the same time. It is the search for universality in the particular of the form. The result however goes beyond this quest, and it goes too far from the architectural border to encroach on that of the street, the urban and landscape border, standing out as a peculiar and isolated element, fully showing itself to the vertical perception. A landmark of the landscape of Barcelona's urban infrastructures, it draws the contours of the light and of the air it contains.

The perception of suspension and aerial floating of the big sphere becomes more daring when one discovers that the building is well-anchored to a basement which is partly hypogeal. The shift from hypogeal to aerial space, the duality between the forms of the basement and of the balloon ready to take flight, emphasise once again the upward line of the overall architectural composition. The opposing dialectics take possession of the project and inflect once more its symbolic value.

At the level of formal-architectural research, the challenge seems to be that of a planner who faces the condition or the perception of the ephemeral: the horizon of the short

5   Gaston Bachelard, *Psicanalisi dell'aria. L'ascesa e la caduta*, Red Edizioni, Milano 2007.

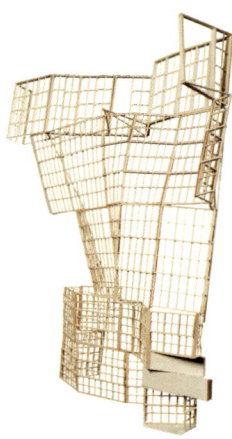

Balsa wood model of Miàs's Nowhere Skyscraper, study model for high-rise buildings.

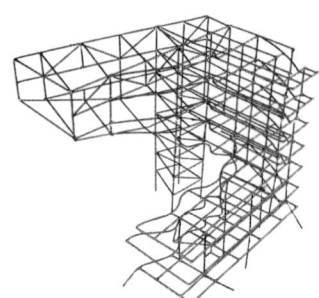

Wire model of Miàs' competition proposal for Córdoba Architectural Association, with the auditorium hovering over the place.

length, in fact, apart from the experimentation with the use of new materials and the organisation of technologically innovative structures, gives a greater and uninhibited expressive capacity.

The sartorial work, covering conclusively iGuzzini Sky with a sinuous fabric which points sensually to the architectural forms, goes in the same direction. It then belongs to that sartorial plastic to which Schelling referred, by describing the figure of the tailor as akin to that of architect.

In this case, the experimental nature of the work is not determined by its short length, but by the awareness of the uniqueness of the chosen form. It indeed takes on linguistic experimentation and manifests itself by the uniqueness of geometric forms and their composition: the power expressed by this combination of contourial conditions and choices does not lie only in the iconic strength of the achievement, but is much more meaningful in terms of the communicative strength, which goes beyond the construction itself.

iGuzzini Sky is an enduring architecture which is, however, as bold as ephemeral and temporary architectures with respect to choices and the solutions adopted. Its formal value as an abstract composition is absolute: it sprouts from forms existing in nature and, just like them, it contains its content within itself. The architect has intentionally chosen this form and he has consciously modified it. So modified, it shines in its own light, it speaks its own language, it conveys the message and excites our senses by the perception of the framing and of the excluding space.

With unusual lightness, this architecture is made up of two meaningful moments: it communicates self and things other than self, as must be if a building is to be representative of something. The position of architecture is not neutral, it rather holds and takes possession of the message to convey. iGuzzini Sky plays, then, the dual role of showing and demonstrating: it shows the stylistic innovation and the technological research of the Italian firm, and it demonstrates how architecture can be, at the same time, content and bearer of a message.

With respect to communication, in fact, this is a case where the classification of the terms to be used, coming from Wittgenstein's *Tractatus Logico Filosoficus*, holds: if the architecture houses objects to be shown—if it is a bearer—the verbs to be applied can be *present*, *exhibit*, *reflect* and *designate*; if the architecture represents the message to convey—if it is content—the terms that can be applied are *assert*, *say* and *name*.

In both cases, clarity and transparency, as synonyms of light and lightness, work together to convey the message more immediately and directly.

iGuzzini Sky, as bearer, presents its own content, that is to say that it shows it by means of the statement of the plastic value of the specific form; it exhibits it by displaying it and offering it to the public in a plain and polished way; it reflects it as the game of lights and mirrors, which sends the light back in order to diffuse it; it designates it, by proposing it as the meeting point of light and form.

iGuzzini Sky, instead, as content, asserts the role of an architecture made up of universal forms, in contemporary society, characterised by a self aesthetics; it tells us that it is still possible to follow the path of research and experimentation to improve the conditions of man's housing; it names the architect as that who does all this.

Miàs's work, in this peculiar sense, is the place where the role of contemporary architecture is definitively played. It becomes a bearer of messages and it burdens itself with a symbolic formal value which goes beyond the brand name it represents. It enters, then, by all rights, the history of spherical architecture, alongside the works of Boullée, Ledoux, Buckminster Fuller, Piano and Leonidov.

Sebastiano d'Urso,
Architect, Researcher and Professor of Architectural and Urban Composition and coordinator of the Composition Section of the Urban Landscape and Mobility LAB at Catania University, Italy

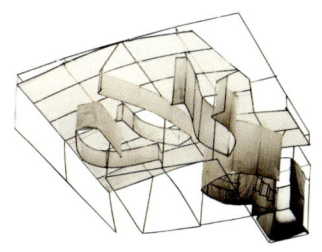

Wire and Japanese paper model of Miàs's Funicular station project in Tibidabo (Barcelona, Spain), studying the ceiling.

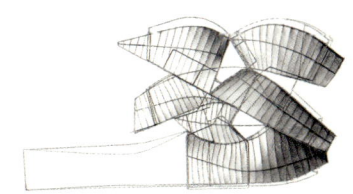

Wire and Japanese paper model of Miàs's Butterfly House project in Besalú (Girona, Spain). The house rises from the ground and hovers over the landscape.

Between the lines

Josep Miàs

I take this brief text as an opportunity to recall Enric Miralles (1955-2000), with whom I was fortunate to share many years of a relationship with the world and with architecture through drawing. Drawing was in fact the medium of our interaction. Ever since, I have continued drawing.

Drawing was and still is, for me, a way to think. Undoubtedly the line, apart from recording and describing our environment, acquires its true meaning when it can invent a new reality, a reality that seeks to establish a discourse of continuity with the past and with the context, and, most of all, with what it can question. And it is the continuity of this simple line that still interests me and that, at the same time, surprises me.

Lines can be continuous, broken, straight or somewhat curved, able to recognise something or simply to recognise themselves, immediately and without either temporal order or sequence. Lines interest me when they can, as they trace their doubtful paths, construct clouds or spaces in the air in search of possible forms. I see this possibility in the drawings of Cozens, where you still can't even imagine what this form in movement and constant state of doubt will become. The iGuzzini project started with a cloud drawn in pencil that sought to hold air inside its lines, and whose superimposition, in varying thicknesses, held the power to suggest and transform itself into a model fashioned from wire; as if we were then suddenly trying to build with the bare minimum of material that would allow us to speak of architecture.

In relation to these first wire sketches I like to mention the drawings and models of Alexander Calder, especially the circus characters and animals. Both these drawings and his wire objects remind us of the precision in drawing, the precision of the line in capturing spaces. From his earliest drawings and wire objects this concern can be sensed. I am extremely interested in this relationship between drawings and space, a relationship born of an attempt to let the air flow. And it is in his mobiles, in their state of repose, in those instants when movement, rather than existing, remains a potential, that all their magic is revealed.

We use the latest digital programmes to define and calculate our architecture, but at the same time we work with wire

Initial sketch for Besalú Butterfly House (Girona, Spain) where lines are superimposed.

models whose origin is in the dialogue with drawing. This project is of a complexity far too great to be undertaken without such sophisticated programmes. But the work with wire in model-making relocates the project at a level of basic, necessary comprehension. In the words of Calder "wire, rods, sheet metal have strength, even in very attenuated forms, and respond quickly to whatever sort of work one may subject them to. Contrasts in mass or weight are feasible, too, according to the gauge, or to the kind of metal used, so that physical laws, as well as aesthetic concepts, can be held to. There is of course a close alliance between physics and aesthetics."

On the other hand, the pencil drawings of Picasso or Ingres introduce thickness. And it is in the superimposition of these lines of varying thicknesses, in this process of superimposition of layers, of superimposed traces, that I seek to discover the project. In Ingres, in particular, the continuous superimpositions are essential to the final definition of the drawing. Our architecture is discovered, it appears, among these superimposed lines, as fine layers, as fine veils, of equal intensity and density. In its earliest stages, the project is drawn in a like manner, superimposing sheets of ruled onion-skin paper, blurring the drawn lines—somewhat imprecise and intentionally so—seeking to discover among those lines that space that remains to be defined. This means defining the project on the basis of a plotting of lines, as if it were a plotting of possibilities.

Throughout the project design process and into its development stage, we see a certain affinity with Blossfeldt, who in the end appears as one of the main inspirations for drawing. His photographs enable us to see the invisible. They are like drawings. They are wilfully neutral descriptive documents capable of explaining their reason for being: their geometry. I don't believe the project was born out of any awareness of these photographs. In any case, I've come back to them, to these invisible geometric constellations of nature, to the invisible lines which signify reality.

Simone Weil speaks of space as a receiver of sound vibrations, which propagate within it as air does inside a musical instrument. Space is a container of sonorous lines, in this

Color drawing
for Besalú
Butterfly House
(Girona, Spain).

39

case, of paths and possibilities. Certainly the centre space around which the iGuzzini project is arranged could be described in these terms, although the term gravity would perhaps be more precise in explaining this large void. With regard to gravity Weil uses the expression "fall upwards", when the gaze, instead of being drawn towards the bottom of this space, flows naturally upwards, as if the building encouraged an ascending movement freed from the intervention of gravity. In fact, the interesting thing is to invert the direction of gravity, in lending the space a natural upwards tendency.

Certainly, the sensation of gravity inside the building is inverted, and the perception of the centre space proposes a clear relationship with the sky. Looking at the sky becomes looking at the bottom of the well. And the other way round; the very sheet of water at the bottom gives us back the sky. Evidently, these considerations come after the fact, but they were certainly there in the first drawings of the courtyard, in the search for a form capable of inverting gravity in order that this lightness which allows the building to hang would be perceived.

We cannot say that the location of the iGuzzini Building lacks points of reference. However, they are not the same geometric points of reference that we might find in a more or less fixed urban area of Barcelona like Poble Nou and specifically in the Plug-in Building in 22@ district. I want to compare these two buildings in order to comment on the above statement. They do in fact share similar programmes, but in two apparently very different contexts. However, both arise from trying to find a geometry of lines in the places where they stand, a set of geometric rules that enable them to belong objectively to the latter. In the case of the 22@ building, the plot and the streets that delimit it trace and suggest the relationship of the building to its immediate urban environment. The building emerges from the standardised drawing of the plot. The pedestrian spaces of Pere IV and Pujades streets run right through the ground floor. And the streets within project onto the streets outside, inviting them to engage in dialogue. The relationships between the different spaces of the building, and even the visual relationships, thus occur along these interior streets, in the manner of urban courtyards.

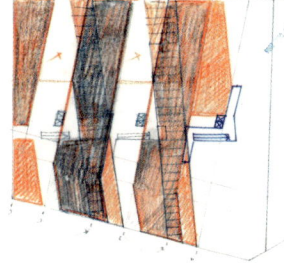

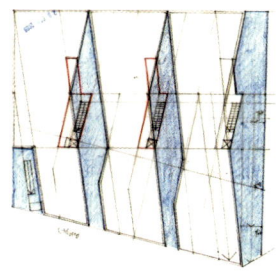

Plug-in Building (Barcelona, Spain). Initial sketch tracing the existing plot, and seeking the hidden lines of a possible geometry.

In iGuzzini, with the volume of the corporate building accounting for the entire buildable space, and conforming to the limits to buildability of the plot, the building succeeds in regaining its own interior space, which acts as an urban courtyard. This courtyard is defined as the space through which the relationship between the work spaces occurs.

On the other hand, the building occupies the site under the assumption of a certain disappearance of any urban layout. Its somewhat spherical form recognises precisely this ambition to avoid having its façade face anything or anyone, and its relationship to its environment arises from the fragility of the landscape itself and the general perception of this building occurring in movement, from the roads that run past it. It sustains itself in its place, or rather, it hangs in delicate balance in the landscape. Access to it will occur naturally, across its vast double-curved square, accentuating its precarious fragility.

I am interested in the interpretation of the physical conditions with which we advance in our projects, a reading superimposed on the drawing, the mental reading of the structural loads imposed on our buildings by gravity. The trick is to avoid having the centre of gravity of the building fall on the line that we can trace once the building is built; to have the gravitational loads run through the voids, through the inaccessible spaces, those which hold the tension that runs through the air. A similar phenomenon occurs in other projects where gravity or, rather, the density resides in the void, like when one tries to draw something that cannot be built. It is between these two worlds, the one you build and the one you draw or you intuit that you're defining, that we want to explore. The force diagrams then appear as an invisible layer. The design seeks to weave another layer, as if playing cat and mouse, in order to discover this new reality. Curiously, it is by tracing literally the load path imposed on us by gravity that we can circumvent it. No doubt building means belonging to this world even when you are much more interested in the world without laws, where architecture can still float.

Josep Miàs,
Architect of iGuzzini BCN HQ

Plug-in Building (Barcelona, Spain). The interior and at once exterior spaces of the building are public spaces open to the city. At the access level, the public is welcome to pass through. These urban courtyards lend the whole building an urban sense.

Barceloneta Market (Barcelona, Spain). Through its undulating surfaces and its volumetry in movement, the building proposes a relationship with a site laid out with military geometry, introducing density into the neighbourhood. The dialogue with the existing building and structure occurs in a situation of enormous complexity, in which the existing building, like its structure, never touches or interacts with the new structure incorporated into it in order to define new spaces.

INTRODUCTION

Pyrenees Golf Club, Fontanals de Cerdanya (Girona, Spain). The section of the covered swimming pool is resolved with a simple girder-pillar, resulting in a structurally complex support where it meets the ground. The building's relationship with its environment occurs through the greatest possible proximity to the ground leaving free an area of contact between environment and ground all along the perimeter, and proposing a 360-degree view of the environment. The building exists in a constant relationship of fragility, adapting reptile-like to the gently undulating topography of the golf course.

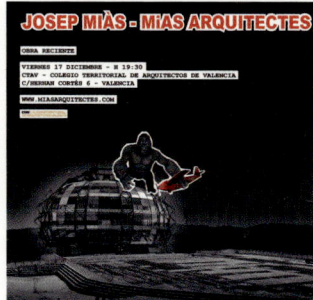

Posters for
conferences
and workshops
with iGuzzini as
a central topic.
The project
invades each of
the places where
it is explained.
Images go
beyond the
project's reality.

Josep Miàs,
International
Lecture Series
at the Bartlett
UCL (London,
UK). Images
of the project
searching for its
place in London:
the City, the
Treasury
Building, Kew
Gardens,
the British
Museum, the
Admiralty Arch,
Langham Place
and Piccadilly
Circus.

iGUZZINI BCN HEADQUARTERS

Metropolitan lighthouse
Vicente Guallart

Barcelona has always been at the forefront of the most cosmopolitan, fastest moving cities in the world, a status it has gained through its economic diversification and history—the manufacturing industry that led nineteenth and twentieth-century Barcelona to open itself up economically to the world abroad—which prevail in a city that has succeeded in integrating seamlessly development and social evolution, grounded in the reality of a world that is becoming increasing clustered around major cities.

And now, in the twenty-first century, cities already account for half the world population; an growing trend, given that worldwide more than one million people move to cities each week. In addition, cities account for roughly 60 to 80% of global energy consumption and, in the near future, the developed cities alone will generate 80% of global economic growth.

In this context, the challenge facing cities today is clear: attain maximum efficiency in urban growth while integrating areas of influx and influence, which, in the case of Barcelona, embrace the metropolitan area. To do this, cities must again be productive but also environmentally friendly, generating synergies with the environment and the opportunities posed by the new information and communication technologies (ICT).

In Barcelona and its metropolitan area, the new technologies play an increasingly prominent role in the wellbeing of its citizens and the infrastructure around them. In this sense, Barcelona, the city where one hundred and fifty years ago Cerdà coined the term *urbanism*, a city which

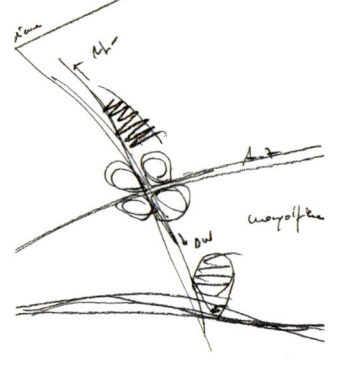

IGUZZINI BCN HEADQUARTERS

is an international benchmark in urban habitat, now conceives a new urban model, able to re-boost its economy and that exploits the new opportunities generated by its surroundings, environmental innovation, ICT, and the talent and willingness of an ever innovative and entrepreneurial society.

The new headquarters of iGuzzini Illuminazione Ibérica, in Sant Cugat del Vallès, is an example of a leading international firm staking on the Barcelona metropolitan area, taking advantage of a location privileged not only in terms of the geographical situation of Barcelona in the Mediterranean and southern Europe, but also of its position on the Triangle of Economic Innovation at the confluence of the River Llobregat logistics area (airport, port, duty-free zone), the River Besòs (22@) and the Vallès districts (industry), an area well connected to road networks and transport.

The new headquarters represents, moreover, a benchmark in architectural terms, a functional building that both meets the company's diverse needs and reflects its capacity for innovation, creativity and design.

In short, a building and a company which help drive the economic regeneration of the metropolitan area, aligned with the City Council's projects to boost the economy of urban innovation in Barcelona and its metropolitan area, bringing together the elements that enable us to boost the economy and project Barcelona internationally.

Vicente Guallart,
Chief architect and director of Urban Habitat,
Barcelona City Council

It is important to try to understand the place, its topography and context. An aerostatic balloon could explain these conditions of fragility of architecture vis-à-vis the place: it will be perceived, its shape recognised, from the shifting perspective of the roads. In this project, the fixed conditions are those of the paths of the roads, where the building no longer needs to refer even to its own site.

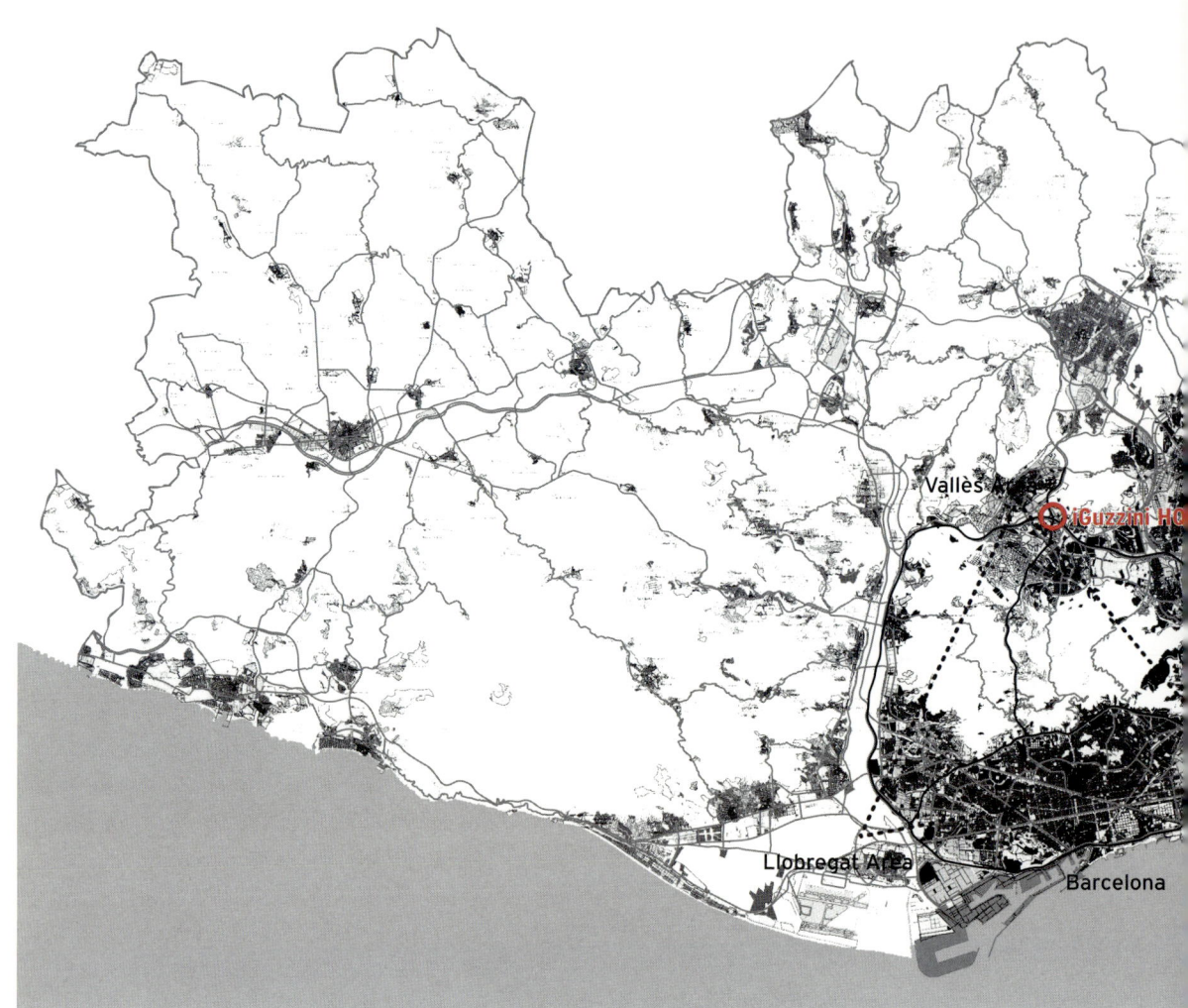

Vallès Á

◯ iGuzzini HQ

Llobregat Area

Barcelona

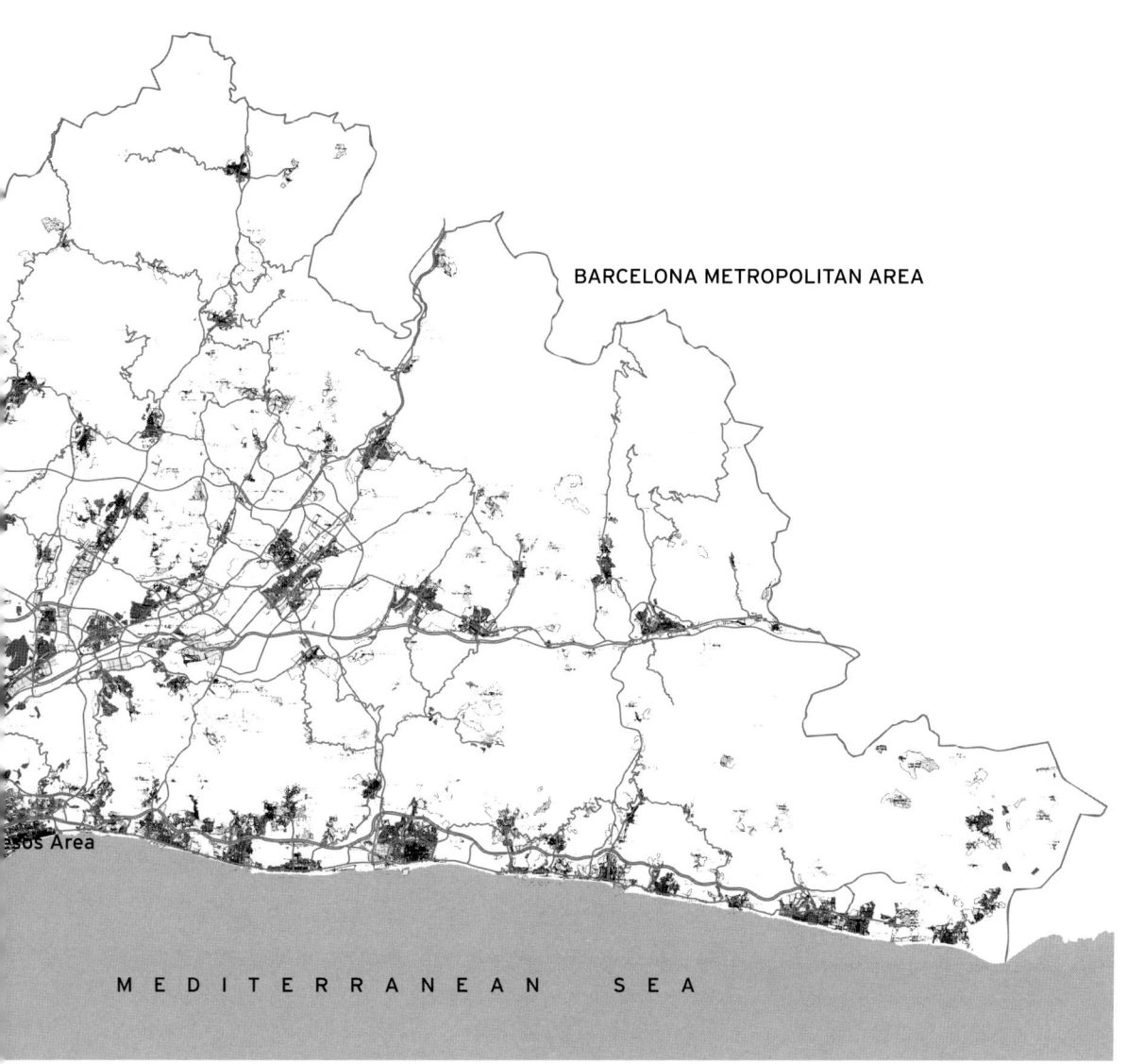

BARCELONA METROPOLITAN AREA

sos Area

M E D I T E R R A N E A N   S E A

The location
of iGuzzini
Illuminazione
Ibérica
Headquarters
occupies one
vertex of
Barcelona's
Economic
Innovation
Triangle, at an
exit/entrance
point of the city.
This location
will bolster its
centrality in the
city's future as
a metropolis.

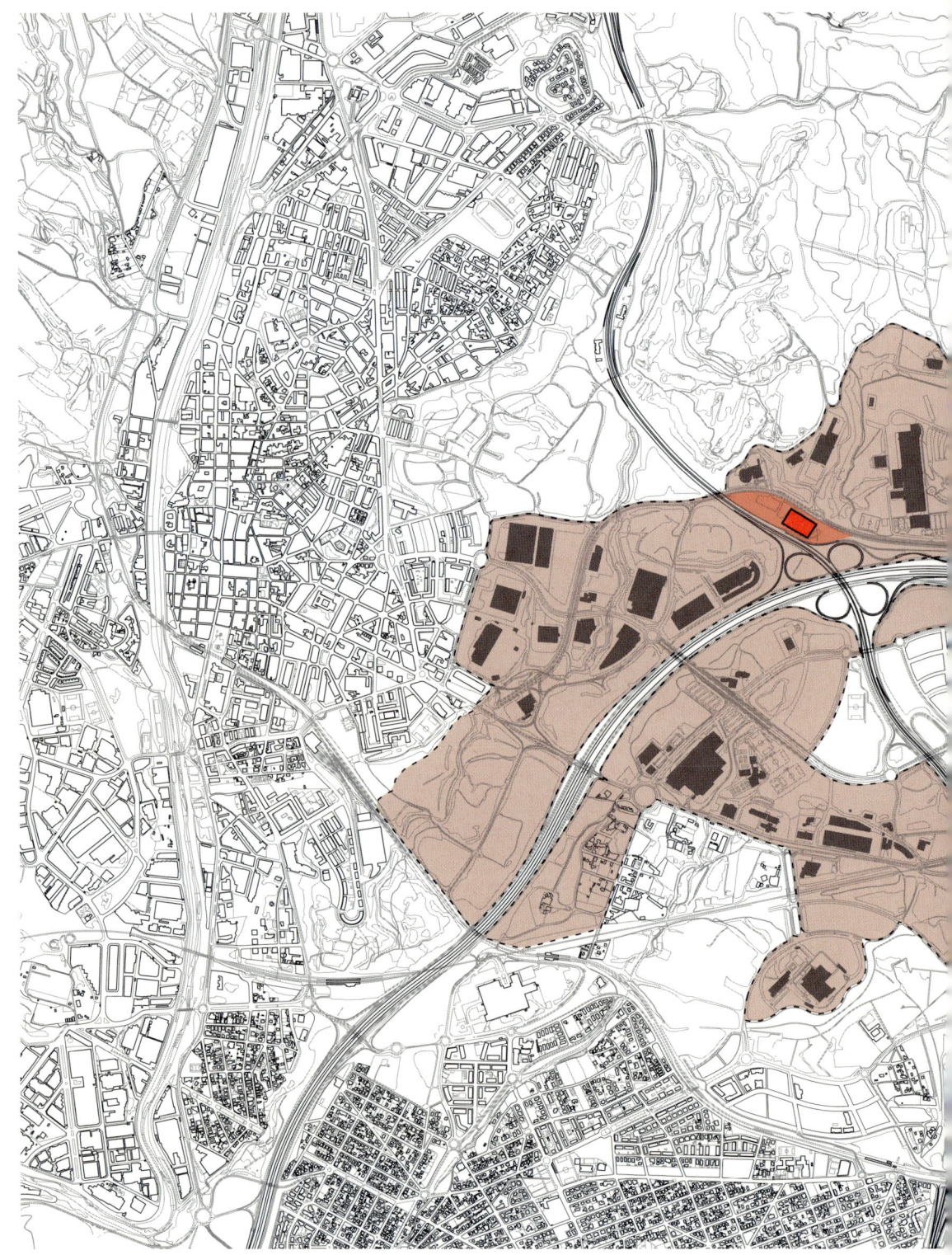

IGUZZINI BCN HEADQUARTERS

Can Sant Joan Technology Park in Sant Cugat del Vallès exemplifies the extremely high level of the services parks attracting the strongest companies in research and development. iGuzzini Illuminazione Ibérica occupies an access point to this area, its formal expression presiding authoritatively over this effort in innovation and environmental balance. The site for the new building is wedged between and visually related to the major access roads to Barcelona. Thus it becomes the point of reference for the Technology Park and a new architectural landmark for the Barcelona metropolitan area.

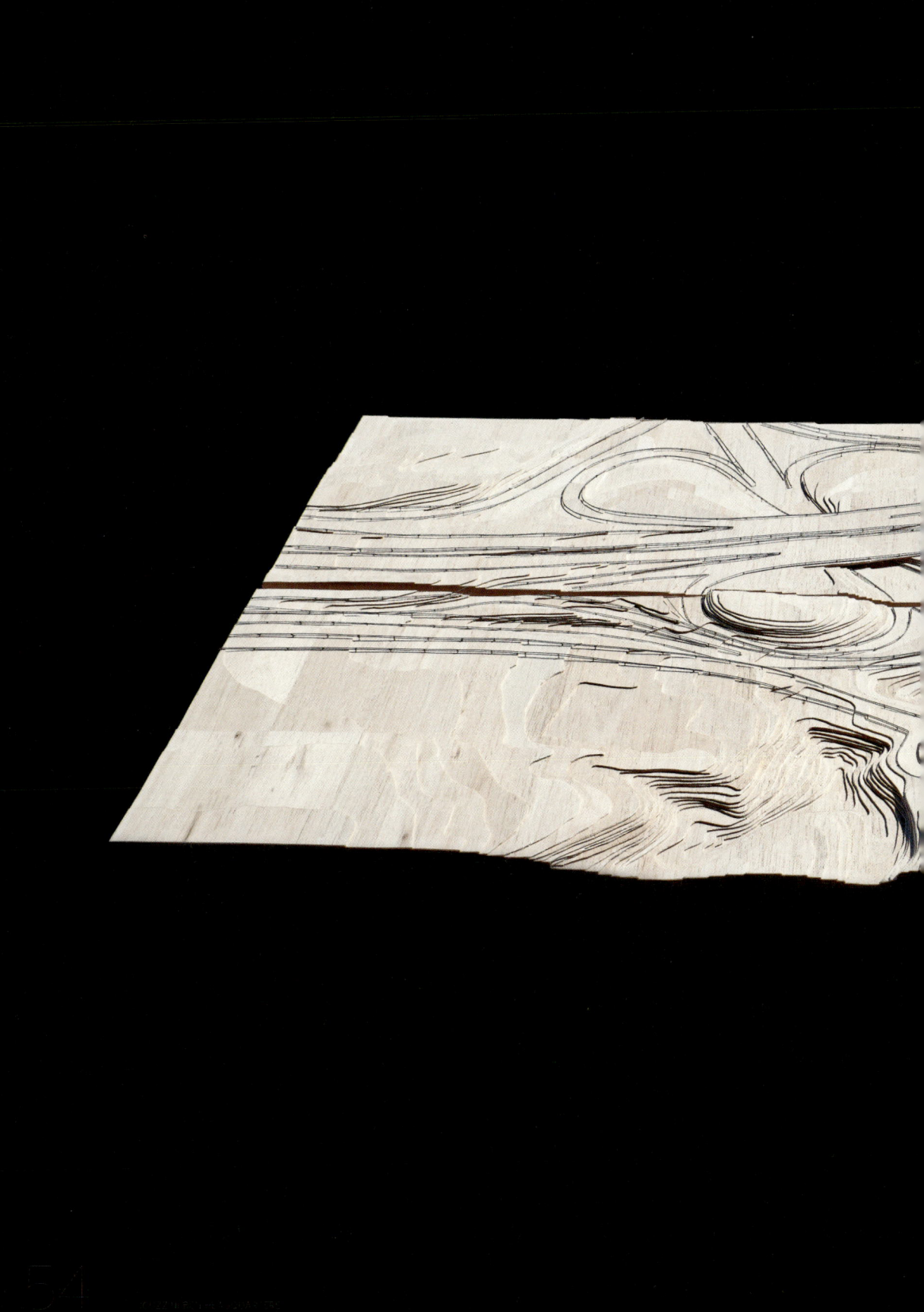

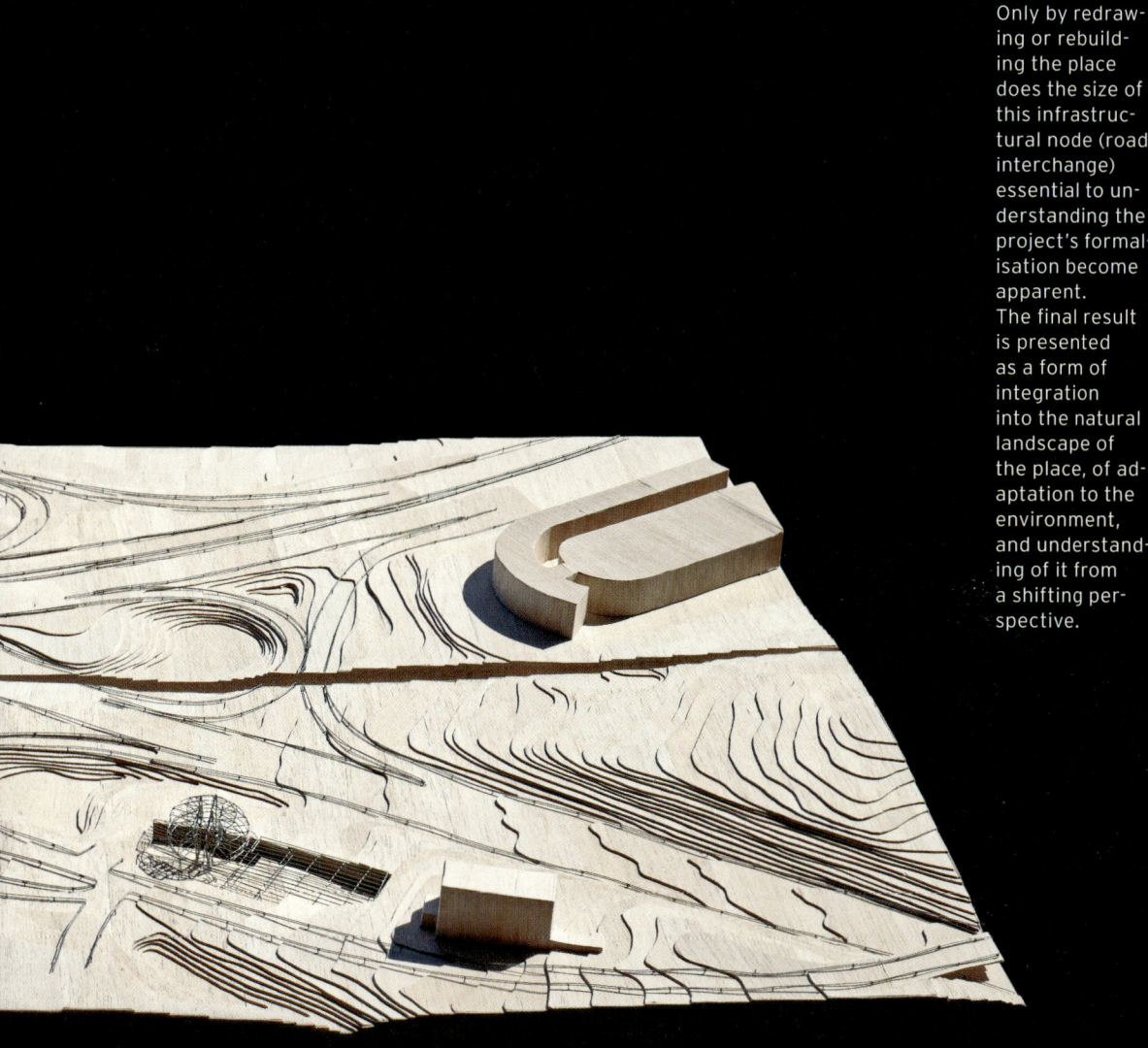

Only by redraw-
ing or rebuild-
ing the place
does the size of
this infrastruc-
tural node (road
interchange)
essential to un-
derstanding the
project's formal-
isation become
apparent.
The final result
is presented
as a form of
integration
into the natural
landscape of
the place, of ad-
aptation to the
environment,
and understand-
ing of it from
a shifting per-
spective.

A project draft Josep Mias

iGuzzini Sky is located at one of the major highway interchanges of the Barcelona area, in an extremely very fragile landscape. In order to avoid modifying the existing topography, a large part of the building's programme is underground while the rest, the office building, stands above the ground, suspended in the air.

iGuzzini Sky is, at heart, an R&D centre for the development of technical knowledge and expertise in lighting systems, the facilities for which are located both inside and outside the building.

Most of the programme is housed in the huge underground container—built with reinforced concrete diaphragm walls, and barely disturbing the natural lay of the site—volume it shares with spaces for stock and distribution, product management, a showroom and a garage. Of these only the stockroom requires natural light, and thus is equipped with some skylights in a roof that also serves as a showroom for outdoor lighting systems.

The north side of the building houses the technical installations and is somewhat offset from the natural terrain to provide direct access for maintenance routines.

Concrete proved the ideal material for the construction of this container, employing conventional concrete containment walls around the perimeter and precast concrete pillars inside. This system also provides high thermal inertia, reducing considerably energy consumption.

The indoor showroom features a large indoor exhibition space for the entire iGuzzini product range and space, including an auditorium, designed as a centre for product presentation and the dissemination and sharing of knowledge.

Another space—known as the *theatre of light*—is dedicated to the simulation of a range of lighting conditions for the purpose of precision testing and design of virtually any sort of system the company makes, including prototype development. The high-ceiling theatre, a key facility in iGuzzini's

- Offices– 3,000 m²
- Toilets– 230 m²
- Technical rooms– 50 m²
- Out. showroom– 2,500 m²
- Hall– 500 m²
- Private rooms–50 m²
- Cafeteria– 190 m²
- Terrace– 180 m²
- Garage– 650 m²
- Meeting rooms– 50 m²
- Warehouse– 1,900 m²
- Auditorium– 180 m²
- Exhibition area– 180 m²
- Int. showroom– 1,000 m²
- Light theatre– 90 m²
- Building services– 500 m²
- Main kitchen– 70 m²

research efforts, is equipped with movable structures, height-adjustable platforms and a high ceiling adaptable to changing needs in the placement of lighting systems.

Like the indoor showroom, the outdoor showroom is designed to provide the optimum setting for the exhibition and testing of the company's entire outdoor product range. It is conceived as a large pixelated space with different interchangeable pieces in order to provide the broadest possible range of supports for product testing and display. Based on systems normally used in the interior of buildings, it features a height-adjustable raised floor for easy access to wiring and a great deal of freedom in the placement of mains connections. The enormous flexibility of this floor makes this large, open showroom one of the most advanced in existence.

Like the underground volume, the corporate office building hovering above it and the landscape, is equipped with the latest technology in technical and climate management and control systems. The principal rationale of its design is to optimise natural light. The building does not seek orientation toward any roadway in particular, but rather avoids imposing this sort of hierarchy on its environment. A large open courtyard framed by the main structure—the pentagonal pillar system from which the building hangs—ensures homogeneous light in the workspaces. This lightwell acts as a centre point of the office spaces and plays a key role in overall energy management of the building. The column system, meanwhile, leaves the work spaces free from structural elements, opening them up to both the courtyard and the surrounding landscape. A sunscreen covers the building only where absolutely necessary. Indeed, this is another rationale of and way of reading the project: as an expression of bare necessity.

Josep Miàs,
Architect of iGuzzini BCN HQ

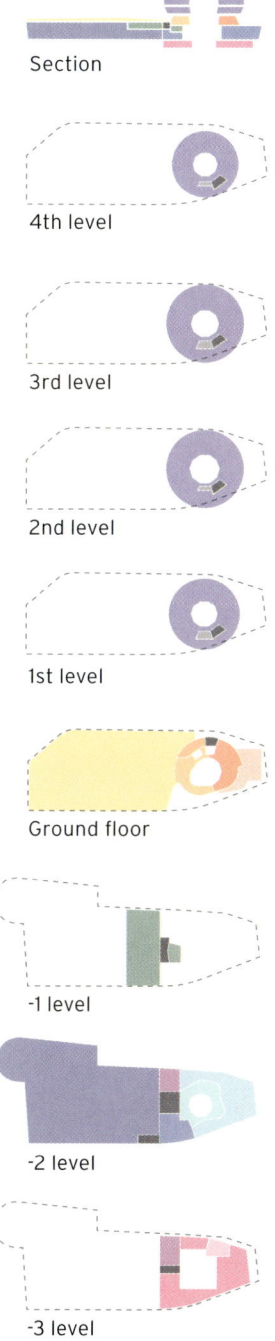

Section

4th level

3rd level

2nd level

1st level

Ground floor

-1 level

-2 level

-3 level

57

This section shows the large underground building designed to meet logistics needs. From inside, a single central pillar that defines an open courtyard will bear the glazed building. The courtyard plays a fundamental role in climate control as well as balancing the light in the offices.

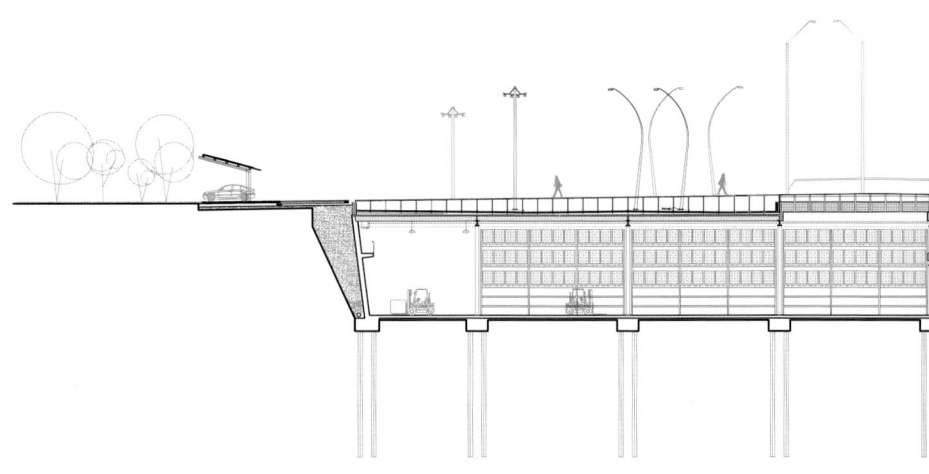

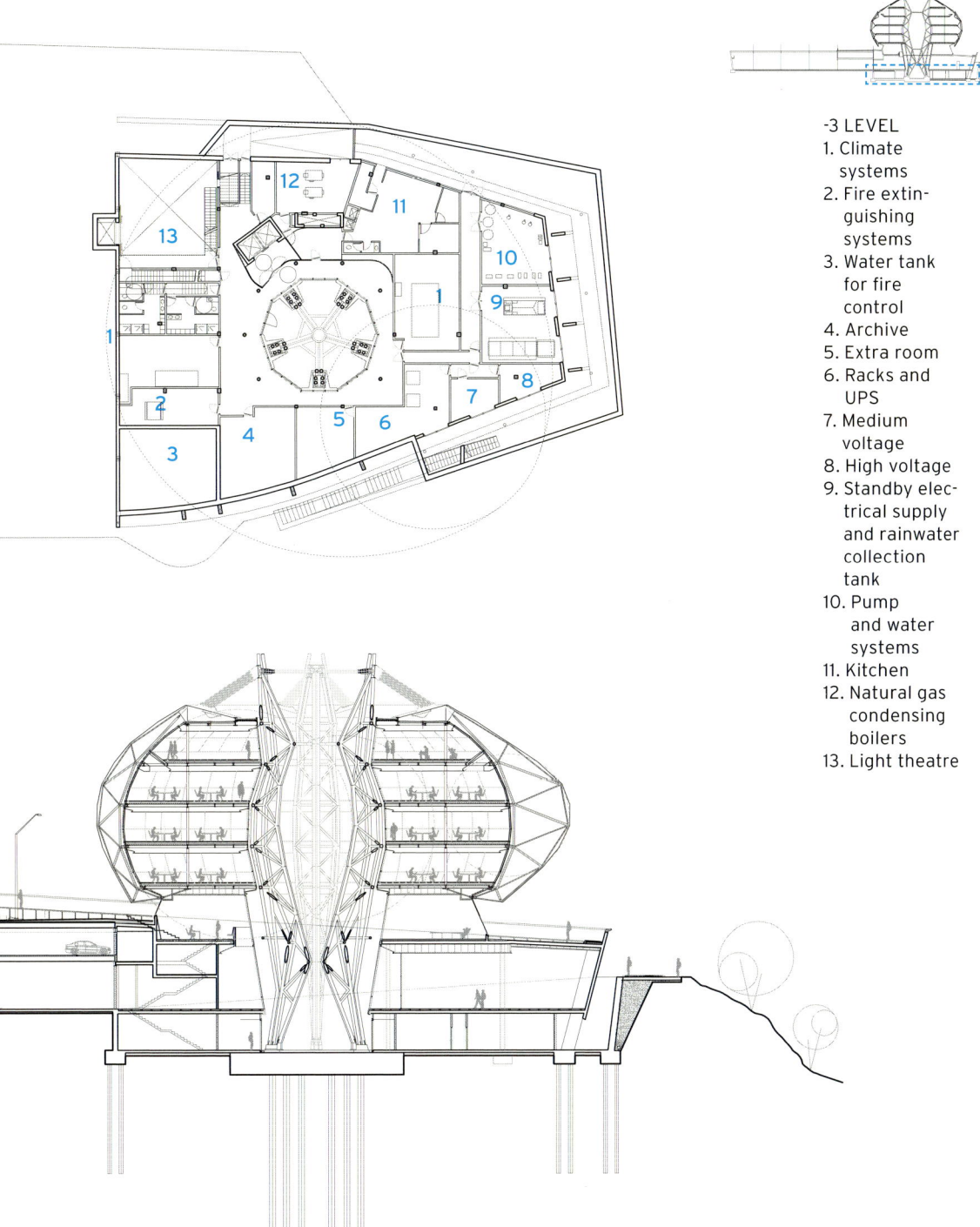

-3 LEVEL
1. Climate systems
2. Fire extinguishing systems
3. Water tank for fire control
4. Archive
5. Extra room
6. Racks and UPS
7. Medium voltage
8. High voltage
9. Standby electrical supply and rainwater collection tank
10. Pump and water systems
11. Kitchen
12. Natural gas condensing boilers
13. Light theatre

59

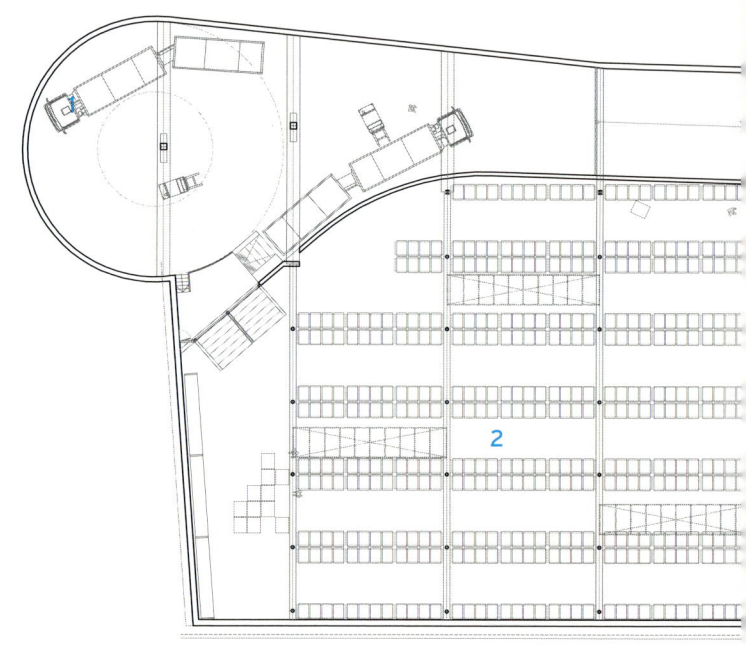

The building
includes an
underground
volume which
fits into the
topography,
with
warehousing
space, garage,
technical
installations
and an indoor
showroom
for lighting
systems. The
place—or this
volume—is
prepared to
receive the
office building,
which will
float over the
landscape.

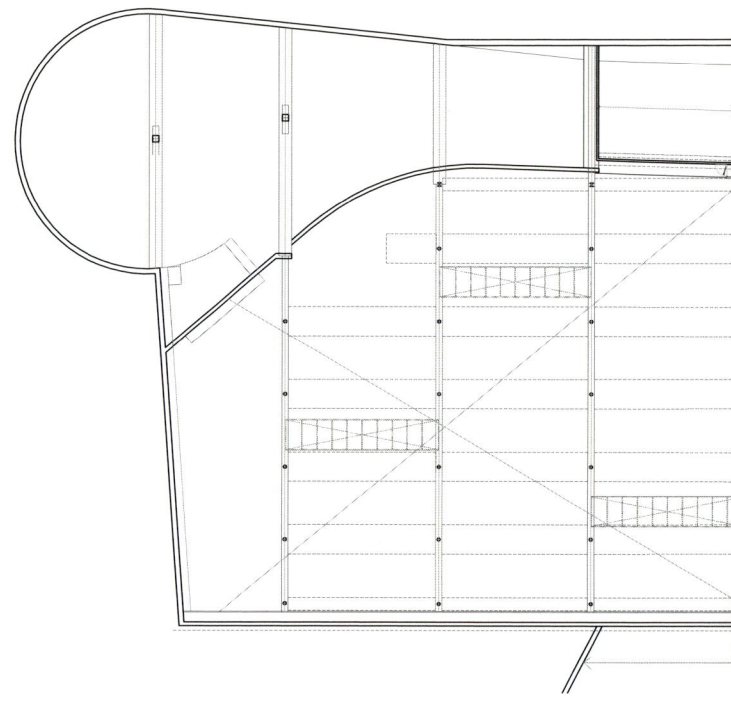

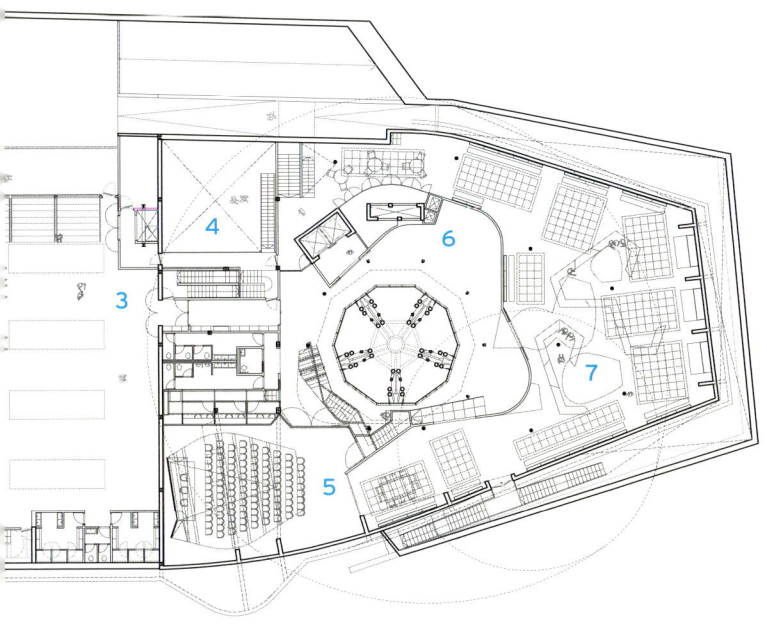

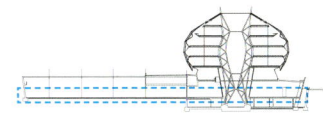

-2 LEVEL
1. Loading and unloading area
2. Warehouse
3. Operations area
4. Light theatre
5. Auditorium
6. Exhibition area
7. Indoor showroom

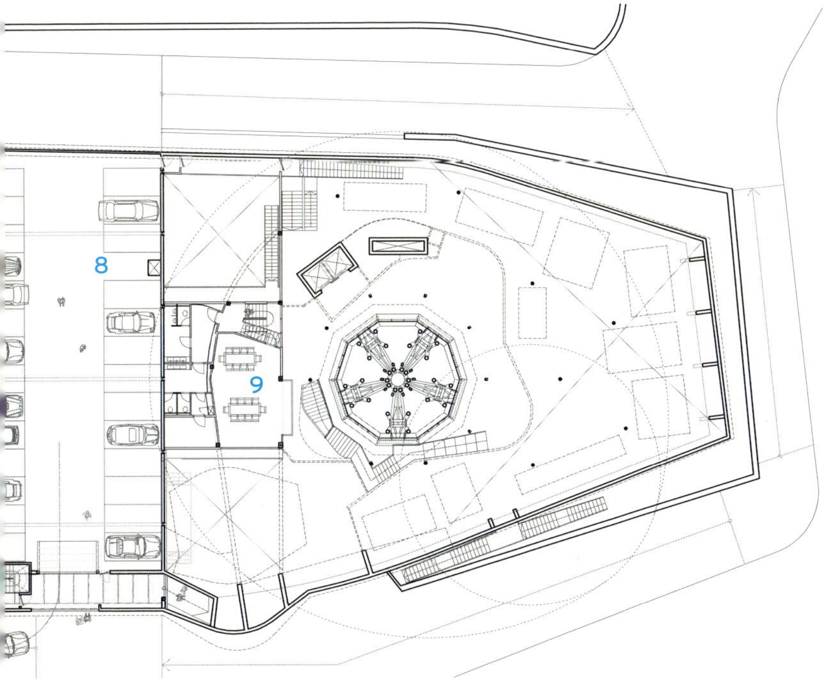

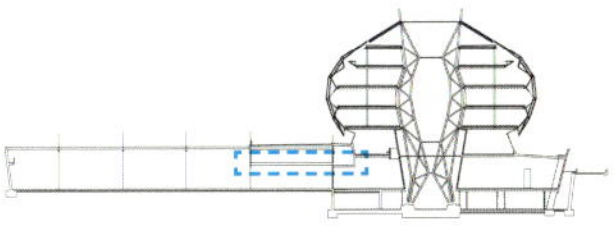

-1 LEVEL
8. Garage
9. Meeting room

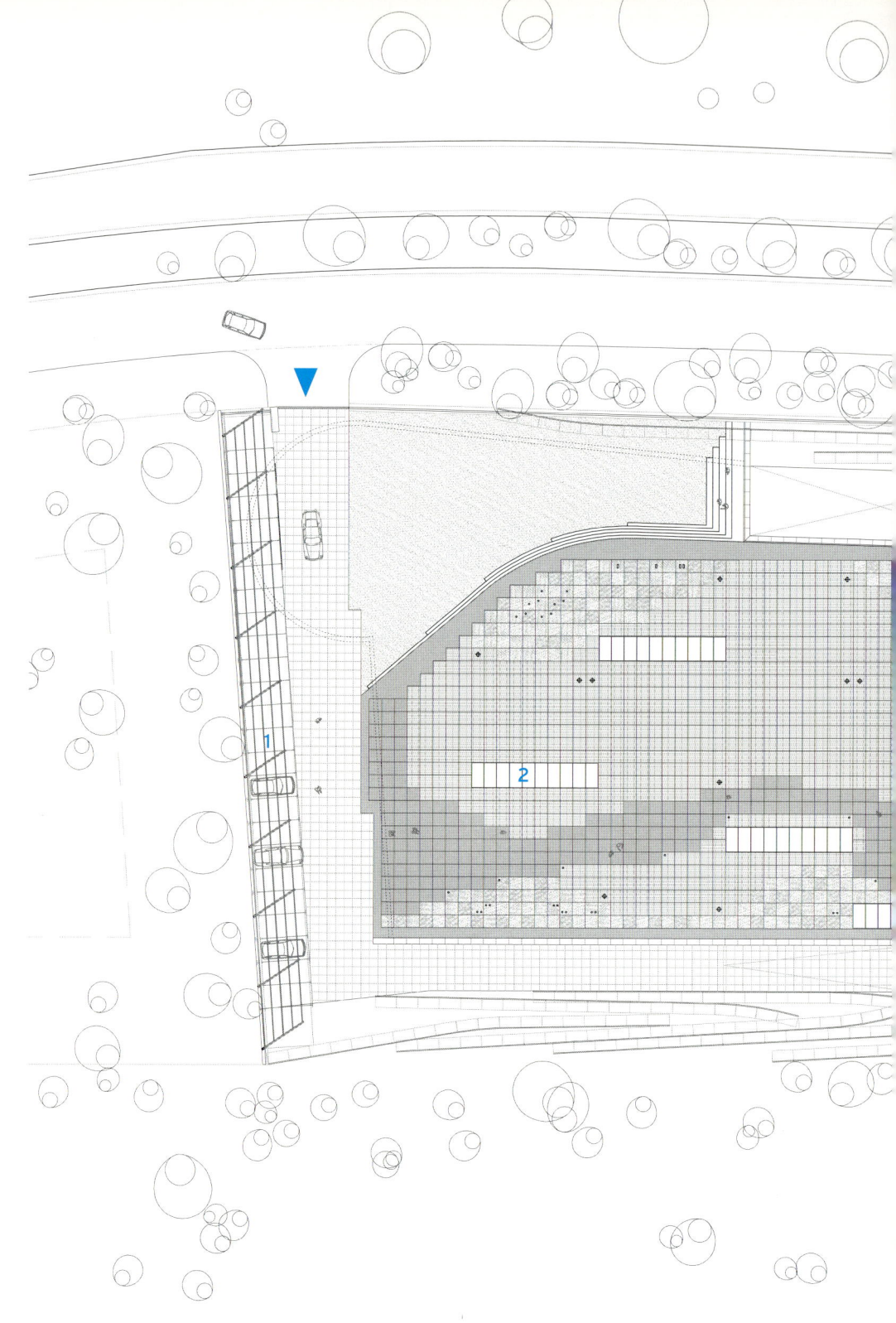

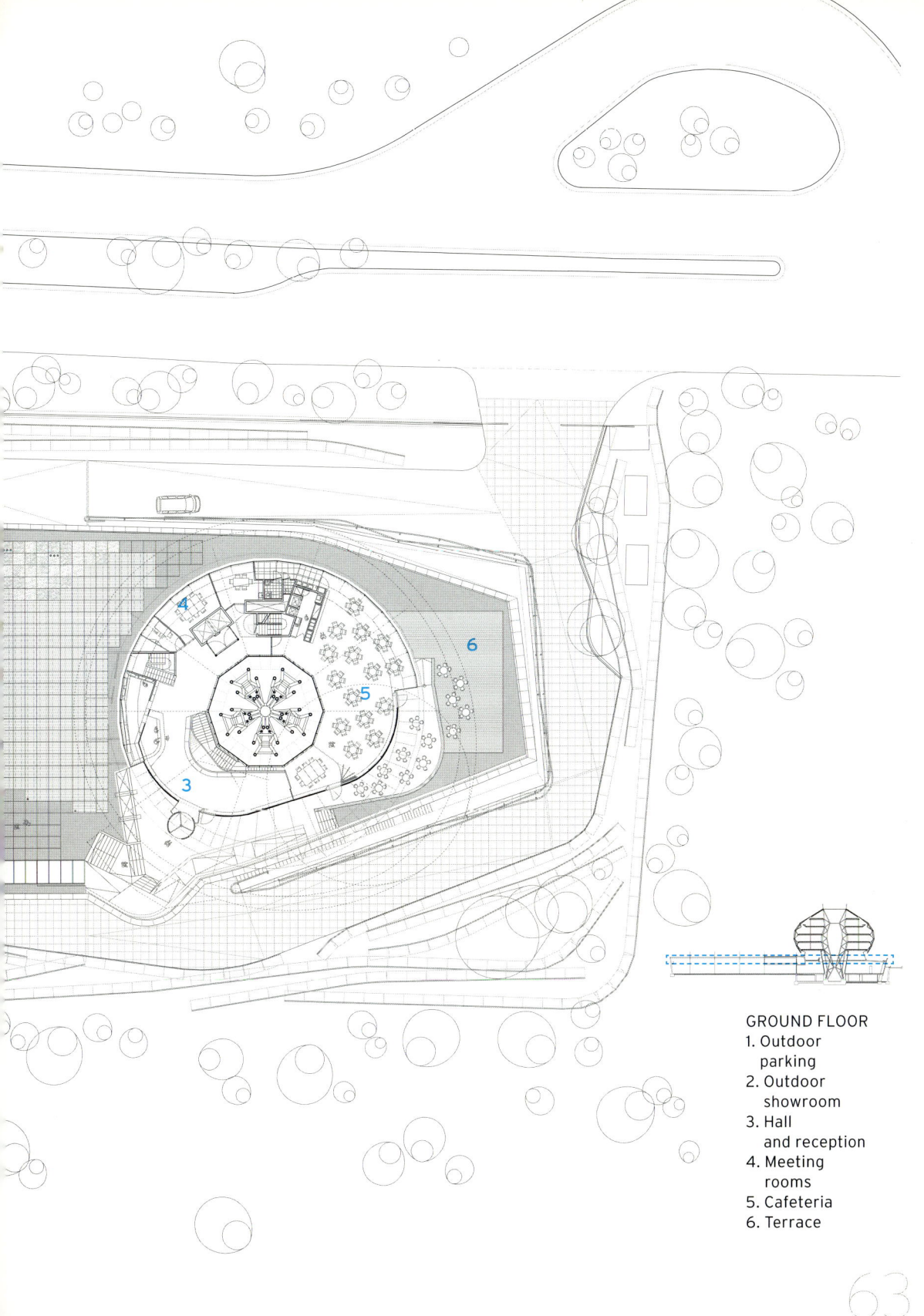

GROUND FLOOR
1. Outdoor
   parking
2. Outdoor
   showroom
3. Hall
   and reception
4. Meeting
   rooms
5. Cafeteria
6. Terrace

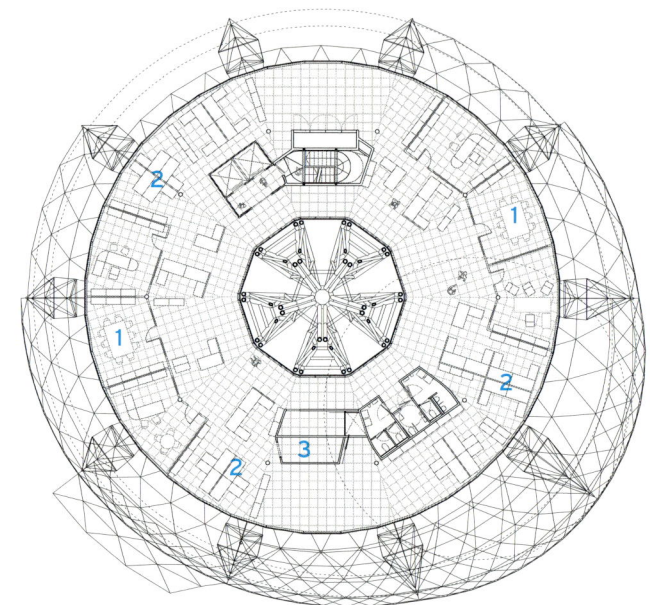

1st level

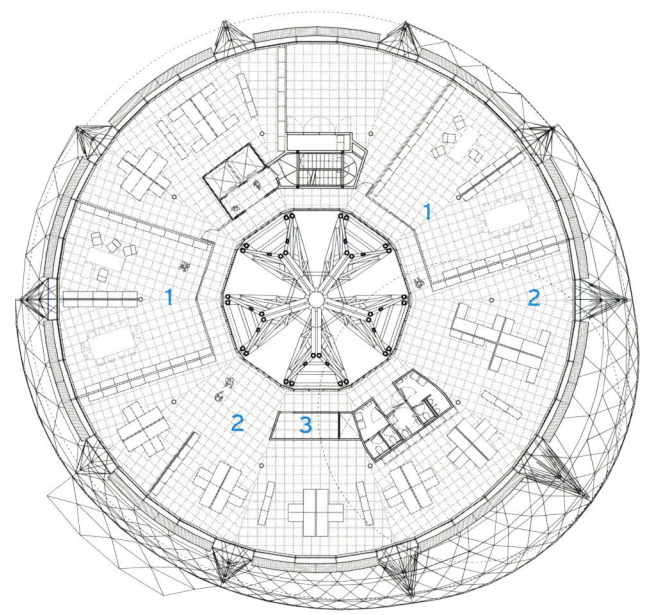

2nd level

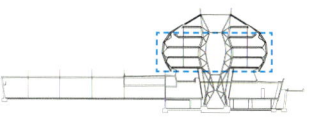

OFFICE LEVELS

1. Private offices
2. Open space offices
3. Technical & service rooms
4. Investigation and learning areas

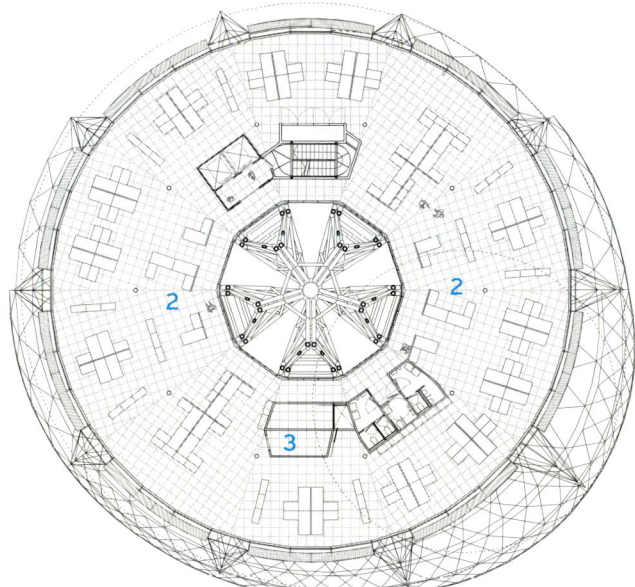

3rd level

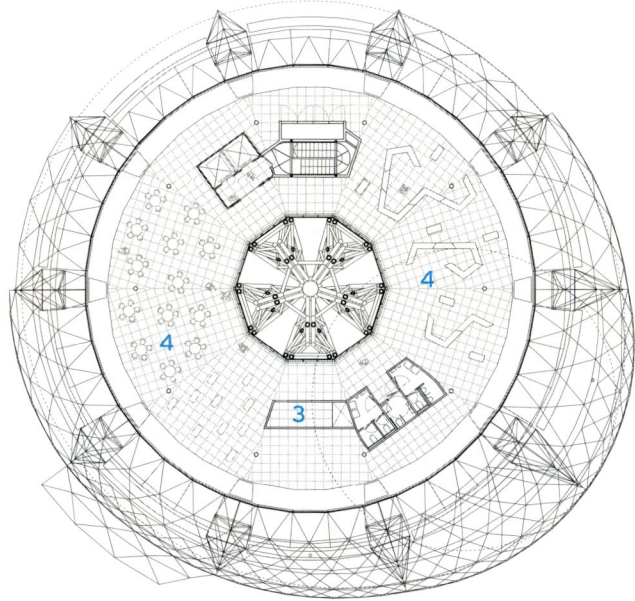

4th level

IGUZZINI BCN HEADQUARTERS

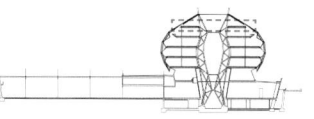

ROOF LEVEL

67

The underground building reconstructs the existing topography. The double curve of its roof, the outdoor showroom, enables the emergence, in a situation of balance, and suspended from a single pillar, of the office building.

IGUZZINI BCN HEADQUARTERS

The glazed building detaches itself from the underground concrete building emerging from the ground. The former building will be hung from its topmost point, the vertices of the five masts that make up the central pillar, which surrounds the open courtyard. Locating the entire structure on the outside enables absolute freedom of distribution in the interior spaces.

71

IGUZZINI BCN HEADQUARTERS

IGUZZINI BCN HEADQUARTERS

IGUZZINI BCN HEADQUARTERS

79

The space between the underground building and the building hung from the central pillar is the public access. The large roof of the logistics building runs beneath the office building.

They represent two different ways of belonging to the site: the first belongs to the ground, the second to the sky. They do not interfere with each other, between there is just air.

Togetherness
Josep Miàs

At a workshop in Sardinia, I had the honour of sitting on a jury with and making the acquaintance of Herman Hertzberger.

Actually, I already knew him from his books *Lessons for Students in Architecture 1*, *Space and the Architect*, *Lessons in Architecture 2* and *Space and Learning*, which Enric Miralles and I read together. Not only I was interested in his architecture, which was depicted in photographs and plans, but in his way of describing other architects' works and the intrinsic debate this engendered. Reading sections of the book out of order led to in-class discussions.

I always approached his architecture from the perspective of its inhabitants: the smile of a kid half leaning on a banister; the gesture of a woman standing by the entrance to a public building, her shopping bag on the floor; or groups of people, some standing and others sitting, talking or working around a table, in a very playful attitude, rather than one of concentration.

Anyhow, architecture seemed indispensable for this to happen. These images and buildings all speak of the human condition, of relationships between people, situations they share and a sense of community.

When he talked, in a lecture he gave, about his most recent projects, mostly schools, his train of thought would return to his well-known ideas, but he insisted on a single concept, *togetherness*, showing how this existed in each of the images of his designs. Once he had shown us this, he went straight onto the next project.

The feeling of togetherness was the main structural idea underlying all his projects, describing carefully the physical conditions of each space, and explaining which activities were possible, for example, on each landing. Actually, stairs were one of the most interesting spaces for him, since they are the most complex architectural space. He also described how people on an upper level interacted with people on a lower level through the open space of the stairwell. In sum, he spoke about spatial relationships as if they were human, seeing, for example, the act of two people crossing paths as an exchange of glances.

He repeatedly stressed that in-between spaces were the places for the most interesting activities, and on empty spaces being the most useful. Empty spaces are considered as a place, like a building is considered as a city. Place is what happens, or where life happens. If you can put a table somewhere, then you have a place. Architecture is, then, the act of accommodating and welcoming people, the act of creating a space for people to meet.

The iGuzzini Building really acquires meaning when occupied. That is when we see that what matters is not what happens but rather to observe what happens. The work spaces participate in this awareness of common space just as they define their own private and personal space. Evidently, the horizontal geometry of the office floors facilitates this relationship between private and public space. The privacy necessary for the management offices is obtained precisely by creating a relationship between them and the surrounding landscape, ie, locating the enclosed offices on the perimeter; looking onto the courtyard is a manner of recognising publicness, since the courtyard is like an unoccupied piazza, an unoccupied public urban space. The spaces in the iGuzzini Building are evidently specialised, but in reality one could talk about a single space, of the meeting of gazes or of intertwined paths of human movement. As if, as Simone Weil might have said, visual exchanges were the building blocks of the edifice. In this sense of belonging to this spatial unit, all the building's intensity is focused on the courtyard. In fact, at that point, the iGuzzini project brings us closer to a certain sort of celebration, as Herman always sought to tell us in his projects. I hope that the iGuzzini Building can continue to be described in these terms, or simply let the inhabitants of these spaces describe the experience of their mere participation in this place.

Josep Miàs,
Architect of iGuzzini BCN HQ

Herman
Hertzberger
and Josep Miàs
driving through
Sardinia.

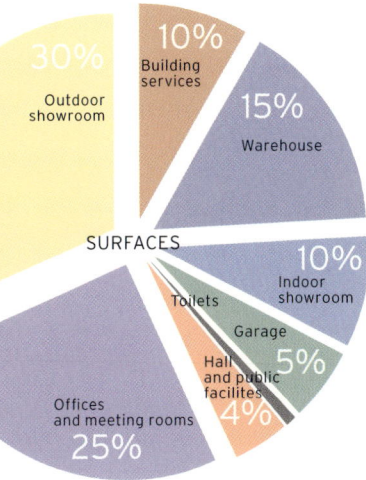

SURFACES

30% Outdoor showroom

10% Building services

15% Warehouse

10% Indoor showroom

Toilets

Garage

Hall and public facilites

5%

4%

Offices and meeting rooms 25%

Light theatre

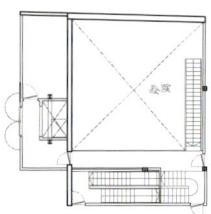

-2 level

The under-
ground building
has dedicated
spaces for
research and
development.
The "Theatre of
Light" is a high
space equipped
for all sorts of
artificial lighting
research.

Auditorium

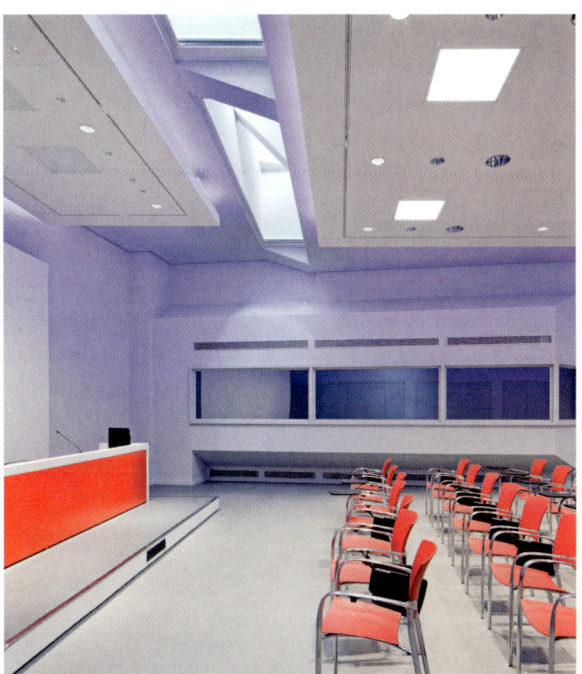

The auditorium, with capacity for 230 people, is equipped with simultaneous translation booths and uses both artificial and natural light. It is used for product presentations and educational and academic activities.

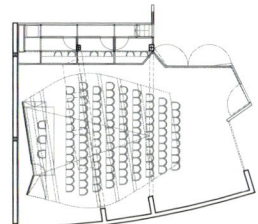

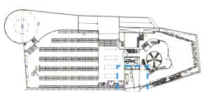

-2 level

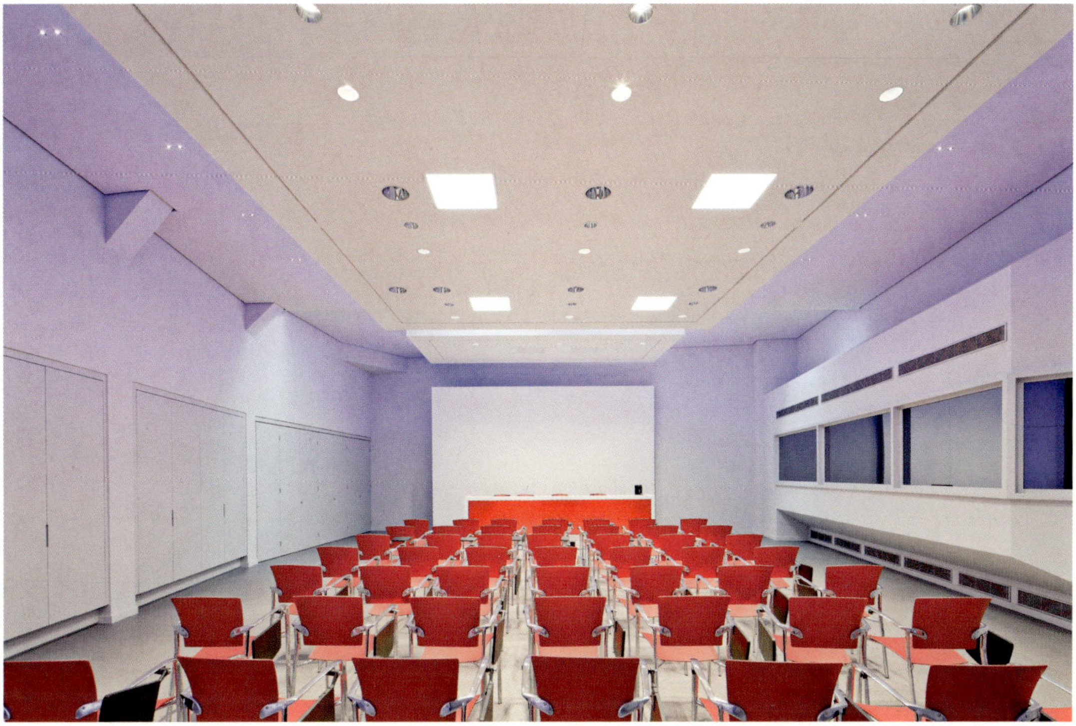

Indoor showroom

IGUZZINI BCN HEADQUARTERS

The indoor
showroom has
various exhibi-
tion and small-
group work
spaces. All com-
pany products
are displayed
interactively. It
also has spaces
for research and
testing prod-
ucts, including
their architec-
tural applica-
tions.

1. Interior light-
   ing system
2. Didactic area
3. Exterior light-
   ing system

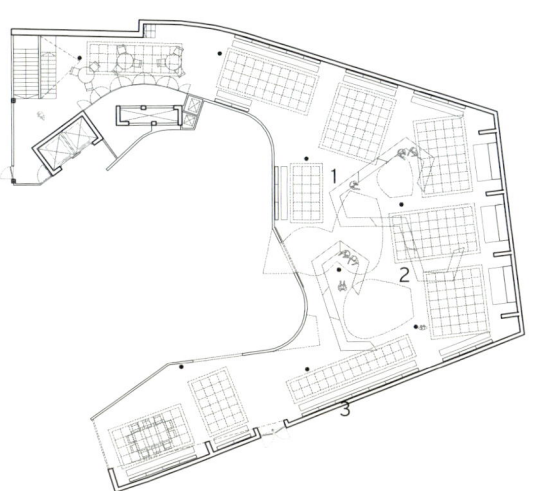

-2 level

87

Warehouse

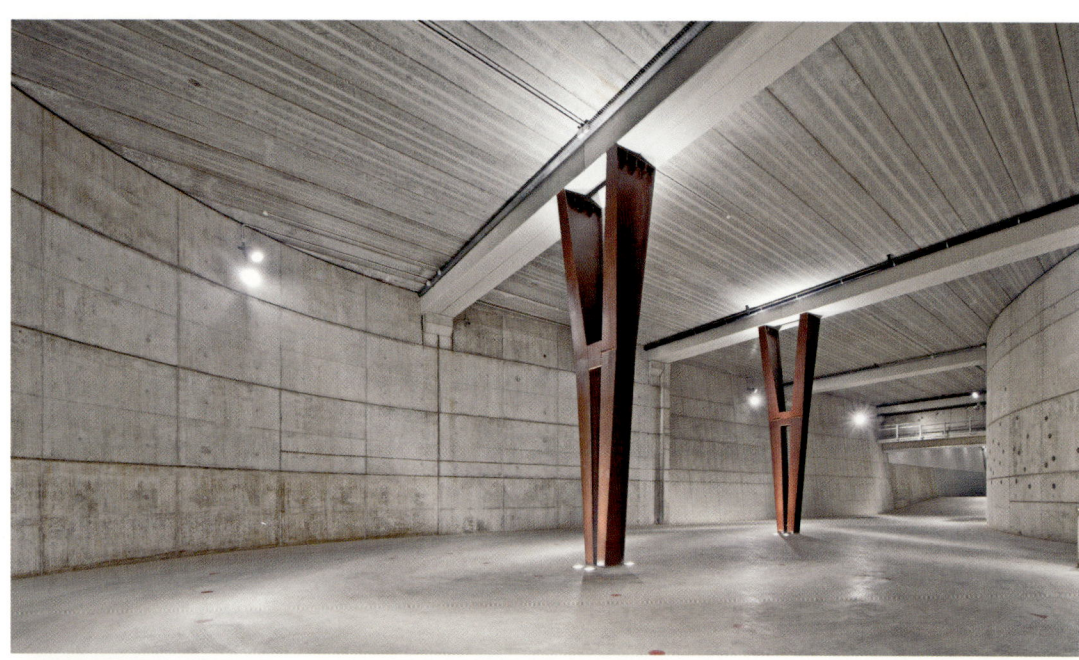

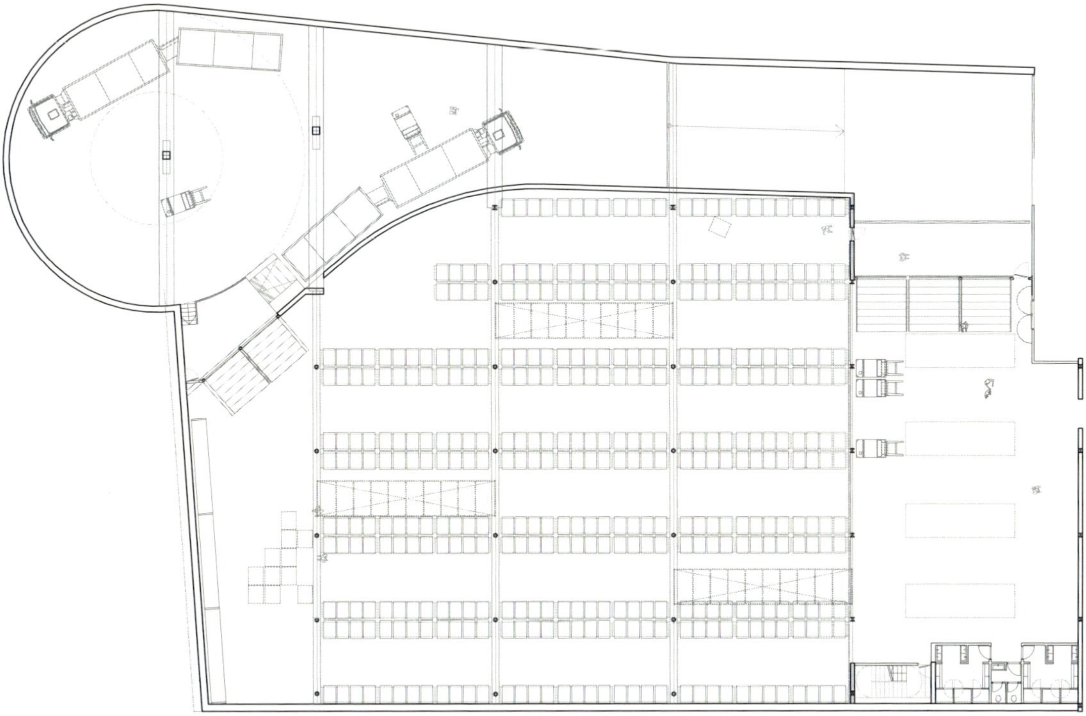

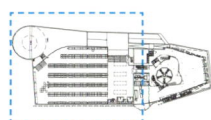

The loading
dock inside
the under-
ground ware-
house is acces-
sible for HGVs.
An intelligent
robotic system
automatically
processes stock
from the Italian
factory. The
warehouse is
lit from above
through the
roof, which dou-
bles as the out-
door showroom;
natural light
is combined
with artificial
lighting.

-2 level

Exhibition area

IGUZZINI BCN HEADQUARTERS

At the point of
contact between
the hanging and
underground
buildings, the
courtyard acts
like a large foyer
for the indoor
showroom. The
staircase leads
to the light
museum on
the lower level,
recognising the
central role of
the courtyard.

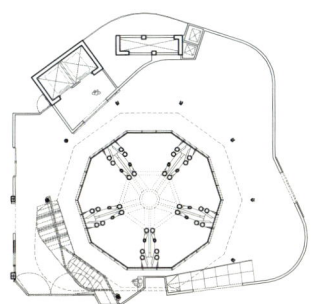

-2 level

Outdoor showroom

The 2,550 m² outdoor show-room is an outdoor-product testing and display space. The prefabricated raised floor facilitates the installation of any outdoor lighting element and accommodates a range of covering materials: concrete, wire mesh, or plants. Its regular-grid support system allows the entire surface and wiring system to be adapted to needs.

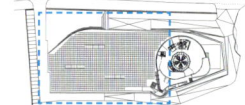

Ground floor

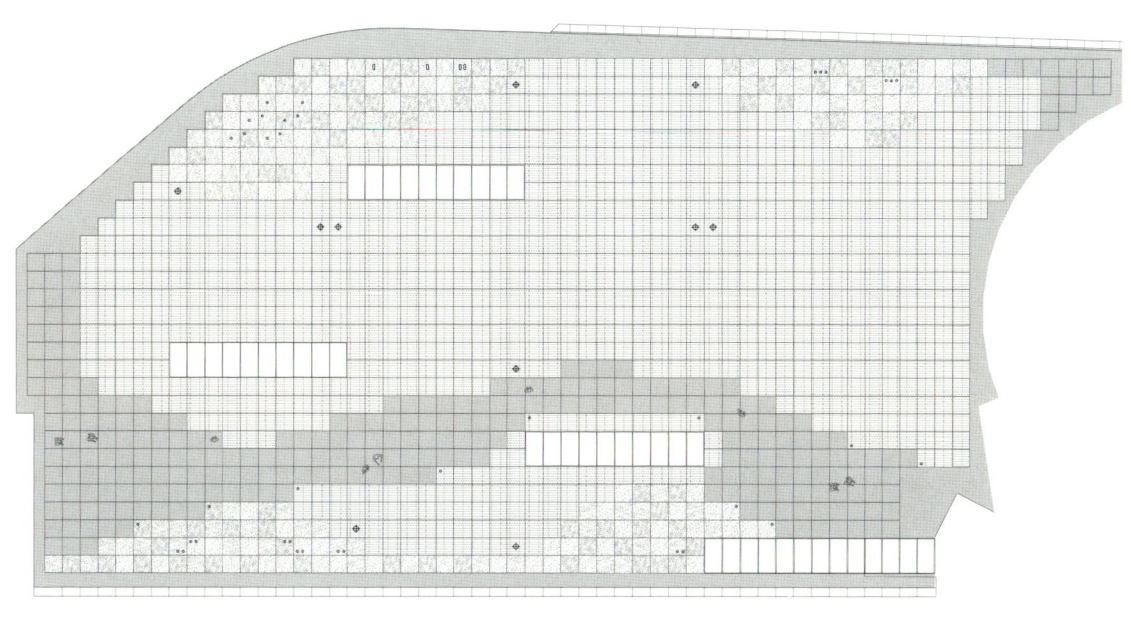

Hall and cafeteria

The entrance space, beneath the hanging building, houses the reception centre, back office and cafeteria. From here there is access up to the offices and down to the indoor showroom, exhibition area, research spaces, auditorium and technical installations. The space expresses the independence between the underground building below and the hanging building above.

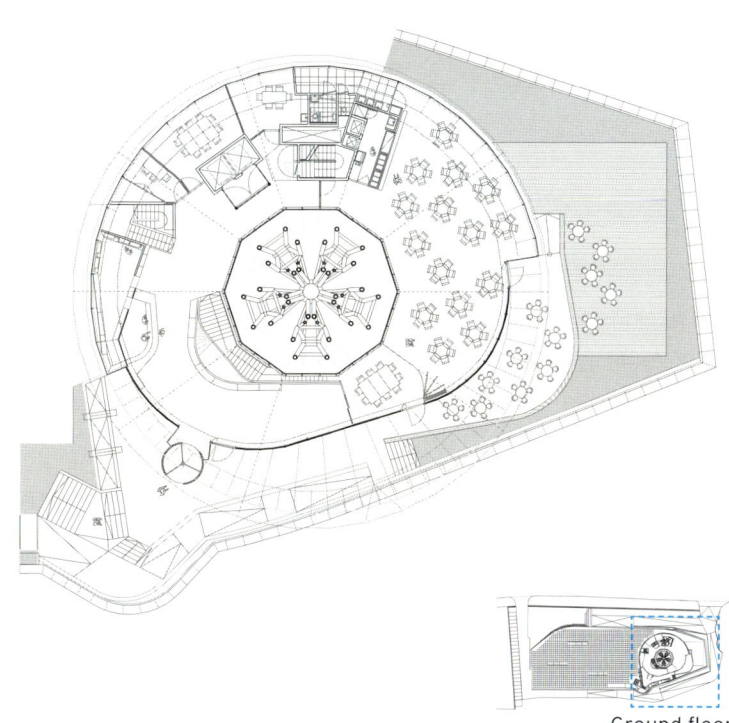

Ground floor

Offices

The four floors
of office space
in the hanging
building link the
exterior with
the courtyard,
enabling natural
light throughout
the day.
Building the
structure into
the courtyard
and exterior
façade, outside
the work areas,
creates open
spaces easily
dividable into
a diversity of
layouts.

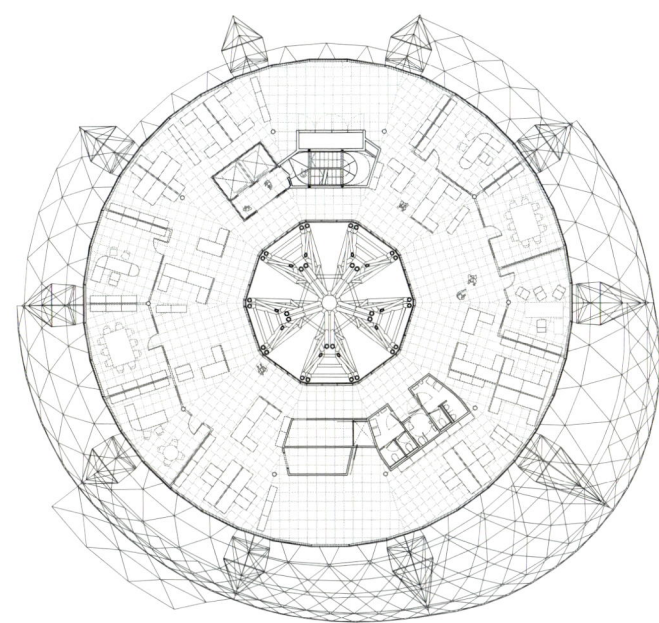

Office type floor

Multipurpose space
for investigation

This space houses light, design and architectural research and development, and operates in partnership with the university. The open plan and raised floor allow flexible placement of installations and complete freedom in designing environments and changing them as needed.

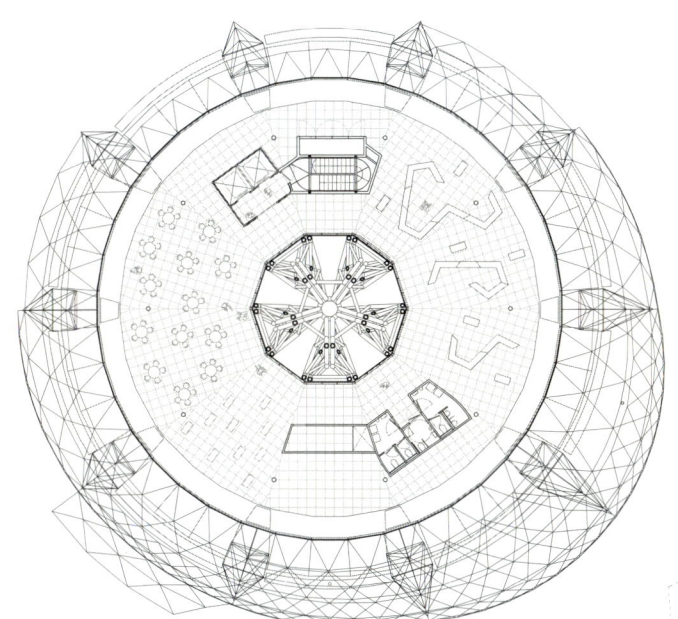

4th level

BEGINNING A PROJECT

Competition abstract Josep Mias

Each new project is an opportunity to return to certain abandoned trains of thought and continue them with renewed focus. Original or not, these thoughts surely take us back to the origin, and from the minds of others to one's own. I like to think that our work has a certain continuity beyond the project itself, and that this continuity occurs not only in a specific context but even goes beyond our own particular realm.

I like to establish certain continuity with those who in their projects seek to discover certain qualities in relation to the place, the topography and specifically the light. Ultimately, this comes down to establishing the geometric conditions that enable us to talk about the place, about relationships with the environment, and where light can be the source of a possible geometry.

Dialogue is then established with certain utopias which seek to explain the world and its complexity, often renouncing gravity, thus suggesting weightlessness and a certain condition of not belonging to this world. In similar terms we speak of collective ambition, of an imaginary world, where the sense of belonging is closer to the sky than to the ground.

Often this means secret work with nature, where we seek to discover its origin in geometry, in the physical conditions of things. Aspirations which, in any case, we strive to transform into drawings, which we redraw over and over in the quest to understand.

iGuzzini Sky does not belong to the ground on which it is deposited. Like a cloud or an aerostatic balloon, it seeks not to dwell on this ground but to belong to heaven. This artefact will seek to describe the light conditions that will enable it to exist, conditions, on the other hand, recognised in a geometric order. Moored to the ground, it will belong to this place, and thus to all others.

Actually, there are forms that can be drawn only once, or buildings that can be built only once. The second one is meaningless. We believed in this opportunity for iGuzzini to assume a form, that of this world with a large shared courtyard at its core.

Geometric study sketch of the generating lines of the façade grid.

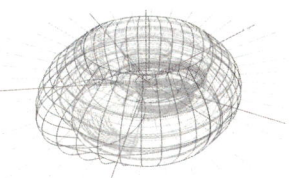
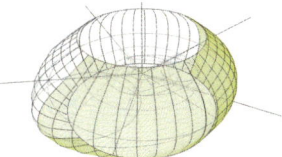

We recognise similar experiences in architectures that represent innovation and when the latter is the objective of research and technological development. The pavilion architectural type, for example, stresses this character of progress and modernity.

iGuzzini Sky is not intended as a display of technological innovation, since as such it would soon be rendered obsolete, its technology quickly superseded, but rather to set an example of the current moment in development towards objective sustainability, in terms of both technology and energy. The building stresses conditions closer to people, of community and ambition, and seeks to survive the test of time because its origin is in the formal search that expresses these conditions.

History endlessly re-examines the examples of architecture which have found in this form or typology a place for its realisation. Establishing certain continuity with the latter, iGuzzini Sky takes this typology further, offering a new concept of the contained space by proposing a central void which incorporates the main structural solution consisting of a pentagonal central pillar from which the building hangs. The incorporation of the latest concepts in technological and energy sustainability likewise affects the spatial design of the building beyond the extensive use made of these new technologies.

Josep Miàs,
Architect of iGuzzini BCN HQ

iGuzzini followed the project throughout; drawings, videos, models and samples were presented at meetings. Photos from one of the meetings to present the project to Adolfo Guzzini in Barcelona.

References
in architecture

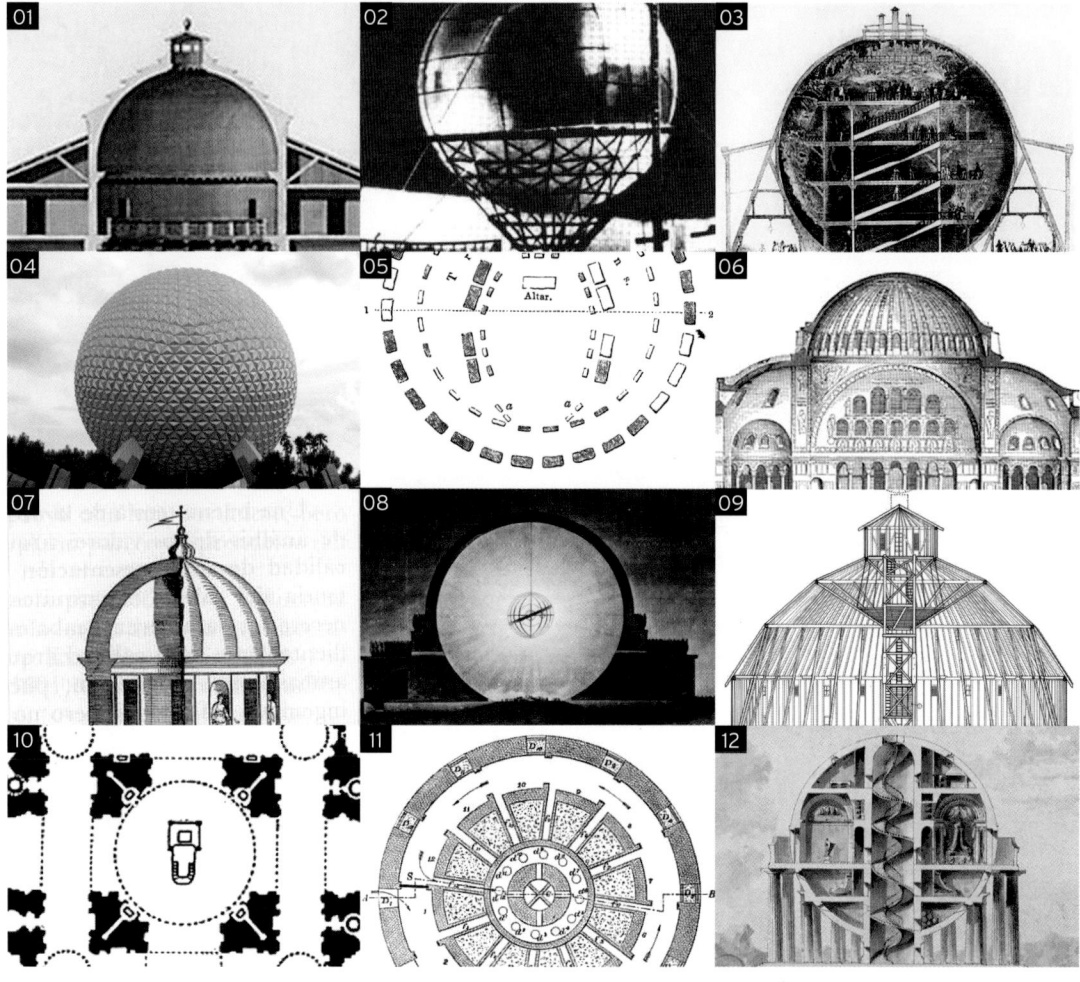

01. Villa Rotonda
(Andrea Palladio)

04. Spaceship Earth (Buckminster
Fuller)

07. Tempietto San Pietro in
Montorio (Donato Bramante)

10. San Pietro cupola
(Michelangelo Buonarroti)

02. Lenin Institute
(Ivan Leonidov)

05. Stonehenge, near Amesbury,
Wiltshire, UK

08. Newton Cenotaph (Étienne-
Louis Boullée)

11. Hoffman Kiln (Friedrich
Hoffman)

03. Great Globe in Leicester
Square (James Wyld)

06. Hagia Sophia (Isidore of
Miletus & Anthemius of Tralles)

09. Littleton Round Barn,
Colorado, USA

12. Design for a House for a
Cosmopolite (Antoine Laurent
Thomas Vaudoyer)

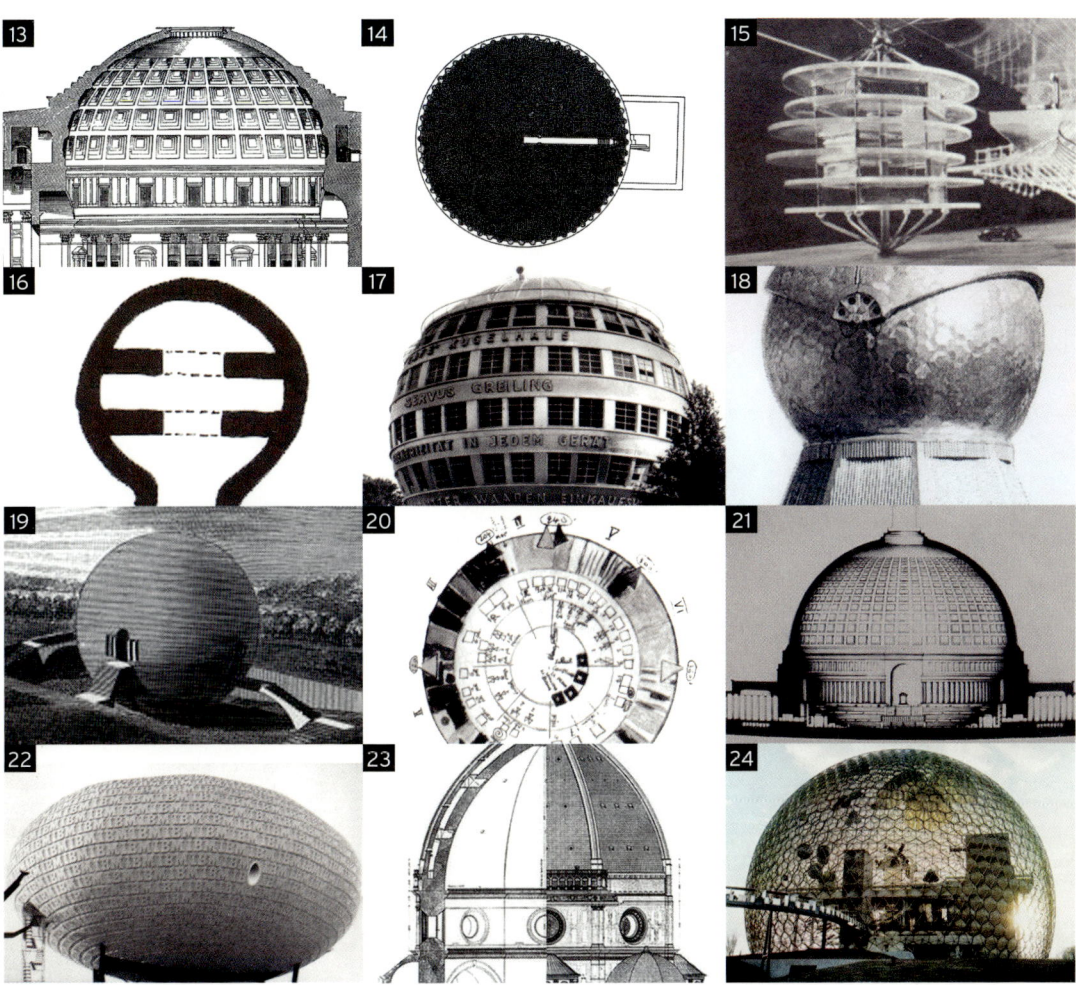

13. Pantheon (attributed to Apollodorus of Damascus)

14. Medracen Mausoleum, near Batna, Argelia

15. New Babylon (Constant Nieuwenhuys)

16. Roman kiln, found all over the Mediterranean countries

17. Kugelhaus in Dresden (Peter Birkenholz)

18. Okno radar near Nurekskoj, Tajikistan

19 House of the Gardener (Claude Nicolas Ledoux)

20. Philips Pavilion diagrams (Le Corbusier)

21. Volkshalle project in Berlin (Albert Speer)

22. IBM pavilion (Charles and Ray Eames)

23. Santa Maria del Fiore cupola (Filippo Brunelleschi)

24. Montréal Biosphere for Montréal '67 (Buckminster Fuller)

Competition project evolution

01. 02. 03. 04. 05. 06. Engravings depicting sea urchins with round and ellipsoidal shapes. **07. 08. 09. 10.** Early study sketches of the deformation of the sphere and base geometry of the masts.

11. Study sketch of the deformation of the courtyard. **12.** Study sketch of the geometry of the central pillar, 4/8 bases. **13. 14. 15. 16.** Sketches studying the inner vertical space and its deformation. Vertical

communication (ramps, staircases, etc). **17. 18. 19.** Study sketches of space division. **20. 21.** Study sketches of the deformation of the surface of the sphere and courtyard. **22.** Study sketch of the

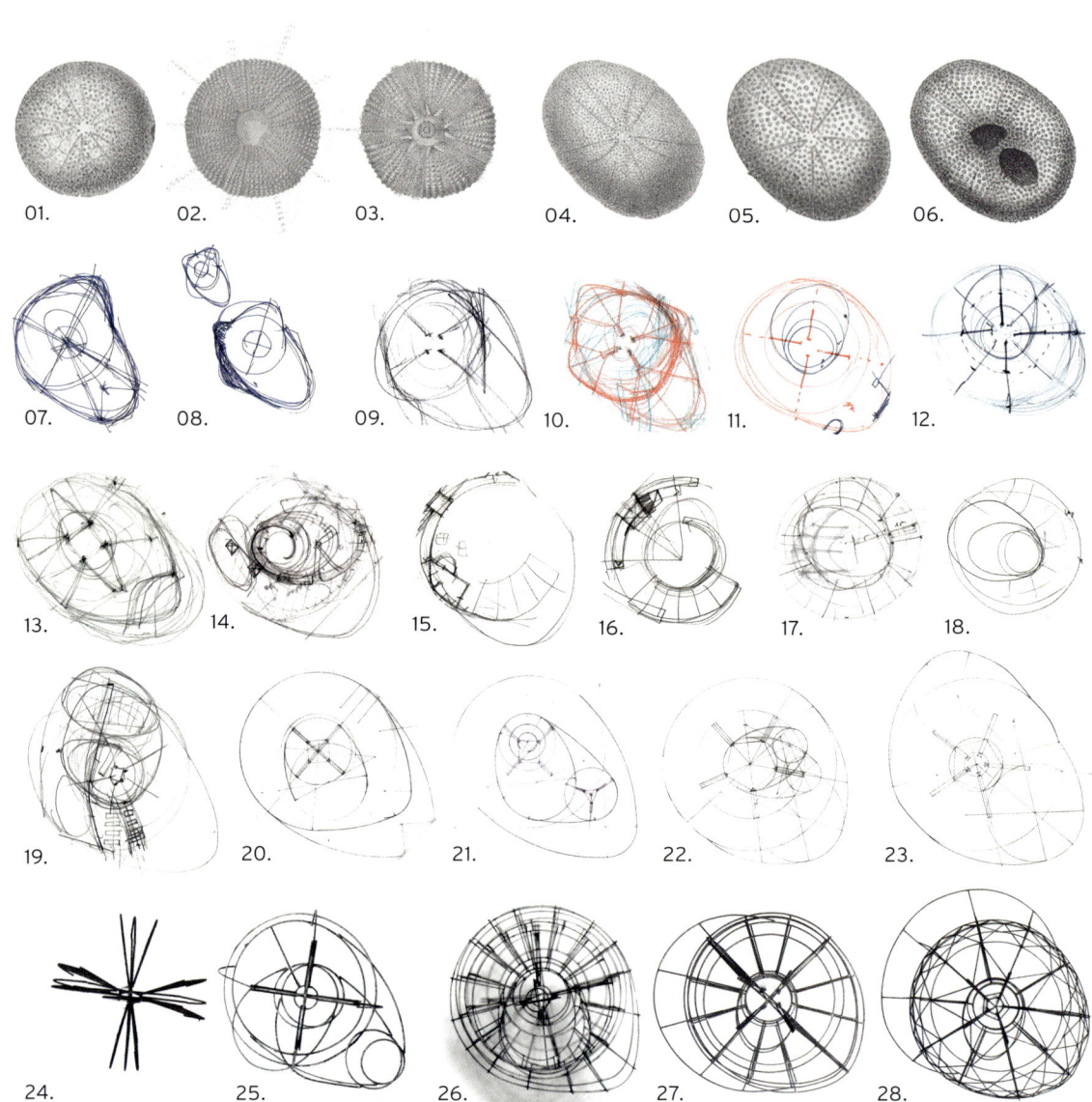

01.
02.
03.
04.
05.
06.

07.
08.
09.
10.
11.
12.

13.
14.
15.
16.
17.
18.

19.
20.
21.
22.
23.

24.
25.
26.
27.
28.

geometry of the pillar, 5 bases.

23. Study sketch of the deformation of the sphere with 5-base pillar geometry.

24. 25. Early study model with 4-base geometry. Scale: 1:300 Material: sol-dered wire.

26. 27. Study models of the volume and the skin deformation with 4-base geometry. Scale: 1:150. Material: sol-dered wire.

28. Study model of the skin grid with 5-base geometry-based and the sun-screen. Scale: 1:150. Material: soldered wire.

29. 30. 31. 32. 33. 34. Engravings depicting sea urchins with round and ellipsoidal shapes.

35. 36. 37. 38. 39. 40. Early study sketches of the relationship between the overall volume and the courtyard.

41. 42. 43. 44. 45. 46. Sectional study sketches of the central pillar and enclosure.

47. 48. 49. 50. 51. Sectional drawings of the overall project made during the competition stage.

52. 53. Early study model with 4-base geometry. Scale: 1:300 Material: sol-dered wire.

54. 55. Study model of the volume and the skin deforma-tion with 4-base geometry. Scale: 1:150. Material: sol-dered wire.

56. Study model of the skin grid with 5-base geometry-based and the sun-screen. Scale: 1:150. Material: soldered wire.

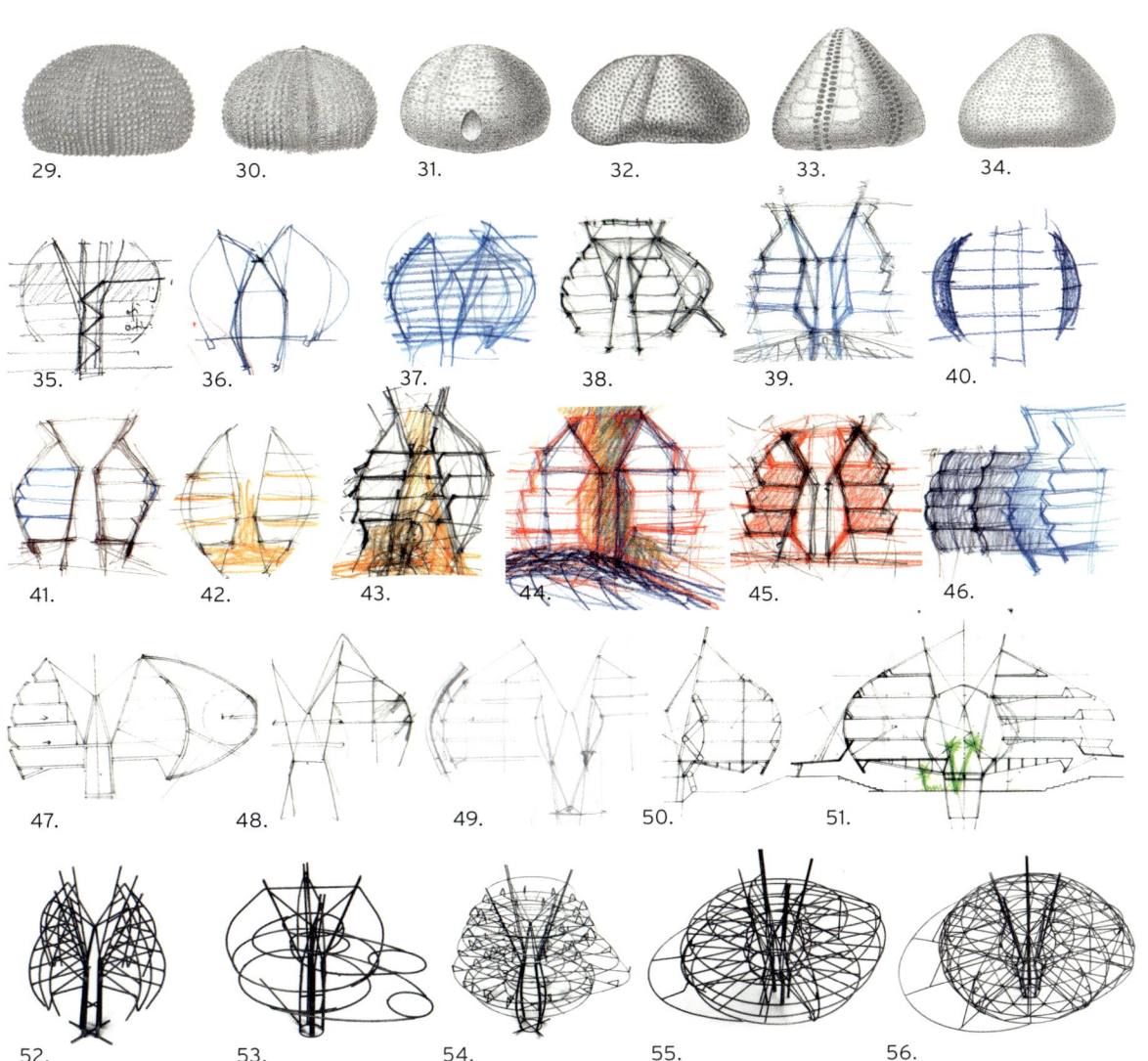

29. 30. 31. 32. 33. 34.

35. 36. 37. 38. 39. 40.

41. 42. 43. 44. 45. 46.

47. 48. 49. 50. 51.

52. 53. 54. 55. 56.

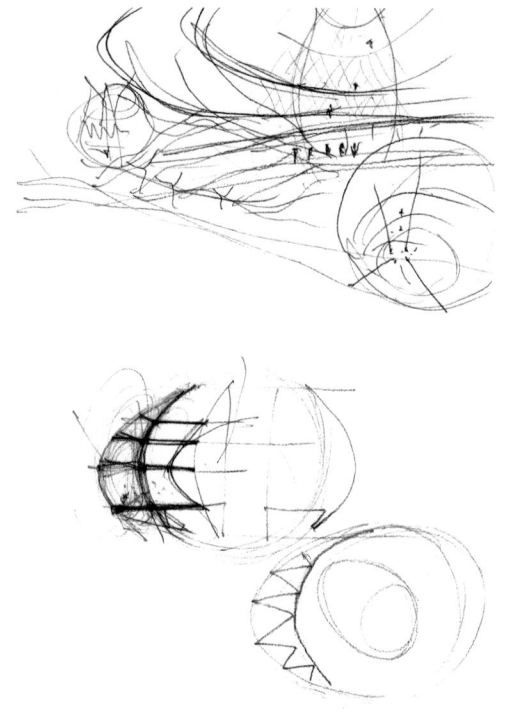

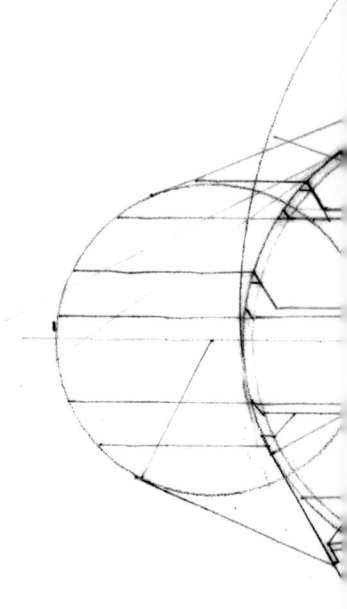

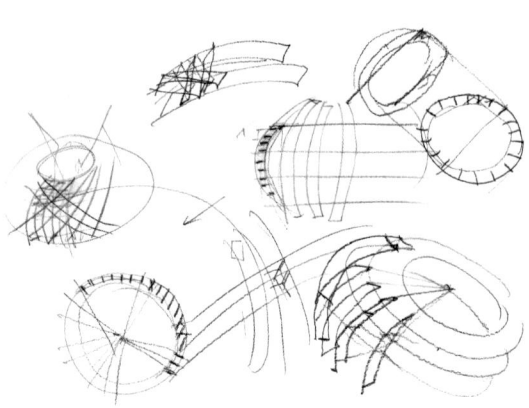

We are interested in geometry. It is the basis of what we do. Form is a result of dialogue with it. The particular form of this building arises from the question why we have five fingers or why the starfish has five arms. There are laws in nature that let you see which numbers work best.

You think about the pillar. And you try out a triangular or hexagonal pillar. And when you arrive at the pentagon. Its geometry let you divide by ten, and by twenty until you arrive at the circumference. As you walk from the centre of the building outwards, you cross 5, 10 and 20-module spaces, and this happens so naturally that you think the central pillar can be no other way.

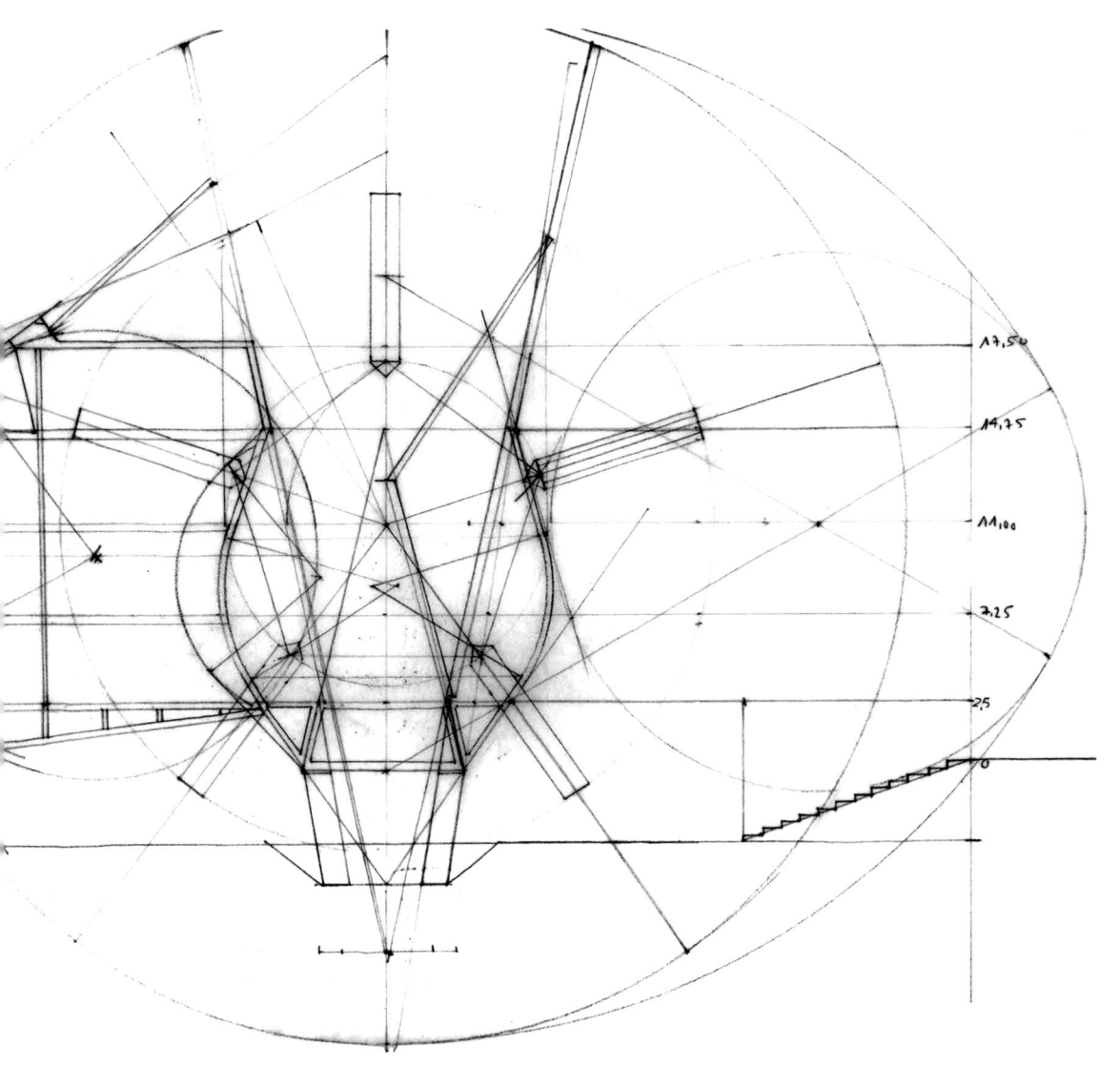

17,50

14,75

11,00

3,25

2,5

0

109

01. Sketch of an aerostatic balloon on the landscape **02. 03. 04. 05.** Study sketches of the structural section of the office building and warehouse. **06. 07. 08.** Study sketches of the contact between the upper volume and the platform. **09.** Study sketch of the relationship between the spherical office and warehouse buildings, where the first hovers above the second. **10.** Competition model. Scale: 1:200. Materials: soldered wire and laser-cut acrylic sheets. **11.** Scale study model of the topography, side view. Scale: 1:400. Material: soldered wire. **12.** Scale study model of the inclusion in the plot, side view. Scale: 1:200. Materials: soldered wire. **13. 14. 15. 16.** Study sketches of spherical volumes aggregation systems. **17. 18.** Preliminary sketches of occupation of the site.

01.

02.

03.

04.

05.

06.

07.

08.

09.

10.

11.

12.

19. Study sketch of the building embedded in the topography.
20. Structural study sketch of the warehouse and skylights.
21. Study sketch of the accesses to the site.
22. Study sketch of the layout of ground floor as it relates to the platform
23. Competition model, overhead view. Scale: 1:200. Material: soldered wire sheets and laser-cut acrylic sheet.
24. Study model of the embedment in the site, overhead view. Scale: 1:200. Material: soldered wire.

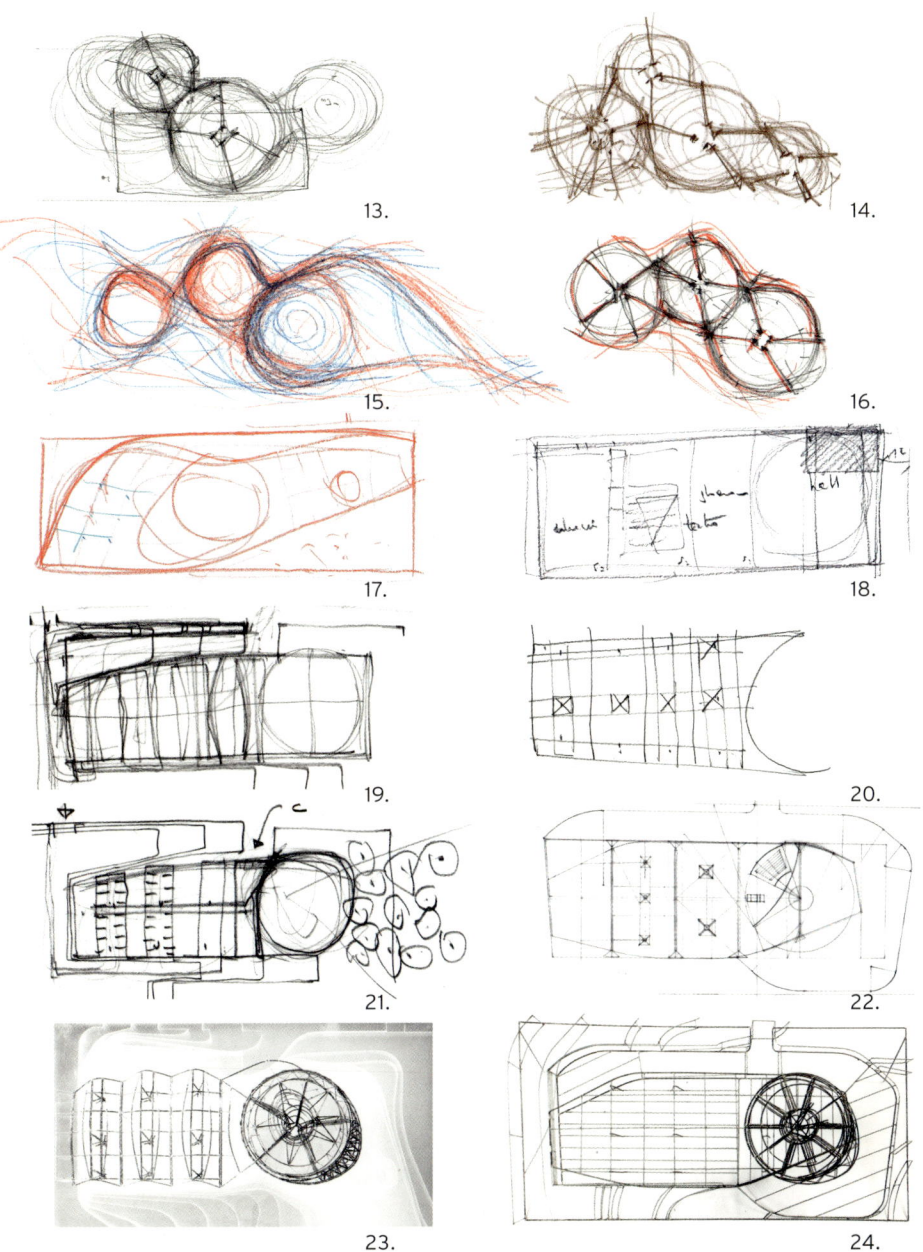

13.

14.

15.

16.

17.

18.

19.

20.

21.

22.

23.

24.

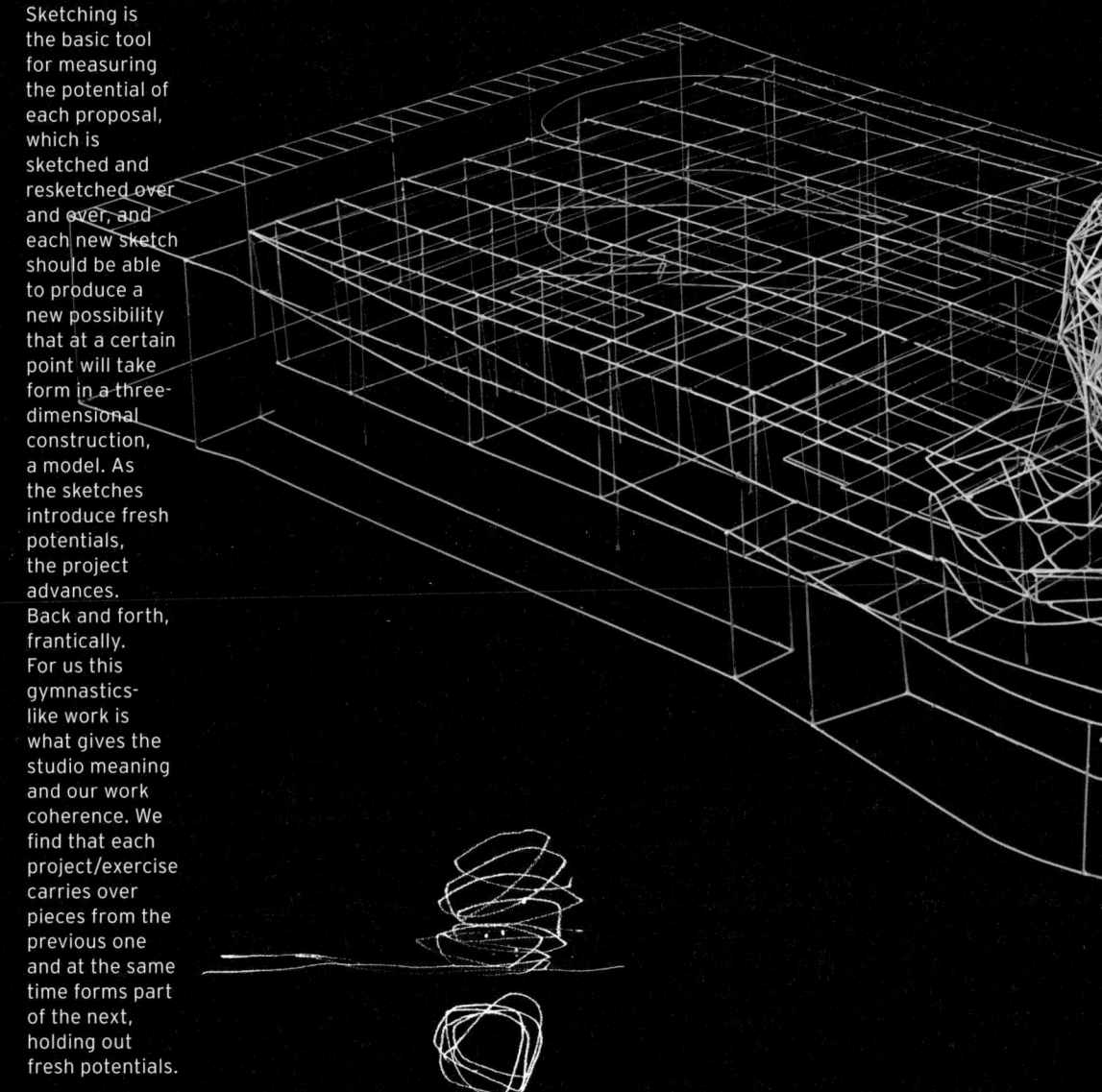

Sketching is
the basic tool
for measuring
the potential of
each proposal,
which is
sketched and
resketched over
and over, and
each new sketch
should be able
to produce a
new possibility
that at a certain
point will take
form in a three-
dimensional
construction,
a model. As
the sketches
introduce fresh
potentials,
the project
advances.
Back and forth,
frantically.
For us this
gymnastics-
like work is
what gives the
studio meaning
and our work
coherence. We
find that each
project/exercise
carries over
pieces from the
previous one
and at the same
time forms part
of the next,
holding out
fresh potentials.

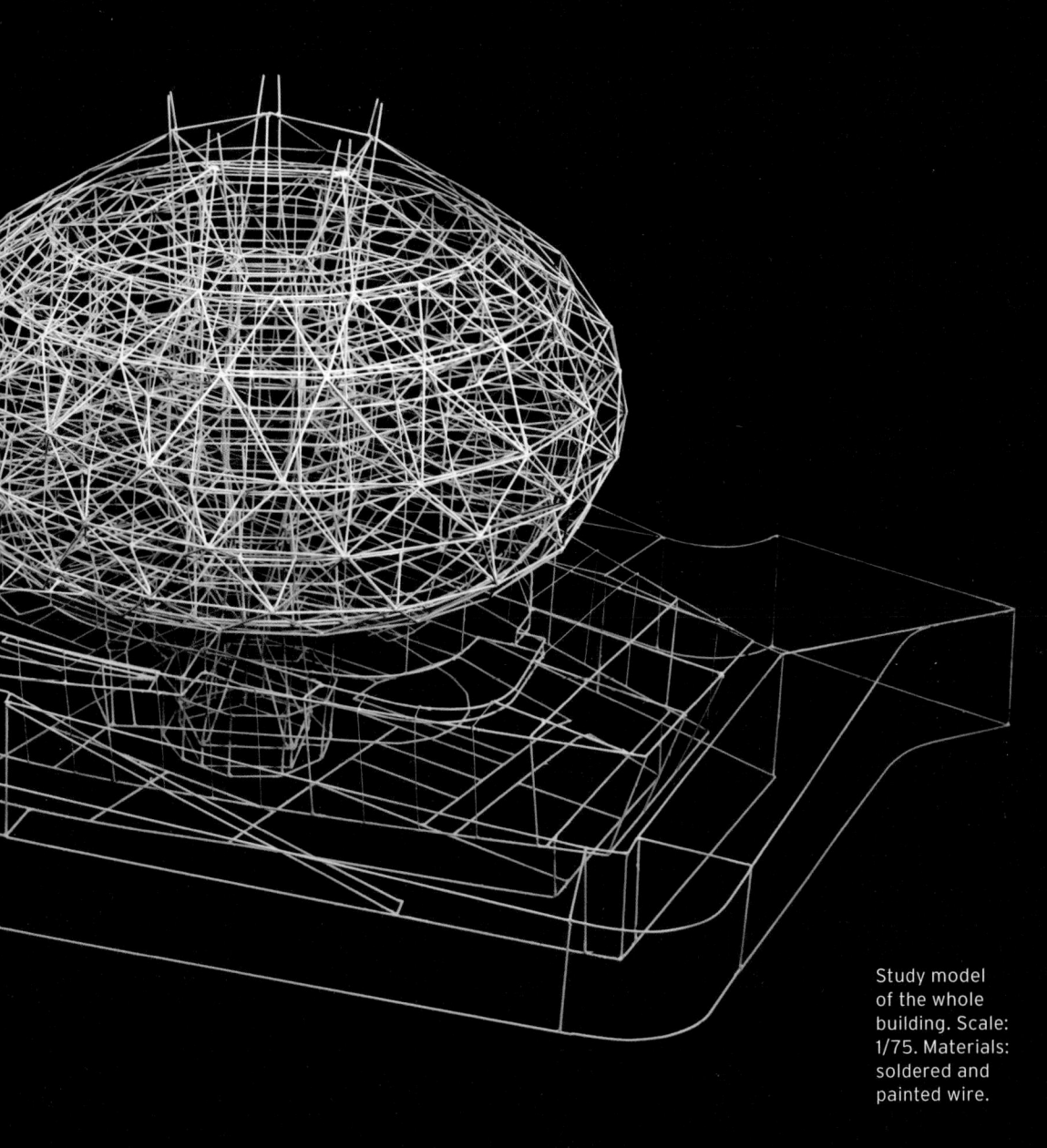

Study model
of the whole
building. Scale:
1/75. Materials:
soldered and
painted wire.

Studies of
enveloping
geometries
starting from
the central
pentagon.

Studies of the
inner space,
or courtyard,
around which
the office floors
are arranged.

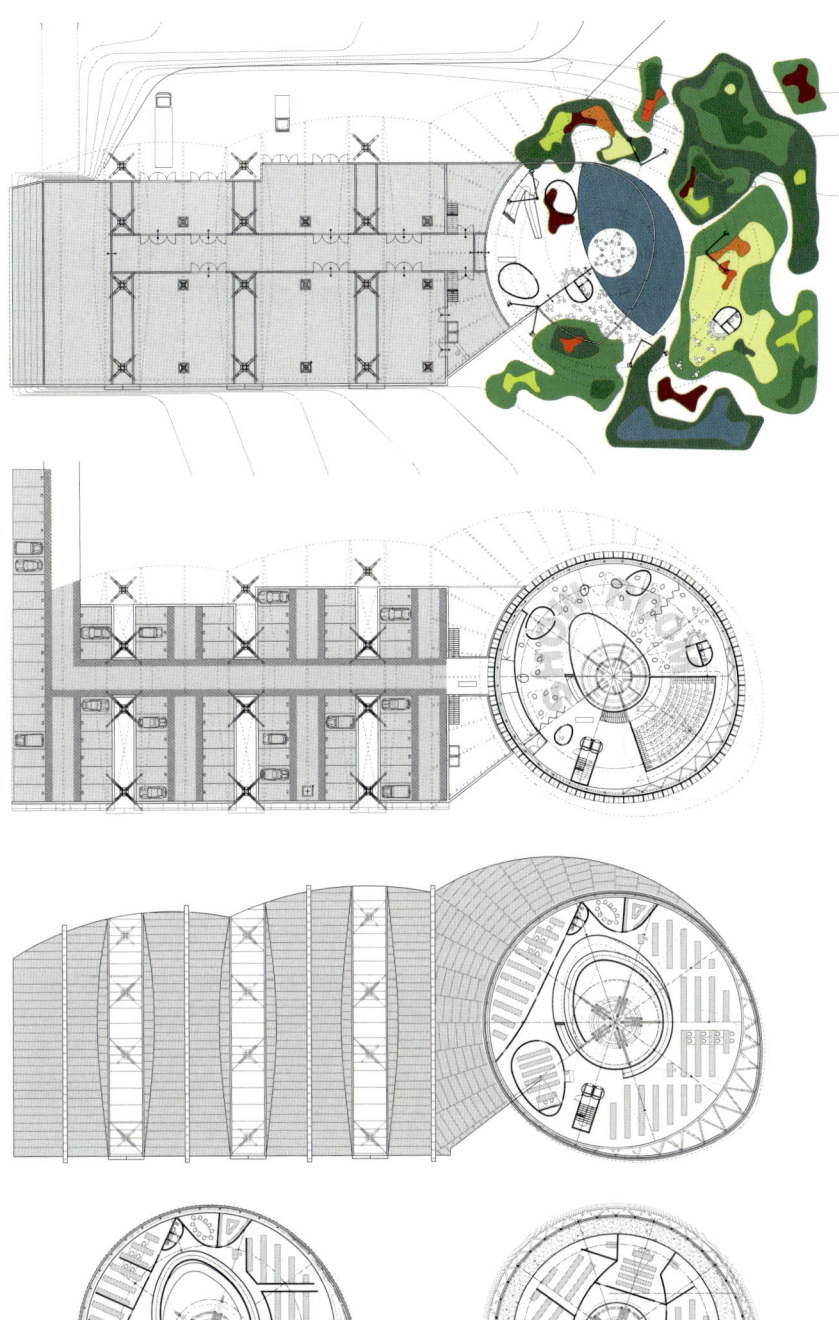

Project plans
in competition
phase.

Exhibiting
the proposal

Draft plans and models were exhibited at the Catalan Architects Association (COAC) Building in Barcelona. The exhibition included videos, sketches and over 150 study and competition models that we produced in defining the building. Competition model. Scale 1:200. Materials: soldered wire and laser-cut acrylic sheets.

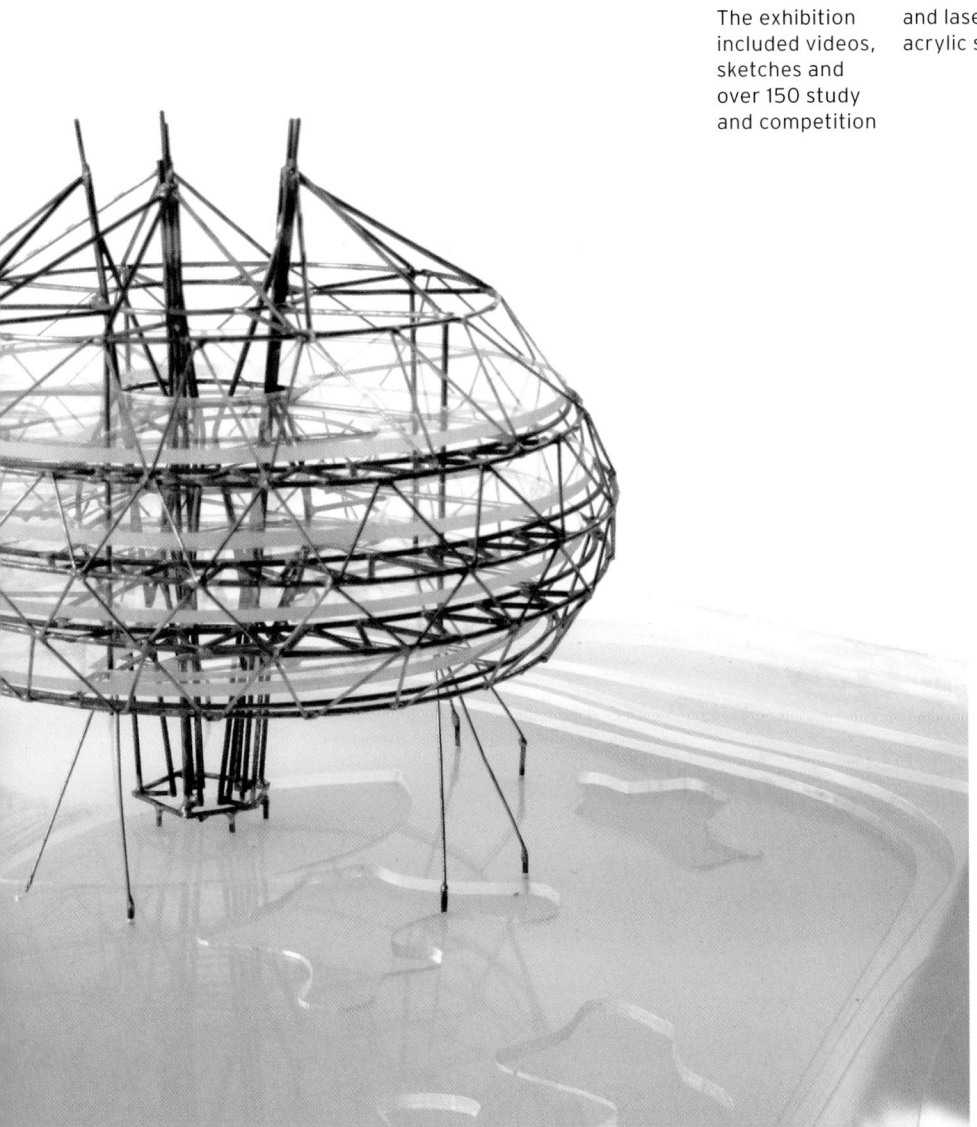

Early morning
on opening day
a 1:10-scale
metal model
is mounted on
top of the COAC
Building in Plaça
de la Catedral,
Barcelona.
This sequence
of photos shows
the installation
of the model.
The precise
location of
this model in
relation to COAC
Building reflects
the location of
the project on
its actual site.
The aerostatic
balloon has
finally managed
to get off the
ground and land
in the centre of
Barcelona.

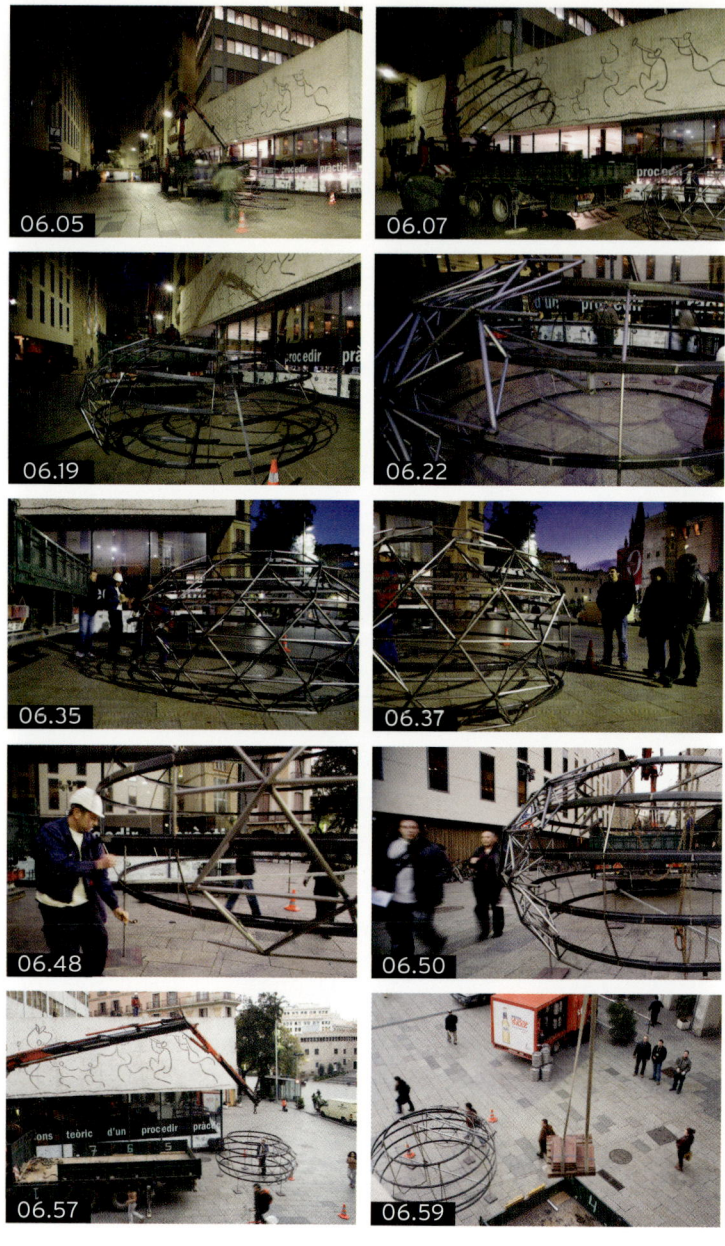

06.05

06.07

06.19

06.22

06.35

06.37

06.48

06.50

06.57

06.59

119

The "Il Cielo iGuzzini" exhibit was not intended to show a finished project, but rather the work and design processes of a project.
It sought to explain the development of an idea from its conception through the successive trials to its materialisation in drawings, showing the intense, painstaking process behind the final definition of an architecture.
The models are displayed in cases that recall those of a natural science museum, evoking the evolution of an exotic beast.

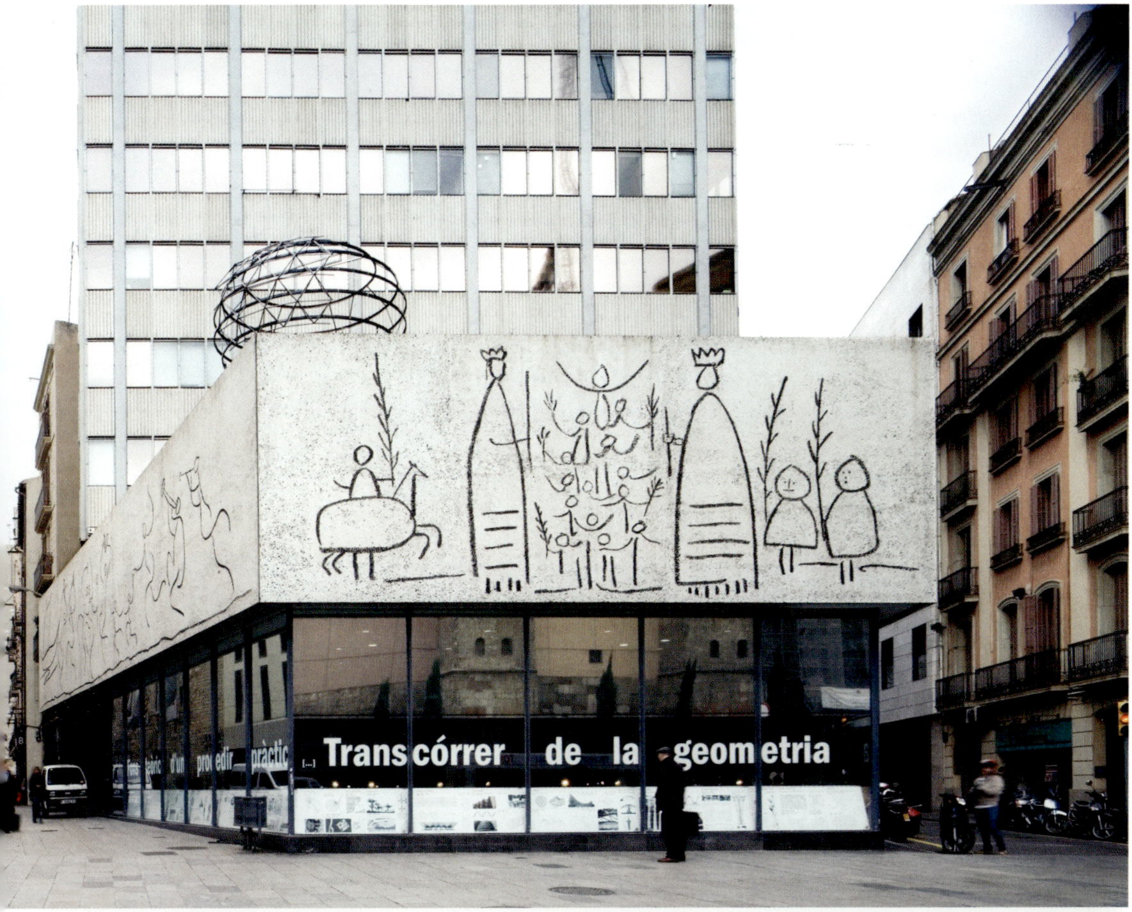
Transcórrer de la geometria

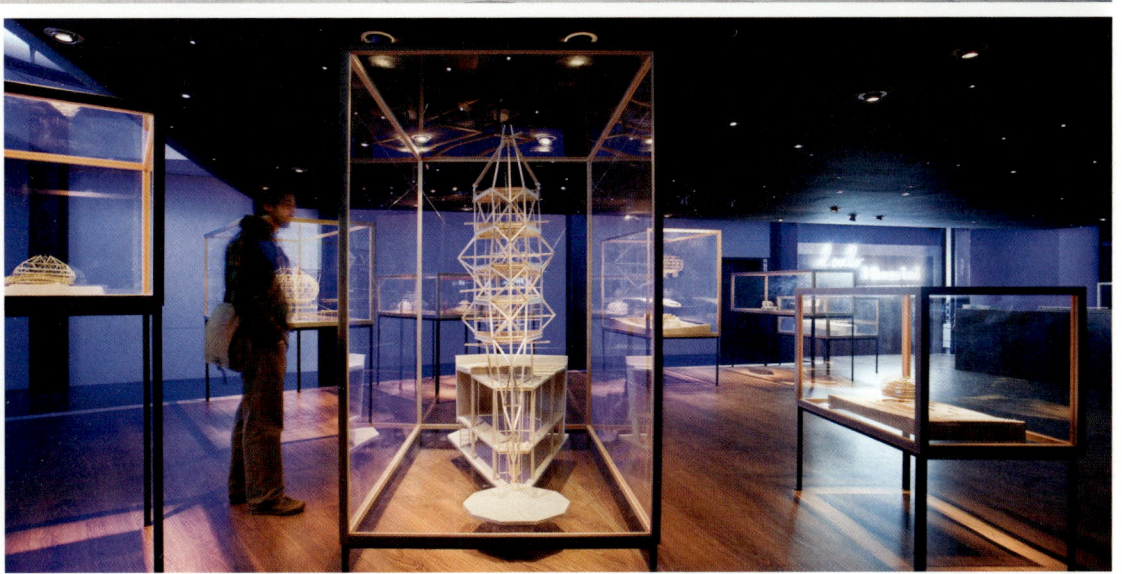

GOING UNDERGROUND

Preparing the landscape
Jorge García de la Cámara

If anything has characterised the recent work of Josep Miàs in his civil–institutional or recreational–projects, it is the stress on awareness of the omnipresent structure that runs through them and makes them possible, and, wherever feasible, a will for topographic manipulation of the environment as an instrument of dialogue with its immediate and distant landscape. Both invariants are for Miàs "foundational" instruments of the project, which always seeks to push them to their limits.

The project for the iGuzzini corporate headquarters responds to a large extent to these two interests that form common threads in the work of Josep Miàs. A strictly formal reading of the project might suggest that the iGuzzini Building marks a turning point in his work. However, careful examination of the project not only confirms that it represents a step firmly rooted in the continuity of the architectural interests found in the bulk of his work. Indeed we can see a step forward in the formal incorporation of new elements in the project that remove it from certain local tectonic tradition very much present in his early work, an evolution that is evident in a strengthening of the objectual character of the building, in its symbolic character in relation to the programme and the specificity of the client, or even in the experimentation with more intangible materials... Nonetheless, in the original conceptual basis and purpose of the iGuzzini project as an intellectual exercise, the architectural invariants of manipulation of the territory and structural omnipresence remain. Thus, the central element, almost the silent point of departure of this project, is not the sphere poised to settle on the ground or break loose into flight. Rather it is, to a great extent, the platform, based upon which the sphere is able to come into play and acquire meaning and identity. The role of this platform is essential to an understanding of the whole.

From a topographical point of view, the platform organises the slope to coordinate an artificial landscape, which, in addition to organising the different needs of access and traffic, in a very subtle deformation in section, tensions its surfacial development in order to enhance, at one end of the site, the apparent instability of the sphere. With this virtually invisible action, the representational character of the iGuzzini headquarters is concentrated and given meaning in the sphere. Thus it acquires a expressive, symbolic condition removed from iconographic intentions, amid the dense web of highways and roads around it.

From a functional standpoint, it accommodates a large part of the technological needs of a complex programme of co-existence between storage, research and display. Inwards, it creates the conditions of artificiality necessary for this work with light, from the most experimental to the strictly exhibitional; and on the outside, like a large plaza-access to the building, it creates the flexibility necessary for the work with and exhibition of light in outdoor spaces.

Thus there is a classic double composition in which, on one hand, a rational, organised, even introverted world contrasts with an organic, unstable and extroverted world; on the other hand, a classic compositional system focused on the use of a large foundation on which to seat a unique building. But what gives it contemporary validity is the committed use current techniques and technologies in its materialisation in terms of construction, structure and energy use.

As for the sphere, it is entirely structure, despite its apparent lightness. By means of a system of tensioners and a three-dimensional surfacial envelope, the floors hang from the complex system of masts which emerges from the subsoil and configures the courtyard that collectivises the entire building. The iGuzzini sphere, its central structure expanded at the surface, the way in which it relates unsteadily to the terrain, recalls the old *gambina*, a manual fishing implement traditional to the Girona coast: a simple unitary structure made from woven reeds, with a central cylindrical body that expands to develop a spherical volume. To make this system work, a simple coupling of weights ensured that the bait would be deposited on the seabed. The secret of the *gambina*, beyond its form and structure, was how it was able to settle into the sea and from there interact and generate attraction. The skills of the craftsman and the fisherman are, in this project, those of Josep Miàs, who knows well that which is of interest in architecture is often found in everyday uses, in the relationships the generate and in the muscles that make them possible.

Jorge García de la Cámara,
Architect, Director of BIArch (Barcelona Institute of Architecture)

Metal cage for fishing in the mediterranean, called *gambina* popularly.

Study model of the outdoor showroom, warehouse volume and their fit into the topography. Scale: 1:100. Materials: balsa wood and soldered wire. Presented at the exhibit "Il Cielo iGuzzini" at the Catalan Architects Association (COAC) Building in Barcelona. The topography of the site was sloped, which was not altered in the architectural proposal: the basement of the building is embedded in the site at its highest point and is exposed as the ground slopes naturally downward.

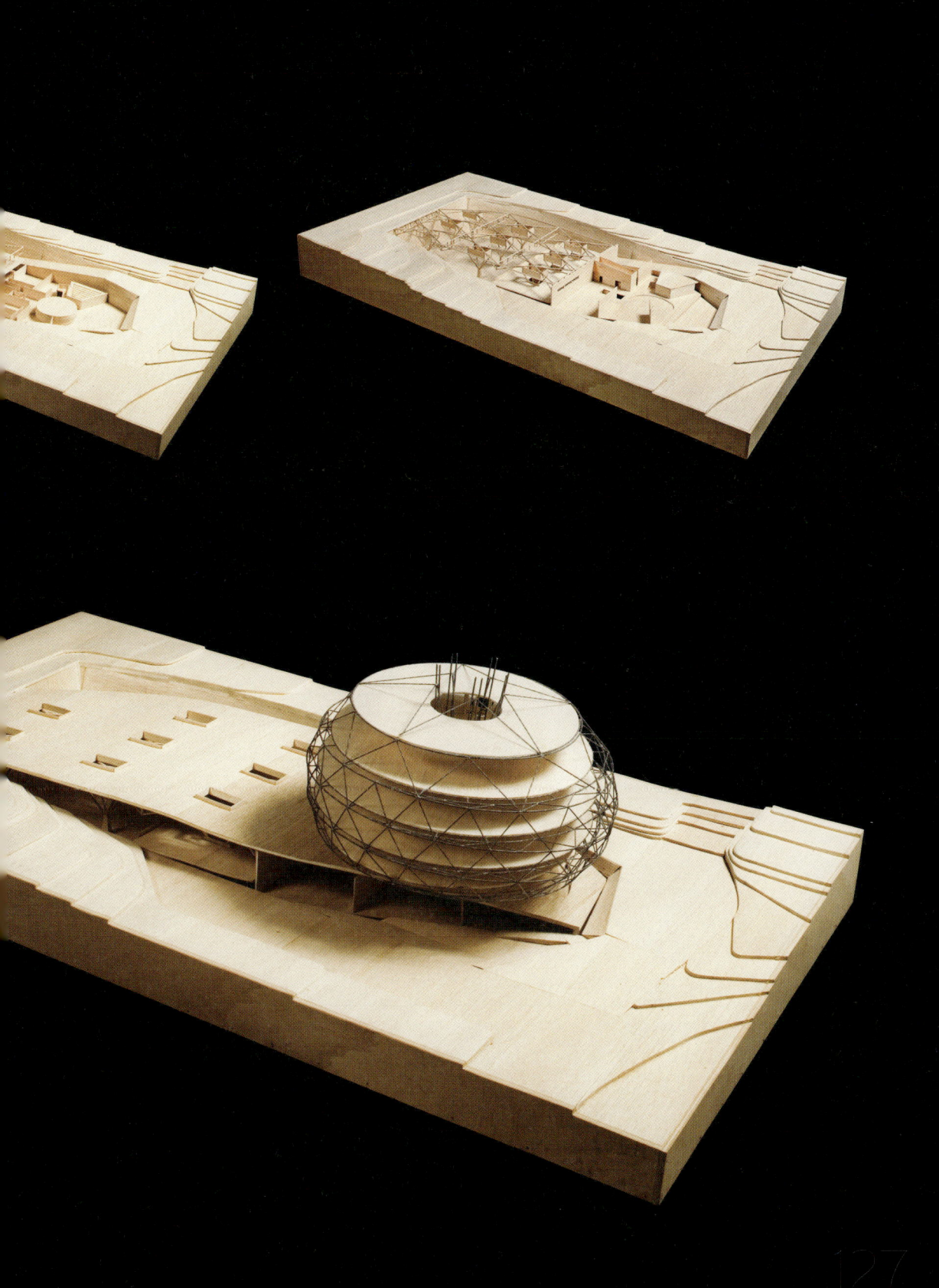

127

Excavation of the site for the large underground part of the building. A total of 40,700 m³ (1,695 truckloads) of earth was removed to lower the ground level by 10 metres. Some earth was put aside for reuse to build green dunes around the building after it was finished.

The type of soil in this area, expansive clay, made a pile foundation necessary, using the CPI-8 system. The system uses continuous flight auger piles, which were driven to depths from 10 m to 16 m. Once the correct depth was reached with the pile driver, the auger is removed at same time as the concrete is pumped in through the central core of the screw, keeping several diameters of the auger tip in the concrete at all times. After pouring the concrete, the reinforcement was inserted to the bottom of the pile by means of a hydraulic vibrator.

131

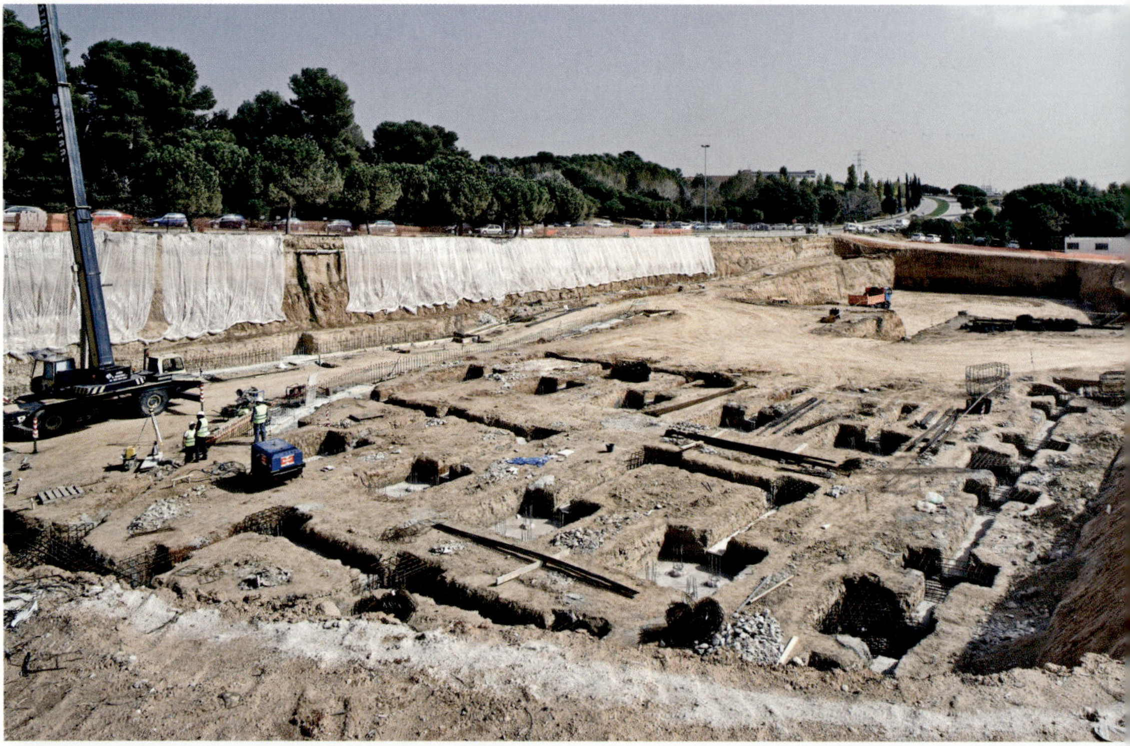

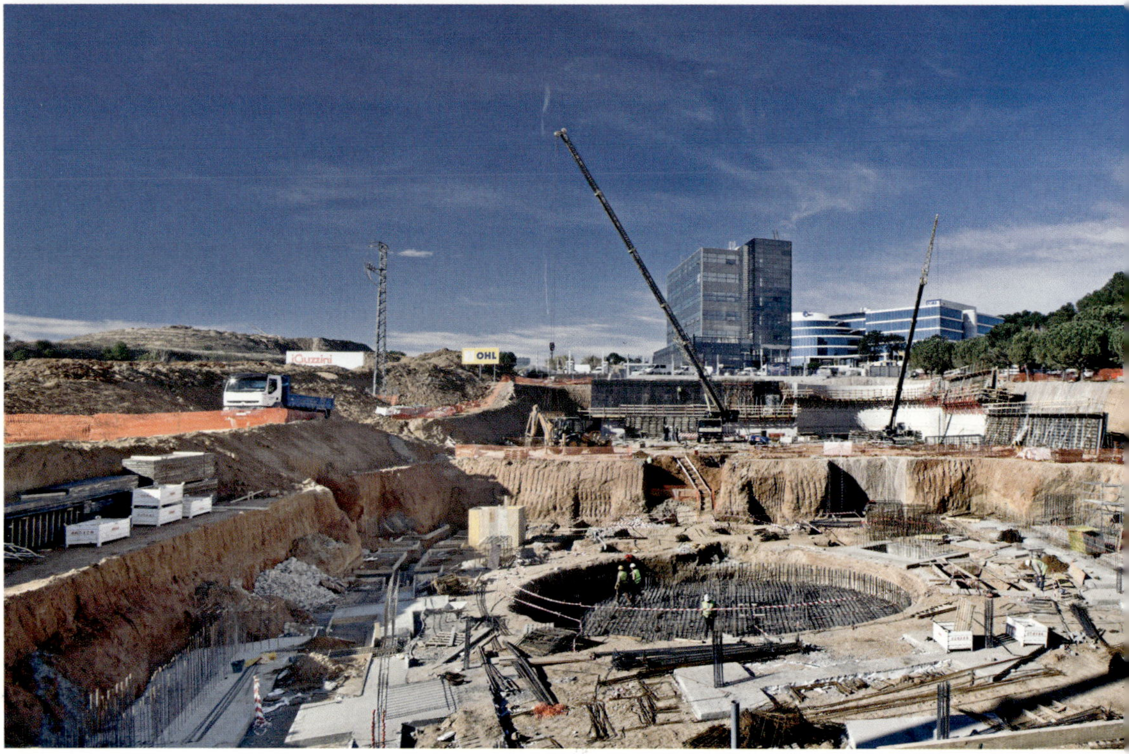
iGuzzini
OHL

In making the piles, 1,100 m³ of concrete were used, while the pile caps consumed another 1,739 m³, for a total of 474 cement-mixer loads.

The total length of the piles is nearly 5 km:
-3,324 lm of 45 cm-diameter piles;
-1,147 lm of 65 cm-diameter piles;
-326 lm of 85 cm-diameter piles.

If we measured the building from the crown of the central pillar to the bottom of the deepest of the piles that ensure its stability, the height would be 54 m, the equivalent of an 18-storey building.

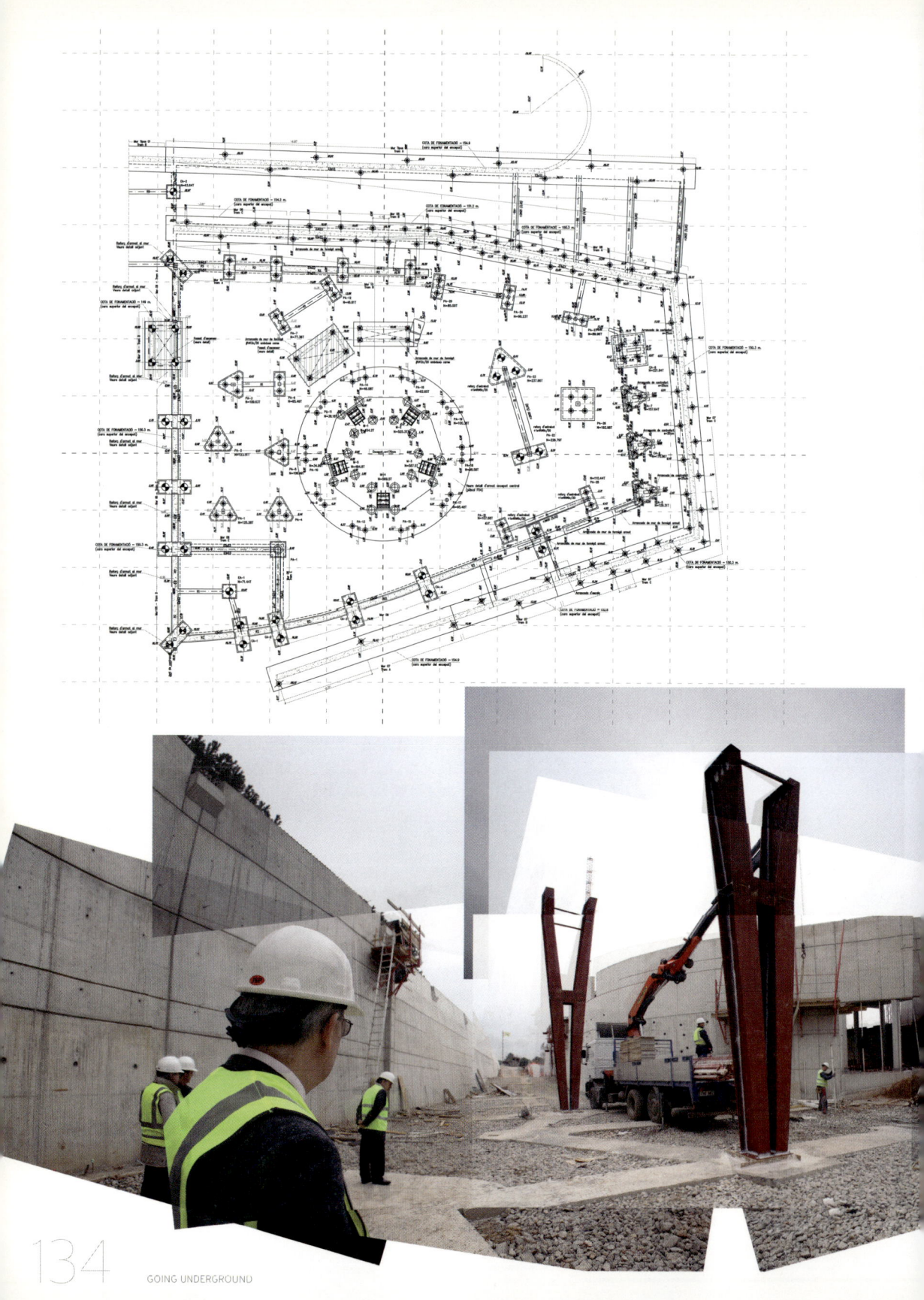

GOING UNDERGROUND

The construction of the containment walls required over 1,000 m³ of concrete and 6,000 m² of double-faced modular formwork.

The warehouse structure is made up of pre-cast concrete pillars and girders and hollow core slabs 50 cm thick and up to 15 m in length. This system enables considerable savings in construction time and above all large spans with few bearing points, meaning increased storage capacity in terms of useful space and greater ease of movement for the electric vehicles used in warehouse operations.

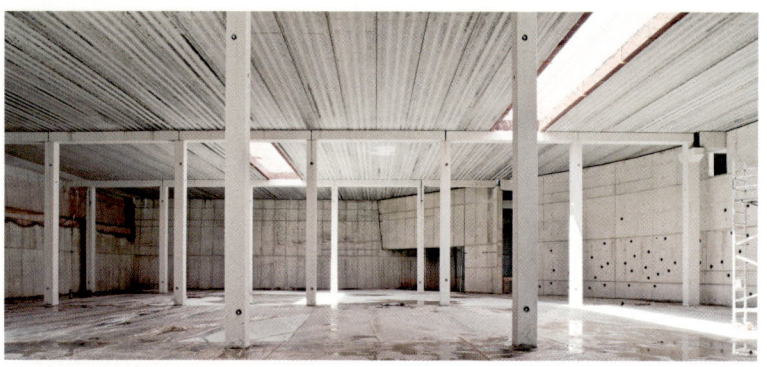

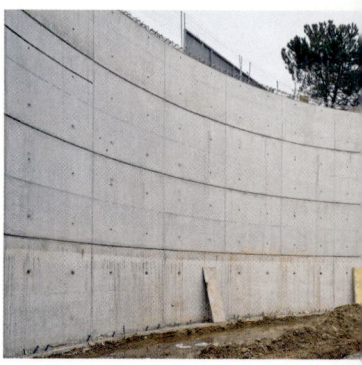

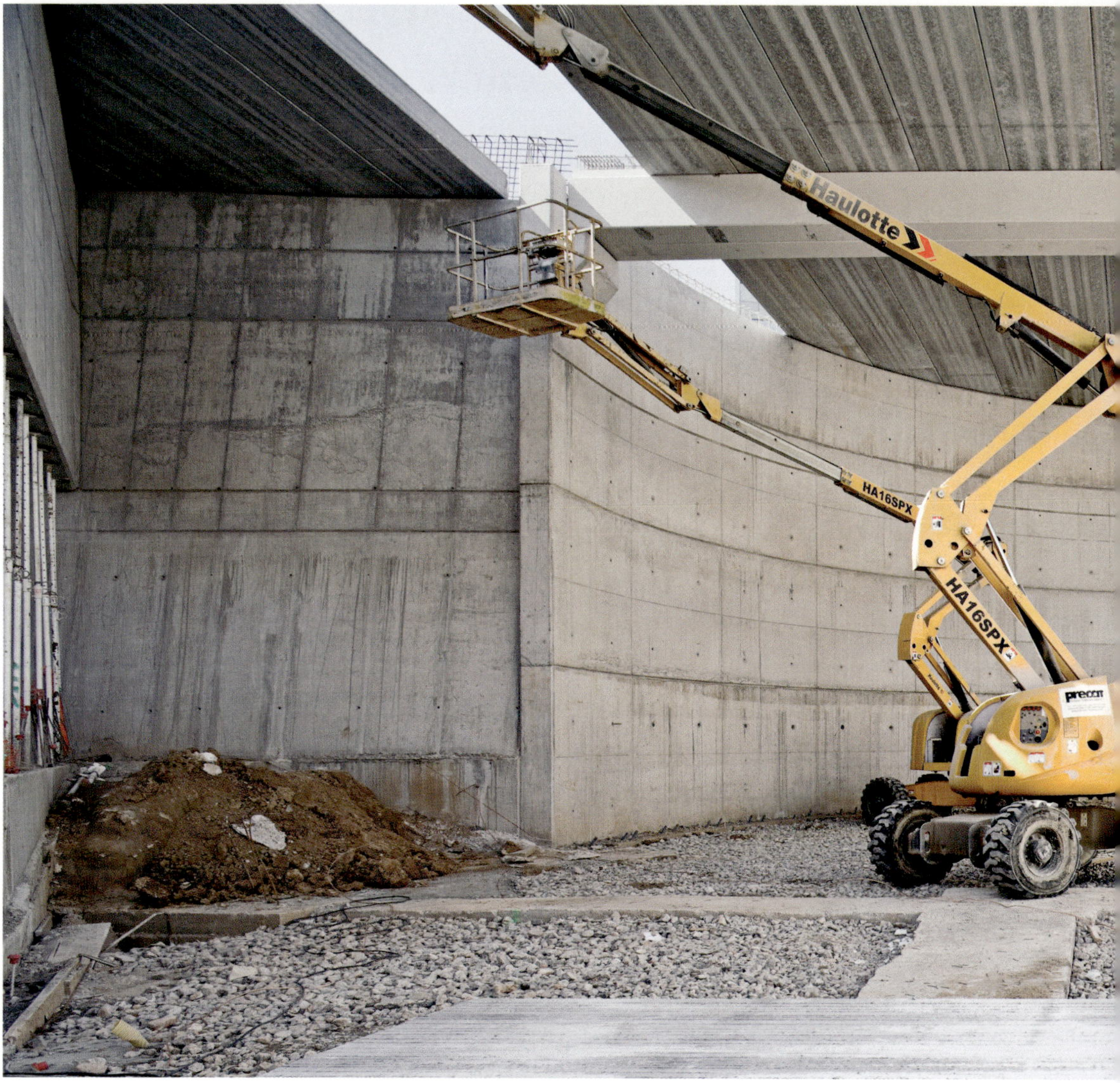
Haulotte
HA16SPX
HA16SPX
precon

The concrete box of the platform, enclosed with slanting concrete structural walls, will be used as a showroom sealed off from natural light. The structural system of central pillar is, on the other hand, completely independent. The pillar is inserted through a hole in the concrete box, which bears the load of the glazed building. Above the hollow-core slab ceiling, the double-curved surface of the outdoor showroom will be laid using a raised metal floor equipped with adjustable pedestals.

SUSPENDING A STRUCTURE

Structural systems
Agustí Obiol

The moment that humankind ceased to appropriate the dwellings supplied ready-made by nature—caves—in order to settle in the most suitable places for subsistence, we found ourselves faced with the need to create our own spaces, to enclose and adapt them to provide us with shelter, safety and comfort. At that very instant, our actions came into direct conflict with the force of gravity.

On the plains, where there are no outstanding natural features to exploit, the most elementary solution is that which consists of lashing a number of branches or logs together at one end and splaying the other end to form a circular directrix; once we have arranged this skeleton with its axis of rotation oriented vertically and filled the gaps with foliage, we have a vernacular cone conforming to a certain type of hut.

If we analyze this "structural scheme" from the contemporary perspective, we can conclude that it is a framework whose principal components work mainly in compression, especially if care is taken to place hoops around it in the manner of parallels, or if the covering material is able to develop a type of performance we now call laminar, the potential local and global moments (bending and turning, respectively) are absorbed through elementary compression/tension mechanisms, with a clear predominance of the former.

But obviously this sort of hut has severe limitations in terms of usability, let alone with regard to increasing its size.

Going beyond this elementary geometry to create more flexible spaces, larger sizes or multiple inhabitable layers inevitably leads to the concept of the flat roof and gives rise to flexural stress.

This stress is not only inevitable but also uneconomic; concentrating on one section the volumes of compression and tension—as must happen if some moment is to be developed—whose triangular distribution leads to only about 50% of the potential of the section being

Hut built from linear elements forming cones. Ona culture.

SUSPENDING A STRUCTURE

used, and limiting the lever arm according to its edge, has a fundamental impact on the "amount of structure" needed to cover a certain span.

That is why, when this variable—the span to cover—exceeds no more than 10 or 15 m, the beam "decomposes" into a truss, and we end up with a collection of tubes and uprights that work almost exclusively in either compression or tension, rather than bearing both types of stress at once and thus allowing us to calibrate the lever arm as we see fit.

Steel, by primarily responding to stress "symmetrically"—ie, virtually identically in tension and compression—is particularly suitable as a material for elements or systems operating under any sort of axial stress.

But this symmetry is not absolute; firstly, because in thin sections compression creates a problem of instability (buckling) that is absent in the case of tension, and, secondly, because we are able to make steel in very thin geometries—above all cables, but also rods—with strengths significantly greater than those of more conventional sections, and, obviously, these geometries so thin they are unable to withstand compression stress.

In any case, optimised response of axial geometries is not a feature of this material alone; with concrete, as well, the structure can be reduced extraordinarily when the form of the latter makes it possible to mobilise funicular polygon structure definition, by composition of forces, rather than having to resort to bending mechanisms, where the above said vector composition is replaced by simple "lateral displacement".

Knowledge of these principles is what makes possible the class of structures known as suspension or tensile. This means creating funicular—in fact, anti-funicular—lines or surfaces in which each individual load is balanced vectorially with the sum of the internal forces developed by the system at the node on which the load acts. The geometric stability of the system is bolstered by the permanent nature of a significant portion of its

Castells are multi-storey human constructions erected on feast days and now the focus of competitions held throughout Catalonia, where they originated. Their structures resemble that of the iGuzzini Building, a central pillar made up of masts.

145

own acting forces (single curvature), or by implementing systems of counterpoised, mutually pre-stressed components (double curvature).

A good example of the first solution is the roof of Dulles Airport in Washington, DC, by Eero Saarinen, while probably the most historically important example of the second variation is the Munich Olympic Stadium, by Frei Otto.

In both cases, we immediately find elements as alien to the tensile network as they are inseparable from its inception, as well as having an evident visual impact: masts. By definition, anything that is suspended needs suspension points, and if the geometry is particularly complex, as in the case of the Munich Stadium, the masts themselves are not enough, rather a second family of "internal" elements, likewise subjected to axial compression, must also be introduced: braces.

All such constructions have in common that the loads follow an upward trajectory, mobilising often "diffuse" mechanisms of tension—especially in double-curve roofs and cantilever spar cable-stayed bridges—before beginning their descent to the ground through a small number of heavily compressed elements. This makes for a triple paradigm: minimise flexural stresses, universalise tension, and concentrate compression on a small number of inevitably rather bulky elements.

Obviously, it is not chance, but the indisputable mechanical efficiency of this type of structure the reason why, in the 1950s, when Myron Goldsmith and Fazlur Khan drew up their ranking of the various structural types they rated this one the best able to cover large spans.

However, all of these arguments become less applicable where we don't have so much freedom to play around with the geometry, since it is from structural geometry that the dominant form of the framework is derived. If we are dealing not with a simple project but a covered multi-storey building, where the floors must conform to a certain regularity, the parabolic paths of tensioned

The main terminal of Dulles International Airport, Washington, DC, with its suspended catenary roof, was designed by Eero Saarinen.

tendons are meaningless.

Still, the basic principles remain: deploy tension as extensively as possible, concentrating the forces of compression, and minimise the volumes of bending, either diminishing or concentrating them; in either case, following the principle of first diffusing the loads upwards, and then concentrating them downwards.

As we have said above, the geometric—and primarily volumetric—constraints to which all of these buildings are subjected are an impediment to the use of "more flexible" mechanisms; the need to redirect the loads from the perimeter to the core—or the other way round, as in the last case examined here—in flat-roofed, vertical-façade buildings makes the use of bending mechanisms to effect this redirection virtually inevitable.

But in the absence of these requirements, we have a new range of possibilities.

In the process of scientific advancement, people have always started by observing the world around them. But later on, in creating their own technological or artistic objects, often they have also used their world as a reference, with the understanding that "natural objects" never cease to adapt, evolving towards broadly optimised forms due to the simple passage of time, through mechanisms of trial and error or, in Darwinian terms, the evolution of the species.

In the field of architectural production countless people have at some point in their work been tempted to follow this path to greater or lesser extent. To name someone both close to home and widely known, we might mention Antoni Gaudí.

Simply observing our environment, specifically the trees of our cities and countryside, we find a good example of the structural pattern that is produced by spreading out from a central core. A tree is, in essence, just that: a main core rising from the earth more or less vertically in order to reach a height at which it can begin to develop and occupy the space immediately around it.

Frei Otto's design for the Munich Olympic Stadium for the 1972 Summer Olympics.

The structural
solution
acquired its final
definition after
multidisciplinary
meetings
between Josep
Miàs, Agustí
Obiol and Josep
Ramon Solé
of BOMA, and
Josep Maria
González
and Jaume
Avellaneda
of the
Construction
Department of
the Polytechnic
University of
Catalonia (UPC).

But, as often happens, from here the possibilities of exploiting certain parallels diminish, and this is because, at least in principle, the stimuli which the growth of a tree and a building respond to are clearly different. While the tree spreads outwards for the sole purpose of capturing the maximum amount of solar radiation through its leaves, the goal of the building is to provide, under this umbrella, inhabitable volumes. Thus the former grows out in all directions in space, while the latter "huddles" around its own core, reversing the path it followed in its growth phase.

This divergence between the goals of either creation, along with the difference in the effects of gravity and wind on them—the tree, relatively lightweight and very exposed, allowing the flow of air through its branches and leaves; the building, far heavier and scarcely exposed due to the enclosure of its interior space—means that the structural patterns to which they adapt are also quite different.

While the building conforms to the aforementioned trinomial—concentrated compression/concentrated bending/diffuse tension—to the very end to the ends of its branches, the tree responds fundamentally by means of bending mechanisms; both its branches and its trunk have much more resistance to simple compression or tension than strictly required to withstand gravitational action.

There is, however one species that does not conform to this paradigm: the weeping willow. This tree, in seeking solar radiation, uses much more efficient mechanisms, hence the extremely high density of its foliage and, even more interesting, its relatively small amount of structure, defined as the ratio between the weight of the wood and the volume occupied.

Instead of projecting boldly outwards, overcoming gravity by bending (but at the risk of being literally torn off in winds of only slightly unusual strength) and leaving a relatively lifeless world at the centre of its crown (where solar radiation cannot penetrate), the branches of the weeping willow decrease rapidly in section as they move away from their starting point on the trunk such that they lose virtually all resistance to bending and act like free-swinging "ties".

Precisely due to this lack of rigidity, the slightest breeze–which can occur during many hours of the day–causes a constant movement of the branches, creating a play of light and shade that allows solar radiation to penetrate to great depths of the tree mass, such that the inner leaves too can thrive. Moreover, the more flexible response to the wind–and we must not forget that this is an essentially dynamic phenomenon and that, therefore, its effects can be controlled, at least in part, "through geometry"–also means less flexural stress on the trunk, thus enabling the optimisation of its mass in relation to the volume of space is occupies.

Thus, as a structural scheme, the weeping willow conforms to the compression/bending/tension trinomial to which we have repeatedly referred.

As happens in these cases, the poetic image of the correlative created by nature never fails to fascinate, but its translation to the realm of human creation is far from straightforward. For the bird that perches on a branch, this is its natural habitat, and the constant movement of its "building" and the air that flows through it–in both cases due to the effect of the breezes–are part of the environment in which it lives. Obviously, this is not applicable to humans.

But, by means of the simple functional occupation of the volume, both problems are solved automatically; in a mere geometric approach, the embedding of horizontal planes that enable people to occupy the space, and the surfacial envelope of the volume, generate a diaphragm effect which restores stability where once there had been movement, at the same time as confinement provides shelter where there had been exposure; moreover, this same diaphragmatic effect of what will

During these intense work sessions the structural solutions previously tested in wire models and the successive floor plan, section and detail drawings were verified.

eventually be the slabs allows the envelope to be configured more accurately, since the ties or tendons do not necessarily need to adopt perfectly vertical geometries, as long as the volumetric treatment conforms to certain norms of symmetry.

Just one weak point remains. The areas where the branches spring from the trunk, which operate based on a mechanism of rapidly diminishing resistance to bending as distance from the trunk increases, are far too flexible for any human construction.

Although we might be tempted to take a small step back in time and revive the hanging-platform schemes of the Torres de Colón in Madrid or the Standard Bank Building in Johannesburg, there is the possibility of retracing a much longer path through time—a few thousand years—to reinterpret the vernacular structure par excellence: the conical hut.

If we take a conical geometry and turn it upside down—such that the vertex is at the bottom and the base at the top—its load-bearing behaviour does not, in essence, change: the generators still work in the same way—basically in compression—while the parallels—the different sections defined by planes perpendicular to the axis—switch from working in compression to working in tension, which, as we pointed out above, is even better and offers more possibilities if made of steel. While this geometry is unstable, there is a simple solution to the problem without inverting the bases again: truncate the cone.

If we set the conical trunk atop a circular, potentially variable-diameter "hollow trunk", and we hang from the perimeter of the upper base our duly reinterpreted willow crown, we obtain a structural scheme in which the transition from compression centred on the trunk to the diffuse tension of the branches depends not on a heavy bending mechanism, but rather on an equally diffuse laminar effect, understood as an axial force enabler along the two primary directions of the surface. In

Building process of the Torres Colón in Madrid, designed by Antonio Lamela and built in 1976.

turn, the truncated cone becomes a means of capturing natural light, which will then spread easily throughout the depth of its core.

Having followed this road through the fundamentals, we finally come to the structural scheme of the iGuzzini Building, in essence, a hanging building that, like the weeping willow, takes a unique approach to the mechanisms of capturing sunlight. While the willow depends on constant movement—a condition which is unacceptable for a human construction—the iGuzzini enables and opens its core in order to allow the light to flow in.

Agustí Obiol,
Ph.D. in Architecture, co-founder of BOMA and Head of Structures Department at ETSAB Barcelona, UPC Barcelona Tech

Standard Bank Building in Johannesburg, designed by HPP Architects and finished in 1970.

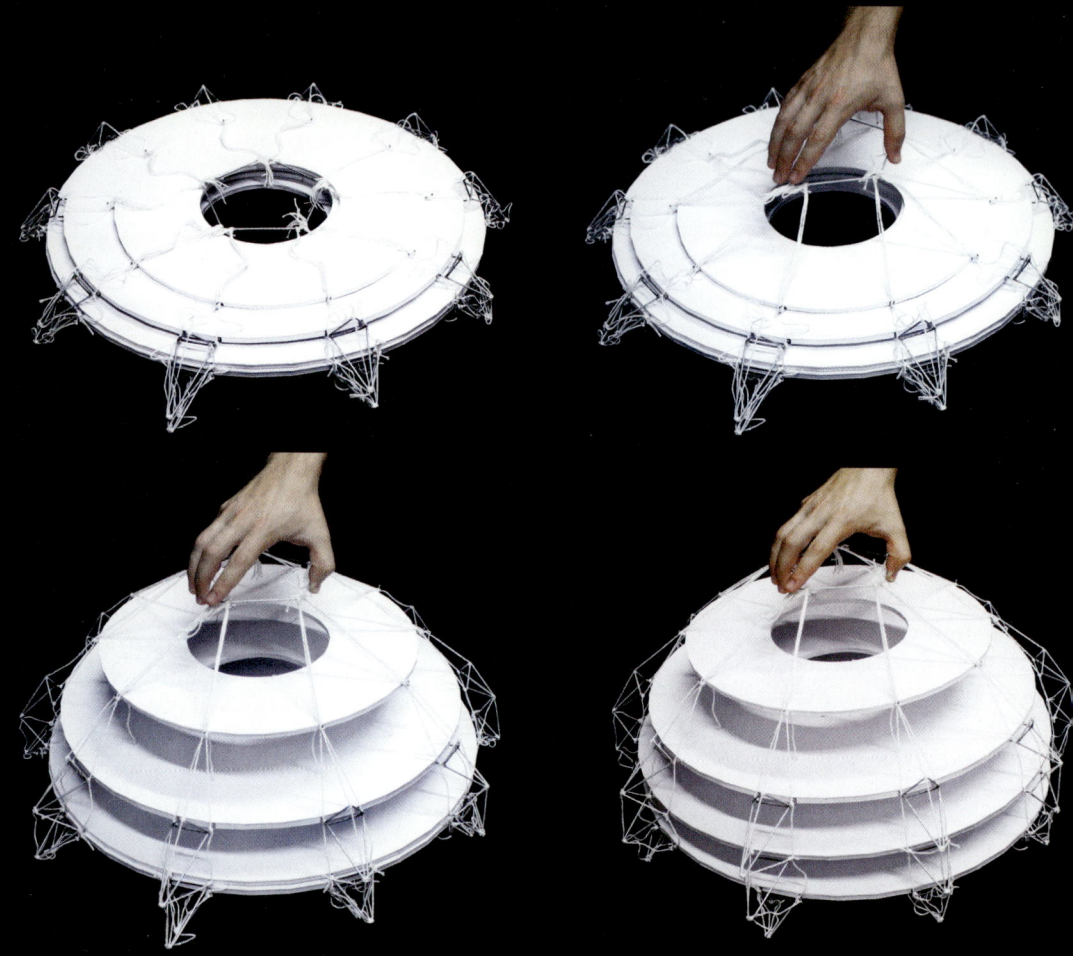

Structurally, the building works contrary to what one would expect: hanging from the top rather than being supported from below. Likewise, once the central pillar was in place, the slabs were added contrary to traditional building practices: from the roof down to the first floor, growing downwards. We built Gaudí-type models in which all the elements that work to pure tension (the inner tie and 90% of the perimeter ribs) are represented by strings. This is how the building works.

152

Axile development
Josep Ramon Solé

Changing the scale of a household item such as a lamp is no trivial matter: the square-cube law is unforgiving. And it is square-cube law that explains, at least to a certain extent, the definition of some of the most significant elements of this project.

This applies firstly to the most primary element of construction, meaning that there is a huge rise in the amount of area needed to balance the volume of load on a single central support (and the effects thereof).

The opening for the courtyard, which runs through the centre of the floors, adds further difficulty to the problem: where to locate the area that defines the support, since a very small but not negligible part of the load from the slabs is received at the perimeter of the courtyard, which measures several metres in diameter.

Divide and rule is a maxim that, properly understood, can also be very useful in structural design. In this sense, the centre support is composed of five identical three-dimensional, grid-shaped pillars, eventually referred to as "masts".

Together, these masts support the heavy load from the building's crown and from the five floor slabs, as we can see from the figure.

The unbalancing of the axial forces of the tubes of a mast in its upper section, seen in Fig. 1, may best be understood by observing the axial forces of the set of five masts in plan-section and including the pentagonal bracing that joins them specifically at their crown, as shown in Fig. 2. As we can see, the amount of tension on the pentagonal tension tightener is comparatively much higher than the axial stress found in all the other elements in the same figure. Mechanics being what it is, simple tension entails a well-known problem that is also one of its main virtues: the sections required for the strict balance of the stress involved are minimal. This fact means that in many cases, as with any top bracing system in a project, we end up determining the section of the ties according to criteria of deformation or, if you will, rigidity.

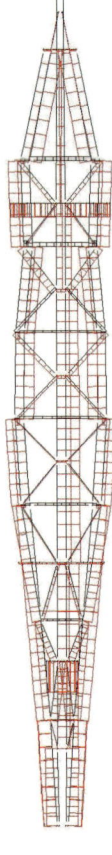

FIGURE 1
This function of axial stresses in one of the masts shows two noteworthy aspects: first, the bulk of the load is received at its crown, since the amount of axial stress at the upper level does not differ much from that at the base, and secondly, the innermost tubes of the masts operate much like the outer tubes, although not from the top.

The outer pentagonal ring dilates, opening outwards, flower-like, under the stresses it bears, and, indeed, this opening had to be carefully designed in order to minimise the flexing of the upper part of the masts. This minimisation should be understood as an aside since the substantial flexural stiffness of the mast means that they play a major role in the control of the opening. It is precisely this localised flexing phenomenon that allows an understanding of the very different axial stress on the tubes at the tops of the five support grids.

The flexural stiffness of the mast, which in this case is at the same time and fortunately resistance to bending, is key to the alternation of loads or in the event to any unanticipated imbalance that might cause a different load input at the vertices of the pentagon, which, executed with ties, would be unable to respond to its own distortion. The mention of the three inner rings also leads us to the defence of the presence of two lower ones, and this leads to comment on another key to the structural design: the curvilinear and staggered trace of each of the masts.

It is easy to imagine that, if you compress a staggered or curvilinear pillar, the geometry of its curvature and folds, once under load, will tend to accentuate, and right away we can say that we have a pillar with a natural tendency to collapse like an accordion. Conversely, if we properly contain the vertices of the folds of a pillar of irregular geometry, where none of the constituent sections deviates too far from verticality, its performance improves dramatically, and we have a pillar practically within the range of performance of a conventional one. That is precisely the function of the two lower rings, a function that, in the sections with floor slabs, is assumed by the latter.

Except for the very minor direct load of the floors on the masts circling the courtyard, the entire gravity load of the structure is transferred to the masts through a series of oblique ties (see Fig. 3). Indeed the problem of the load transfer is precisely their obliqueness. It is worth noting a couple of aspects related to the two sets of upper ties.

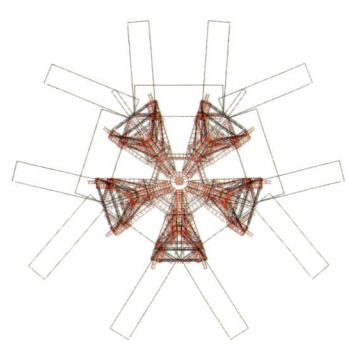

FIGURE 2

Horizontal projection of the structure including the five masts, with the upper stiffening ring, and the series of oblique ties. Note the dark rectangles that define the upper bracing pentagon: the greater the breadth of the rectangle the greater the tension on the corresponding tie.

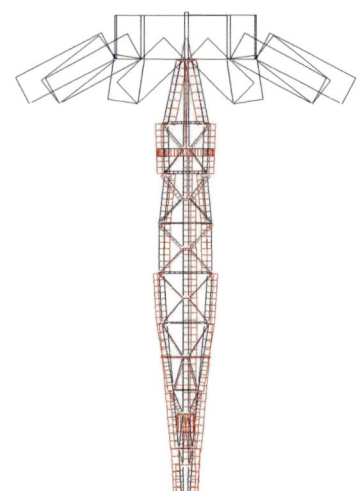

FIGURE 3
Returning to the load path of the ties, it is interesting to examine in isolation one of the five masts that form the central support in figure 7. In this way we can identify more clearly the series of ten oblique ties that transfer the load to the top of the structure and in which we can also see the tensile stresses, defined by the dark rectangles.

The first leads us to the problem of the amount of area needed, the square-cube law. And again, *divide and rule*: each rod represented by the calculation model actually consists of ten solid rods 75 mm in diameter. This decision is based simply on the desire to have the structure perceived in a certain way; rigidity is ensured by a set of ten rods per theoretical tie equal to a single (undoubtedly tubular) rod of much greater diameter, but the relation to the space is completely different.

The second aspect is how the load transfer between the two sets of ties is resolved, as seen in the detailed schemes in page 200.

Let's return now to the loading of the series of oblique ties. In Fig. 4 we can see the gap, measuring some 180 cm, between the upper ends of the inner ties, coincident with the top slab, and the lower ends of the oblique ties. This gap means that the aforementioned vertical load deflection also occurs without the coincidence of the nearest slab, leading to the appearance of one of the most unique elements of the project: the steel gussets that help compensate the load deflection with the nearby roof slab.

Thus, the laminar performance of the top floor, ie, the roof of the fourth floor, is critical to an understanding of the overall performance of the support grid.

The laminar performance of this slab is, although to a lesser extent, matched by the remaining slabs of the building; first, due to the geometry of the masts, as we have explained above, and, second, due the geometry of the sharply curvilinear, three-dimensional ribs which brace the structure on the outside.

If we observe the deformation of the ribs under gravity load in relation to the deformation of one of the slabs (Fig. 5), in this case the roof of the second floor, we can see how the innermost vertical rods of the ribs hang straight down in contact with the floor due to the constraining effect of the floor itself.

If we now turn our attention to the axial function of the roof rods (Fig. 9) we can see clearly the shoring effect on the radial rods or on the nearly radial pairs into which they fork in the outer opening. This forking is meant precisely to constrain effectively the pair of chords that make up the inner side of the outer ribs, transferring to them the corresponding vertical load.

In the latter load diagram we can see another effect: the annular rods are working in tension (dark lined rectangles) while the radials are under heavy compression. To understand this apparent contradiction it is enough to recall the geometry of the masts in this part of the building; their curvature at this point causes, under the heavy load they bear, a dilation effect on the perimeter of the courtyard which is transferred by the radial rods to all the rings. In other words, the heavy compression of the radial rods is due more to the dilation effect of the masts on the courtyard than on the contraction of the ribs on the perimeter of the floor.

The diagonal rods have no real or direct correspondence with the built structure, rather they are part of the analysis model to simulate the bracing effect that the continuous reinforced concrete sheet of the slabs, incorporating composite decking, confer on the grid of real rods properly joined to the beams with bolts. The role of these virtual rods, which barely work under balanced loads, is exactly the same as that of the diagonal rods of the fourth floor, but to a much lesser extent, which explains why, at the four lower floors, their actual deployment by means of specific sections was not deemed necessary.

The rings perform very effectively as restrainers, so the functions of the theoretical deformation of the roof seen in perspective (Fig. 10) show, as noted above, basically vertical displacements.

With regard to the vertical displacements, it is important to point out the heavy deformation of the central nodes where they take the load from the inner ties, at least when compared to the nodes joining the roof to the masts on the perimeter of the courtyard.

In the end, this deformational behaviour affected the size

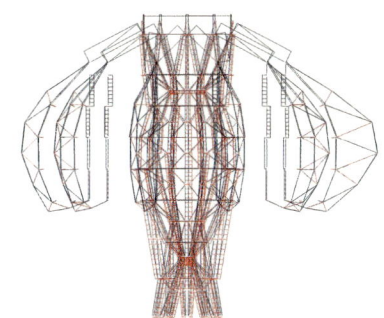

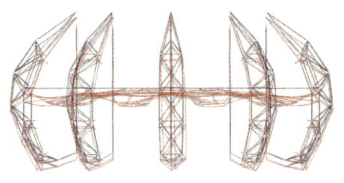

FIGURE 4 and 5
The oblique ties receive, at their lower end, the load from the two series of constructive elements, ten outer three-dimensional grids and ten inner vertical ties.
The progressive increase in tension in the inner vertical ties signals the presence of the slabs and evidences their performance contrary to that of a standard pillar, despite their verticality.

157

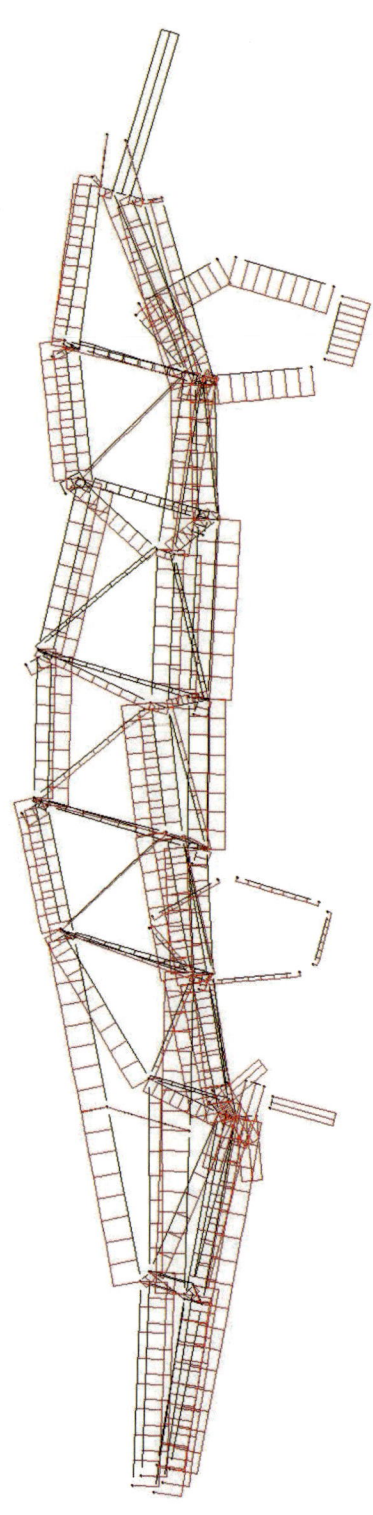

FIGURE 6
The upper flexion of the masts disappears, and with it the axial difference, when each of the masts comes into contact with both the top slab and the first of the three inner rings, as can be seen in figure 7, since the double contact allows a couple to develop, thus cancelling out the flexion.

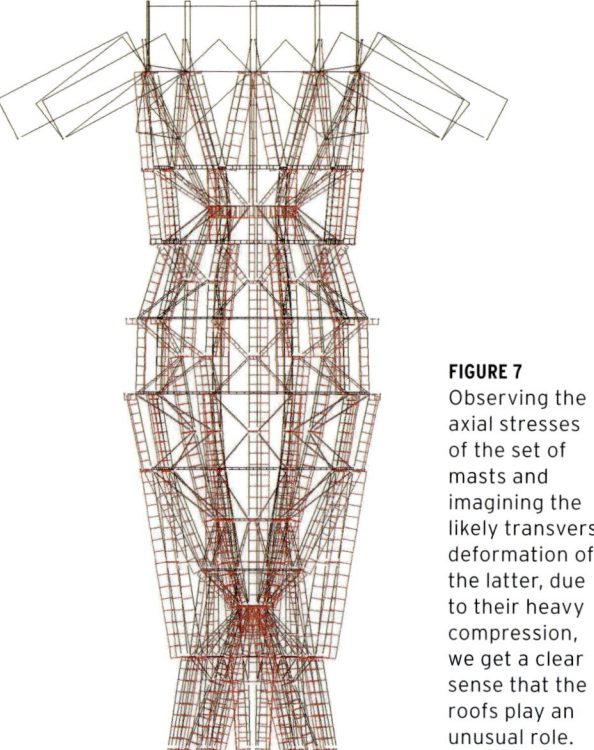

FIGURE 7
Observing the axial stresses of the set of masts and imagining the likely transverse deformation of the latter, due to their heavy compression, we get a clear sense that the roofs play an unusual role.

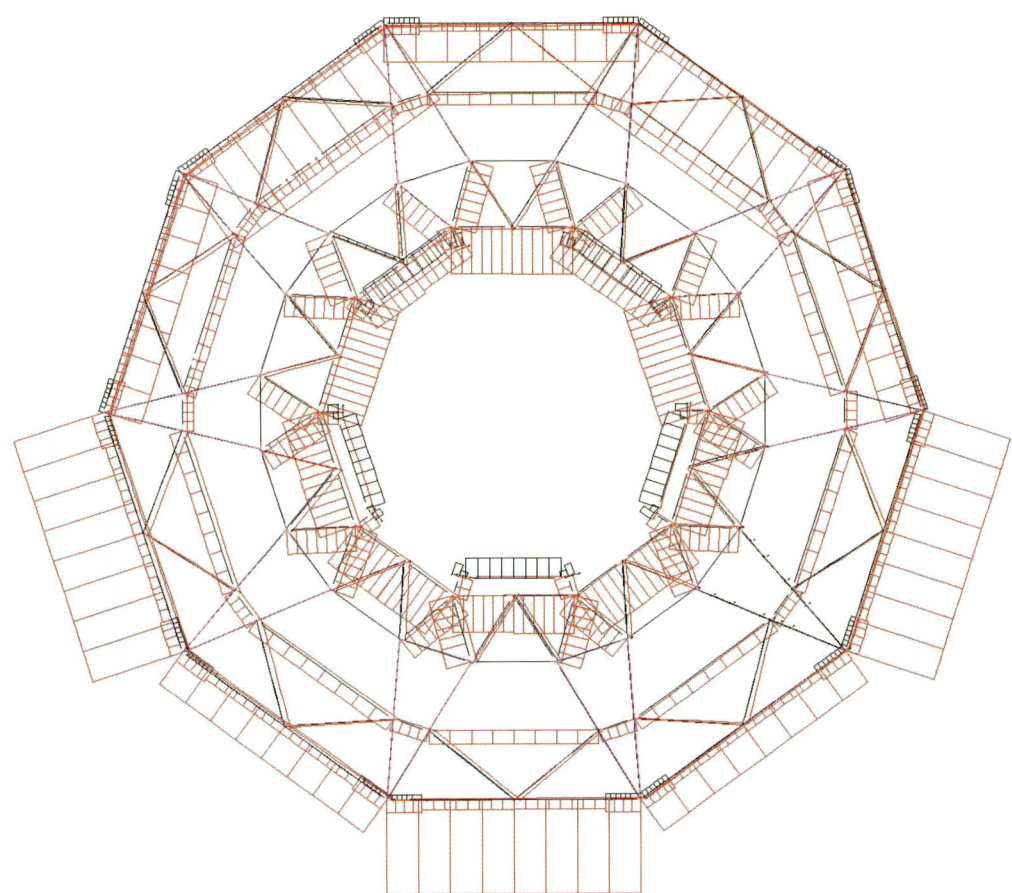

FIGURE 8
Leaving aside the few rods in the inner part that appear to be in tension because they pertain to the masts, we can see that the annular rods logically form regular compression rings, with the exception of the outer ring. The outer ring shows an understanding of rhythmic variation; essentially this variation is due to the fact that the horizontal projection of the oblique ties is non-radial, causing the appearance of annular components of force at the joints with the gussets. Because they are modelled using finite elements, the traces of the gussets do not carry an axial force associated with this representation, which also occurs with the second ring. In this plan we can also see two sets of rods that are neither radial or annular, and that, within the framework of a problem eminently circumferential, could be called diagonal. The axial stresses of the two sets of diagonal rods, with the obvious exception of those located in the innermost part that prop the axis of the gussets against the vertices of the perimeter of the courtyard, are rather negligible. The justification for these diagonal rods can only be understood in terms of phenomena of unbalanced loads, either due to disturbances inherent in the regular use of the building or the minimum imbalances inherent in any resistant system.

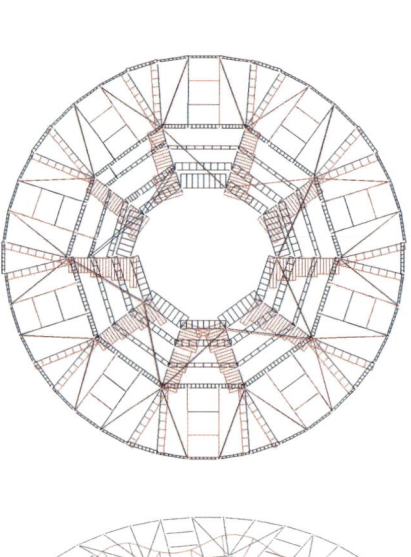

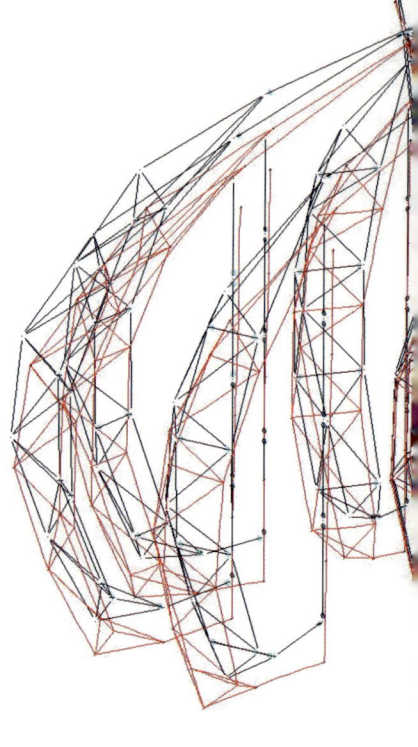

FIGURE 9 and 10

of the upper oblique ties, as well as the size of their pentagonal tightening ring, since it is the rigidity of the upper brace that essentially deals with the gravity load path of the inner ties, as shown in Figs. 11 and 13.

To better interpret this behaviour, it is worth noting the gravity load path of the upper end of the inner ties and, at the same time, try to discern the geometry of the deformation that must occur in the upright triangles which virtually enclose the oblique ties, with the gussets and masts.

Josep Ramon Solé,
Architect, former partner of BOMA and co-founder
of Windmill Structural Consultants

FIGURE 11, 12 and 13

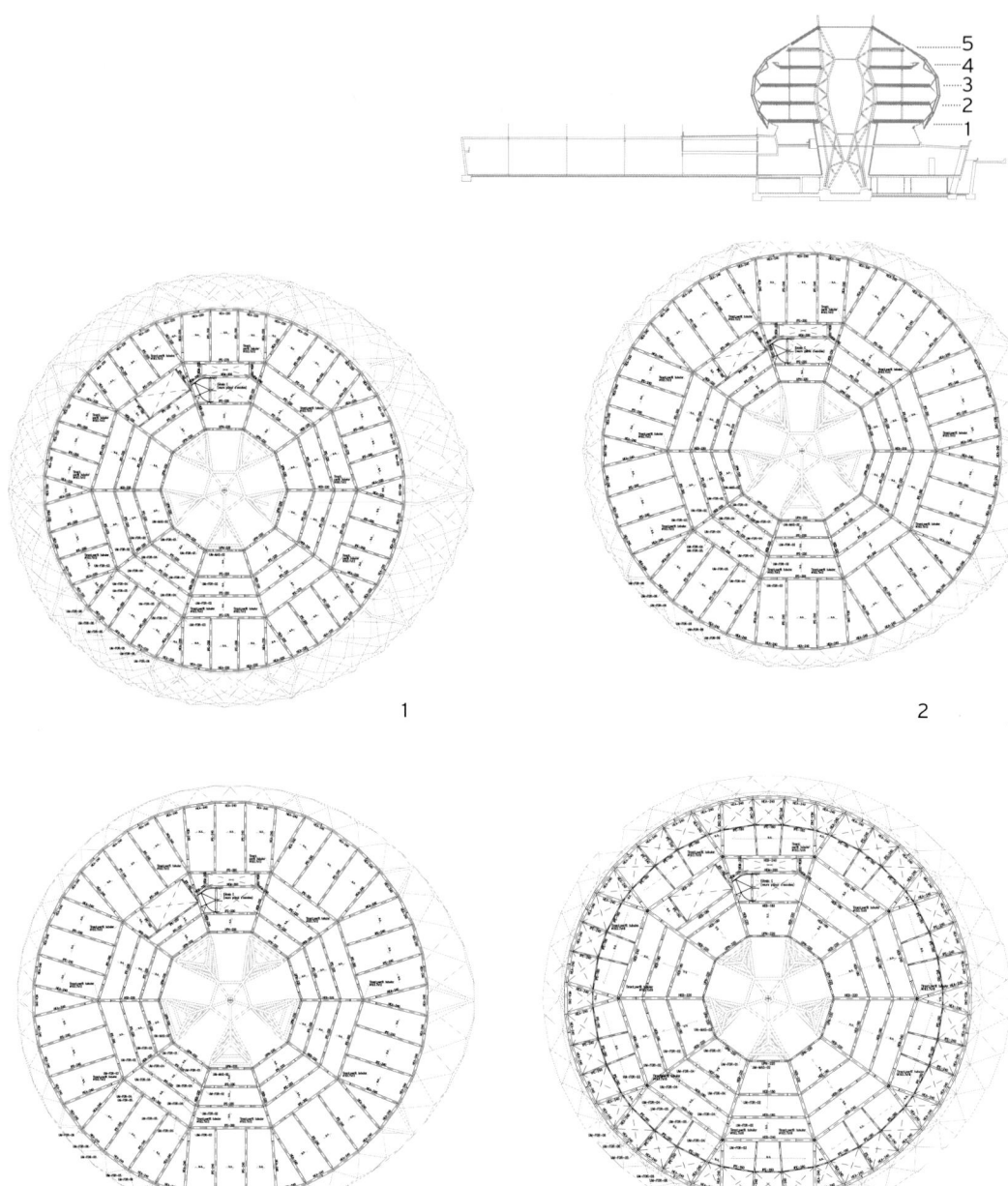

1

2

3

4

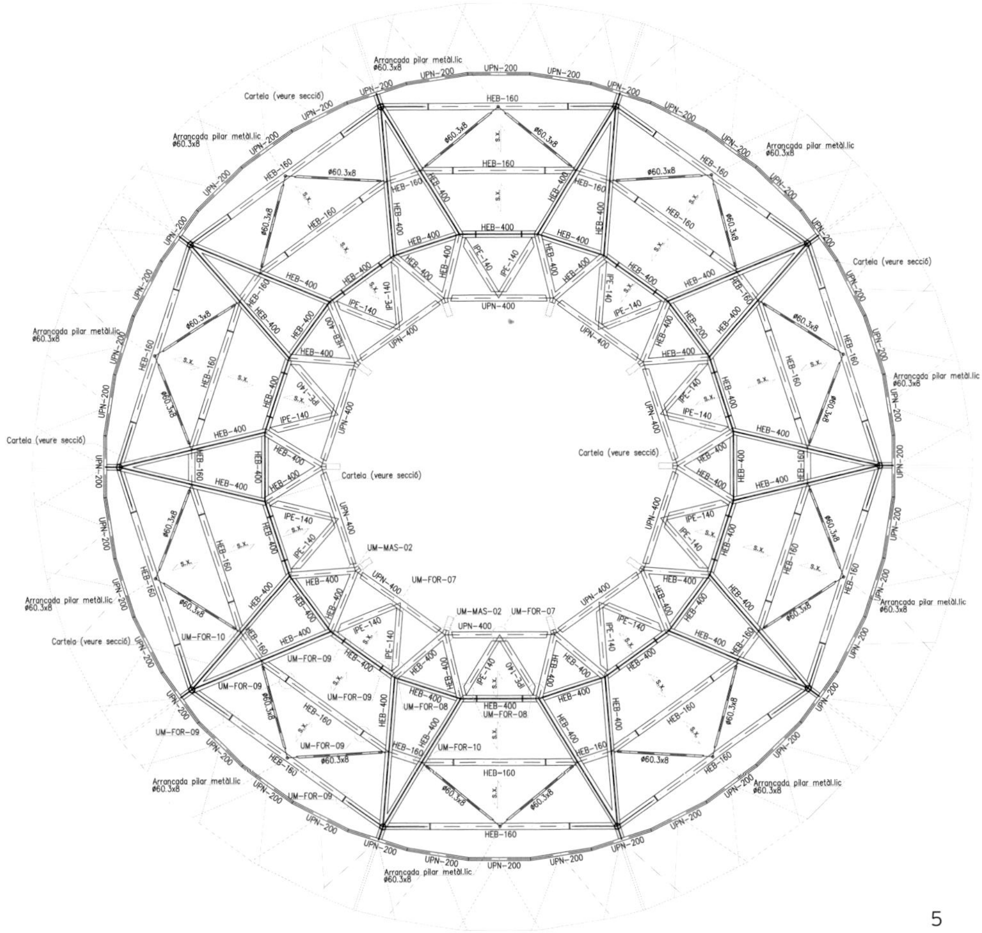

5

The five slabs have diameters ranging from 30 to 35 m. The peculiar design of the roof slab is due to its greater compression load compared to the other slabs. In making the slabs, 205 metric tons of steel structure were used. Of this amount nearly half, 90 metric tons, went into the roof slab with its ten gusset plates.

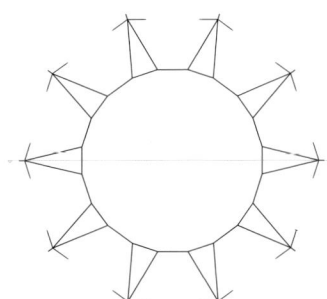

Gusset scheme

Central
pillar

SUSPENDING A STRUCTURE

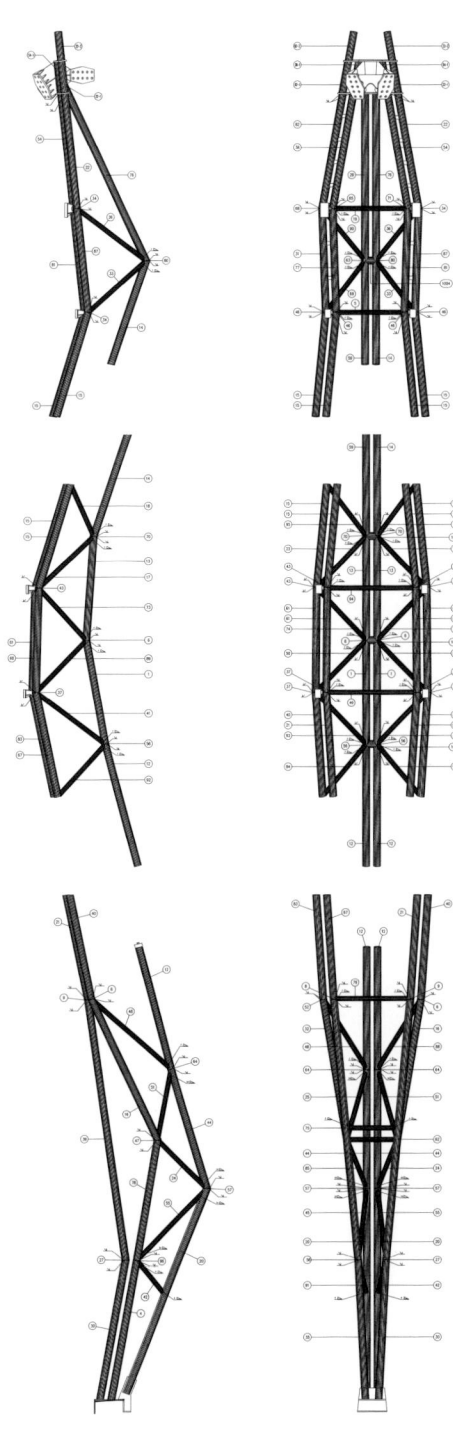

The central pillar is made up of five masts. Each mast is made up of three pairs of 273 mm-diameter tubes, forming a triangle. The reason for the doubling of these chords is architectural: in order to ensure the transparency of the main structural element, maximum tube diameter is 30 cm. If calculations show that a tube requires a larger section than this, it is replaced by two smaller section tubes, to perform the same structural function. Each mast was prefabricated in three separate parts and then assembled on-site in order to optimise assembly time and achieve maximum precision.

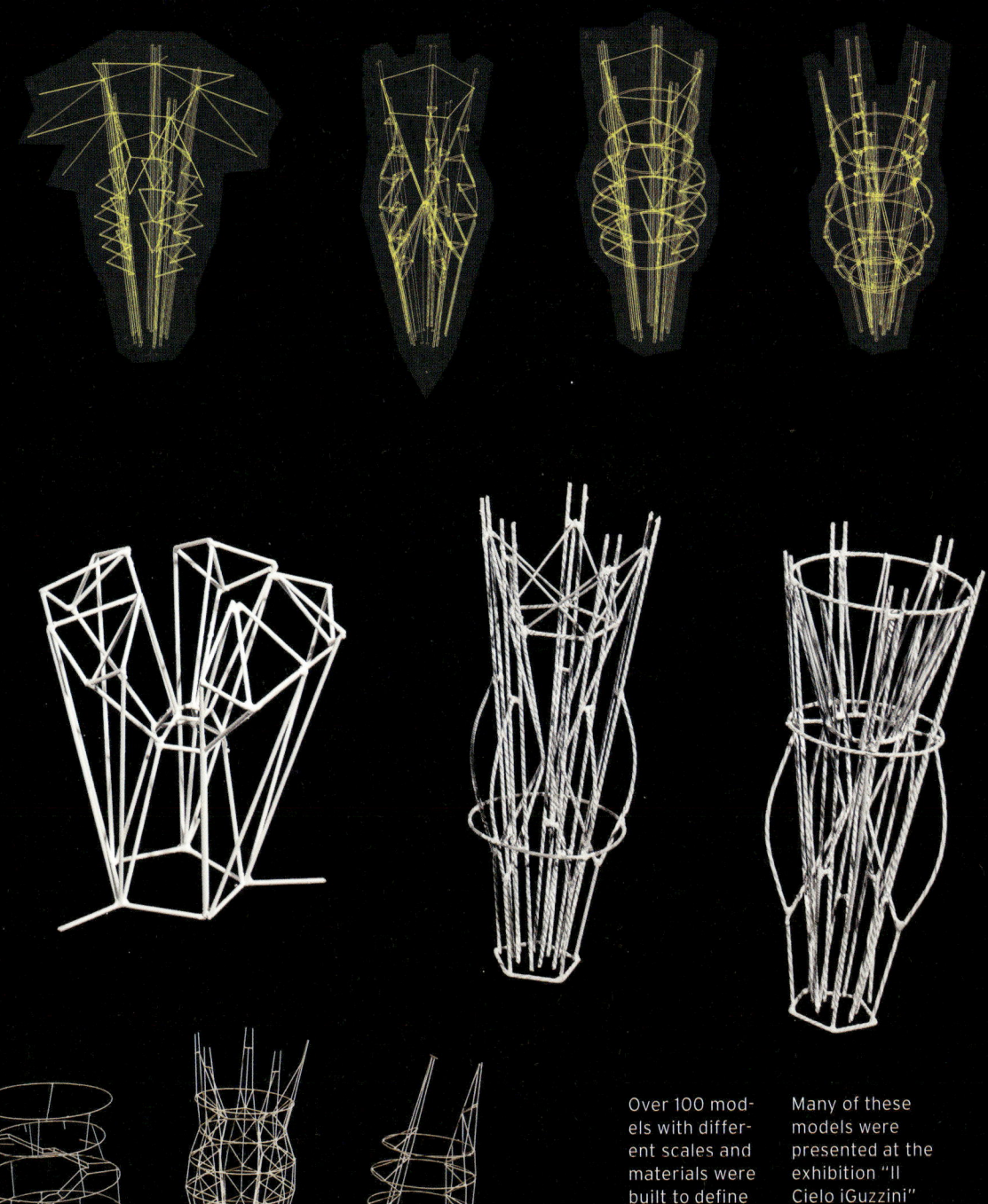

Over 100 models with different scales and materials were built to define the geometry of the central pillar and test the geometry of the structural solutions.

Many of these models were presented at the exhibition "Il Cielo iGuzzini" at the Catalan Architects Association (COAC) in Barcelona.

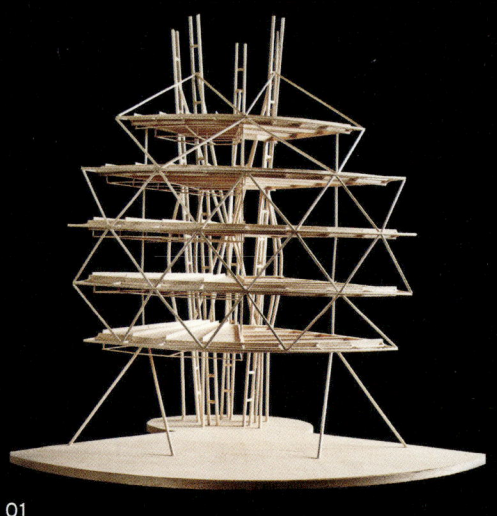

01

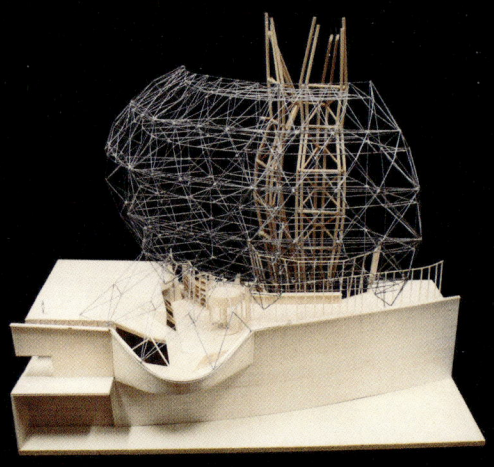

02

01. Study model of construction details. Scale 1:50. Materials: balsa wood sheets and rods. Presented at the exhibition "Il Cielo iGuzzini" at the COAC Building in Barcelona.

02. 03. 04. Study model of the central pillar. Scale: 1:75. Materials: laser-cut acrylic, soldered wire and copper tubes. Shown at La Arquería de los Nuevos Ministerios, Madrid, for the exhibition "35+ Construyendo en Democracia, 35 años de Arquitectura Española".

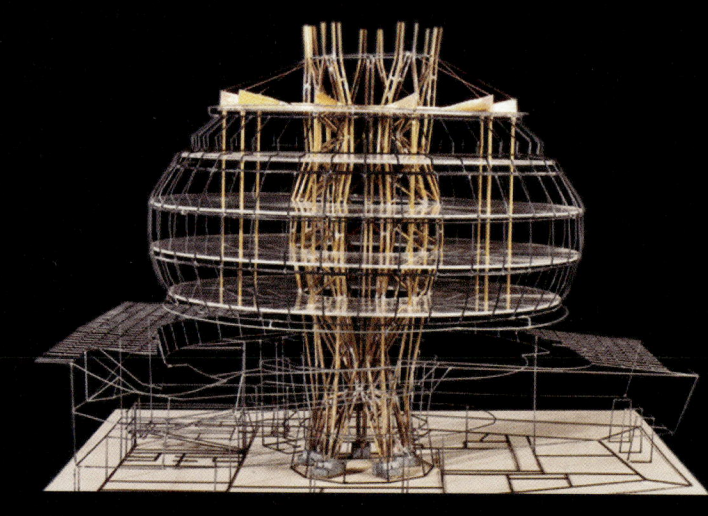

03

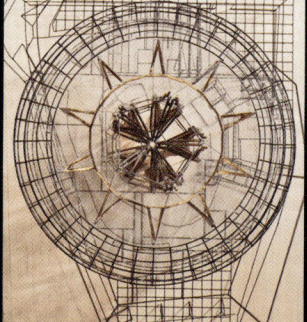

04

Study model of the construction details of the platform, central pillar and skin. Scale: 1:20. Materials: balsa wood sheets and rods. Presented at the exhibition "Il Cielo iGuzzini", COAC building, Barcelona.

Model of the central pillar with grey colour gradients. Colouring of this kind accentuates the slenderness of the structural element. Scale: 1:30. Material: balsa wood rods, putty and paint. Shown at iGuzzini Illuminazione Ibérica S.A. headquarters in Barcelona. On the right, view of the MiAS Architects model-making shop in Barcelona during the construction of this model.

We never make this sort of spatial constructions of finished projects, since more up-to-date means do a much better job of showing the final outcome. We only make models for purposes of our own understanding and as an aide in finding the internal consistency of the project itself.

SUSPENDING A STRUCTURE

The pile cap of the central pillar is a reinforced concrete cylinder 1.80 m deep and 16 m in diameter. This one base element took 31 metric tons of iron and 318 m³– the equivalent of 53 truckloads– of concrete to make. Beneath the cap forty piles, 85 cm and 65 cm in diameter, and reaching a depth of 16 m, anchor the pile cap to the ground.

The five
masts of the
pillar were
prefabricated
in a specialised
metal shop from
high-strength
S355 steel
tubing, each
one according
to the same
specifications,
and in three
parts to
optimise
transport time
and costs.
The tubes are
joined with a
round plate
butt-welded
perpendicularly
to the axis of
the tube.

SUSPENDING A STRUCTURE

As each section
of the mast was
finished in the
shop, it was de-
livered by spe-
cial transport
to the worksite,
where it was at-
tached to cables
according to its
centre of gravity
and lifted into
position by a
large-tonnage
crane.

177

The mast is joined to the foundation by means of a concrete pedestal, through which protrude 26 high-bond steel bolts, 25 mm in diameter by 3 m long, lathed to measure, and also joined to the lower pile cap. Once in position, the base plate of the mast is fitted to the steel bolts protruding from the pedestal. After each stage of assembly, the mast section is fixed in its final position by tightening down the levelling nuts, with the aide of surveying instruments for maximum precision.

SUSPENDING A STRUCTURE

Once the first section of each mast was in place, the next section, equipped with pieces specifically designed for this purpose, was joined to it. The joining of the different sections was the only welding done on site, and, like all other welding, was inspected ultrasonically. All welds, both on site and in shop, were inspected in this way, by an external laboratory, a job which took 194 days in all. In the absence of other spatial references, the position of the second section was constantly checked with laser survey equipment. The masts were built with plates for joining them to the slab beams, and thus it was imperative to position these elements within a tolerance of +/- 10 mm in three dimensions with respect to the theoretical position. Although made of 1,600 lm of tubing, from base to crown the central pillar measures just 36 m. Each mast weighs 37,270 kg, thus the total weight of the central pillar is over 186 metric tons.

SUSPENDING A STRUCTURE

SUSPENDING A STRUCTURE

Once the third section was brought to the worksite and properly positioned, following the same procedure as in the second section, the mast was complete. The five masts were joined together at the crown by means of a tubular top ring to form the pillar.

Work on the
central pil-
lar, both in the
workshop and
on site, went on
around the clock
in order to meet
scheduling.

Once the central pillar was in finished, work began on the slabs. The slabs are made of bolted metal beams and reinforced composite decking joined with a total of 4,200 high-strength bolts up to 3 cm in diameter. This type of dry solution, in addition to saving construction time and structural weight, avoids the need for auxiliary formwork structures. Until the outer ribs were mounted, the outer edge of the slabs was hung from the pillar with temporary ties.

SUSPENDING A STRUCTURE

The slabs contain 3,350 m² of composite decking, 1 mm thick by 6 cm along the edge, combined with 7 cm of concrete. The two materials, steel and concrete, were joined by means of 11,500 special Nelson connectors. Once the fittings and steel decking of the slab was in place, the concrete was poured, working from the fourth floor down to the first, with a waiting period of one week between each floor.

This enabled the ties to be loaded with the weight of the slabs one at a time and the structure to gradually acquire tension.

The five identical masts of the central pillar are joined together by means of four rings: three, under compression, in the lower part and one at the top, which works in only in tension and distributes and balances the eccentric load of each mast. The top ring is made of fifty post-tensioned, high-tensile-strength stainless bars and was tested at the Federal Institute for Materials Testing and Research in Dübendorf, Switzerland.

Another hundred braces of this type work in tension to transfer the weight loads from the slabs to the central pillar. In order to do this, the roof slab is joined to the top of each mast with forty braces, and custom designed and manufactured metal fittings were required to accommodate so many bars in such a small space.

A glossary of wildlife
Silvia Brandi

"And Adam gave names to all cattle, and to the fowl of the air, and to every beast of the field."
Genesis 2:20

By all indications, it didn't look like it was going to be your average job. Starting with the form (how could you call this contraption a "building"?), on to a construction process like nothing ever seen before (hanging from the top and growing downwards) and finally an array of indescribable bits and gadgets that despite of their impeccable structural logic and careful design looked more like debris from a Martian spacecraft passing over Barcelona than components destined to find their place in a piece of architecture.

So, before the construction of the building turned into the *Tower of Babel*, its sundry bits and pieces, in a process half a game half pragmatic need, spontaneously acquired names and gradually became domesticated and came to have life and meaning.

At first, like in many other projects, any apparatus, invention, or detail that had enough personality to warrant a name was called the *Animal*. Things got complicated when "the animals" began to be many and the need arose to put everything in order. And the worksite became a zoo.

01.

The first thing that cried out for a sobriquet was none other than the "sphere" pertaining to the office building, for it was not proper sphere, one side being somewhat squashed, deformed, and no term in Euclidean geometry was able to describe it properly.

First it was called the *Aerostatic Balloon*, with Leonidov's proposal in mind, to reflect the ephemeral, lighter-than-air look of something that is there but at any moment might cast off and float away.

02.

But before anyone could get a grasp of the whole thing, it was the children of the project team members who, inspired by the abstract wire models presented at a large exhibition before construction began, started to sketch the building, and rightly so, as a Spaceship that had just landed, with exhaust still coming out of the jet engines. Once the works were underway, the building became, less poetically, the *Artichoke* (or the *Mushroom*) when the outer structural ribs, the *Bananas* (01), appeared in the façade. These *Bananas*, which couldn't have been better named, carry upwards the weight–transferred by means of metal pieces called *Shields*–of the outer ends of the slabs, while the loads from inner ends are carried upwards by means of vertical ties.

To ensure rigidity, the ties were mounted in-workshop in accordance with their role in the five-floor structure, and were delivered to the worksite in one piece, including the nodal beam joints. And at this point the worksite was invaded by *Spiders* (02), since at these nodes converge three-dimensionally five beams and two ties, one above and one below. Someone noticed that the form of this node was also vaguely anthropomorphic and the works foreman, who travelled every day to the metal workshop on his endless mission of welding control, dubbed this piece his *Assistant* (02).

The *Bananas* and ties pass the loads on to the *Ferraris* (03), the designation for the ten imposing pieces under compression that make up the roof slab. They earned their name both for their shape, not unlike the car, and for the sophistication in the details–thus the roof became a garage for high-performance cars.

The ten *Ferraris* in turn pass the entire load, through post-tensioned bars, on to the five *Bats* (04) fluttering about the mast tops, complex elements which redistribute and balance the loads from the entire building through a system of tensioned rods called the *Diamond* (05) in honour of its form and the preciousness of its function, which is to keep the building from opening outwards like a *Flower*. From here the loads are transmitted evenly to the masts.

The five steel masts were prefabricated off-site and each is made up of a large number of tubes joined together to

03.

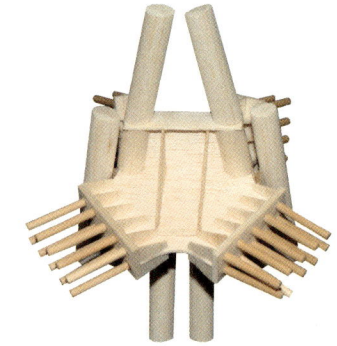

04.

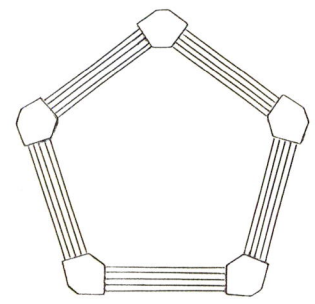

05.

06.

07.

form a sort of complex backbone. Each bar is sized using a CNC laser cutter, leaving them weld-ready and shaped, according to the welders, like a *Shark's Mouth*.

Tube after tube that strange animal the central pillar finally touches the ground on all five legs, each with its own *Shoe* (06), that is, the concrete piece which, by means of a system of *Asparagus*, adjusts the position of each mast and anchors it to the foundation.

Once the main structure was in place, and as the south-facing façade began to swell with the assembly of the sunscreen structure, the building's *Pregnancy* began to show. When the time came to mount the fabric skin, which was also brought to the worksite in one enormous piece, the well-rehearsed *Bridal Dressing Ceremony* took place.

Finally, once the fabric was fixed to the vertices of the triangular structure of the sunscreen, it lay tensioned and sharp-pointed, and the next day the building appeared in the paper as the *Sea Urchin*.

The lower part of the building, despite being a closed concrete box, inspired equally varied designations. With its sloping walls like a great ship, the box itself became a *Fellinian Cruise Ship* rising from the waters, while the elaborate and delicate steel crowning piece balanced atop the wall enclosing this volume, became the *Little Bird* (07).

Through all this, undisturbed, the *Two Personas* (08) continued to bear, arms raised, the roof of the delivery vehicle roundabout.

It was the ambition to probe the boundaries of architectural exploration, in search of the unknown, that lead us to solutions that did not exist, and therefore still unnamed.

The reference to the animal world, or at least to a common vocabulary, so alien to the aseptic initials and iron-clad numbers with which modernity is so want to define inventions, became a wondrous and entirely fitting idiom, without interference from the usual tech-speak,

without detracting from the seriousness and professional-
ism of the design and construction processes.
Thus, as in an Arcimboldo painting where everything leads
into quite another thing, the reading incites doubt and the
interpretations multiply, and in this way we find the space
and pretext for discovering more.
Let sheet metal fly, let the structural ribs make hunger,
let the iron sing:

E' del poeta il fin la meraviglia,
parlo dell'eccellente e non del goffo,
chi non sa far stupir, vada alla striglia!
(da *La Murtoleide: Fischiate* del cav. Marino, 1642)

Silvia Brandi,
Architect,
Project Leader of iGuzzini BCN HQ

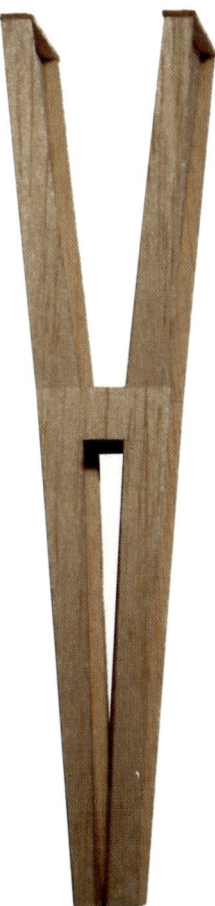

08.

SUSPENDING A STRUCTURE

View of the
metalworking
shop during the
manufacture of
the *Ferraris* and
Bananas.

The *Bats*

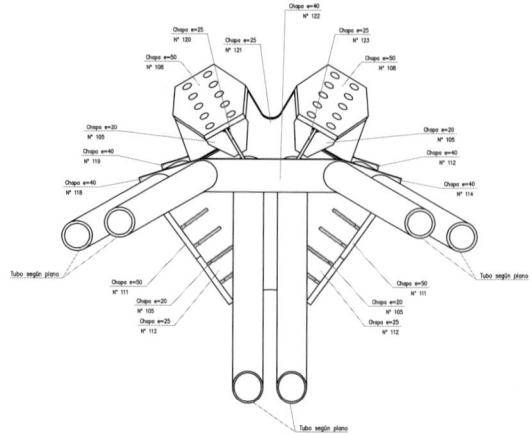

The *Bat* perches atop the pillar, and takes the load from the ten sets of ties and redistributes it to the five masts. This beam-like element transfers the load between the two sets of upper ties and measures 180 cm on edge. Its dimensions are determined by several factors:
– Geometry, due to the space occupied by the ties and their different orientations;
– To ensure its correct tension state;
– The stiffness of the tubes that form the two inner chords of the masts.

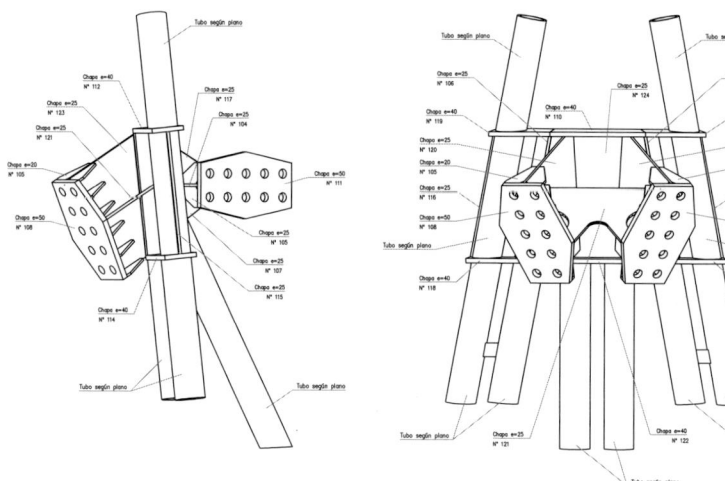

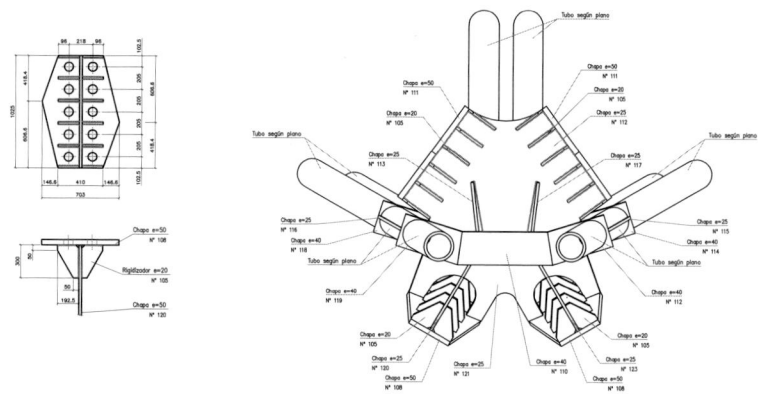

Each of the five *Bats* contains 4,250 kg of S355JR steel. Due to the thickness of these plates, ranging from 25 to 50 mm, they were cut with a numerical control flame cutter.

The metal struc-
tural elements
are protected
with EI 90 fire-
resistant paint.
However, by
adding sprin-
klers at the
upper inner ring
a real fire resist-
ance
of EI 120 is
achieved.

The *Ferraris*

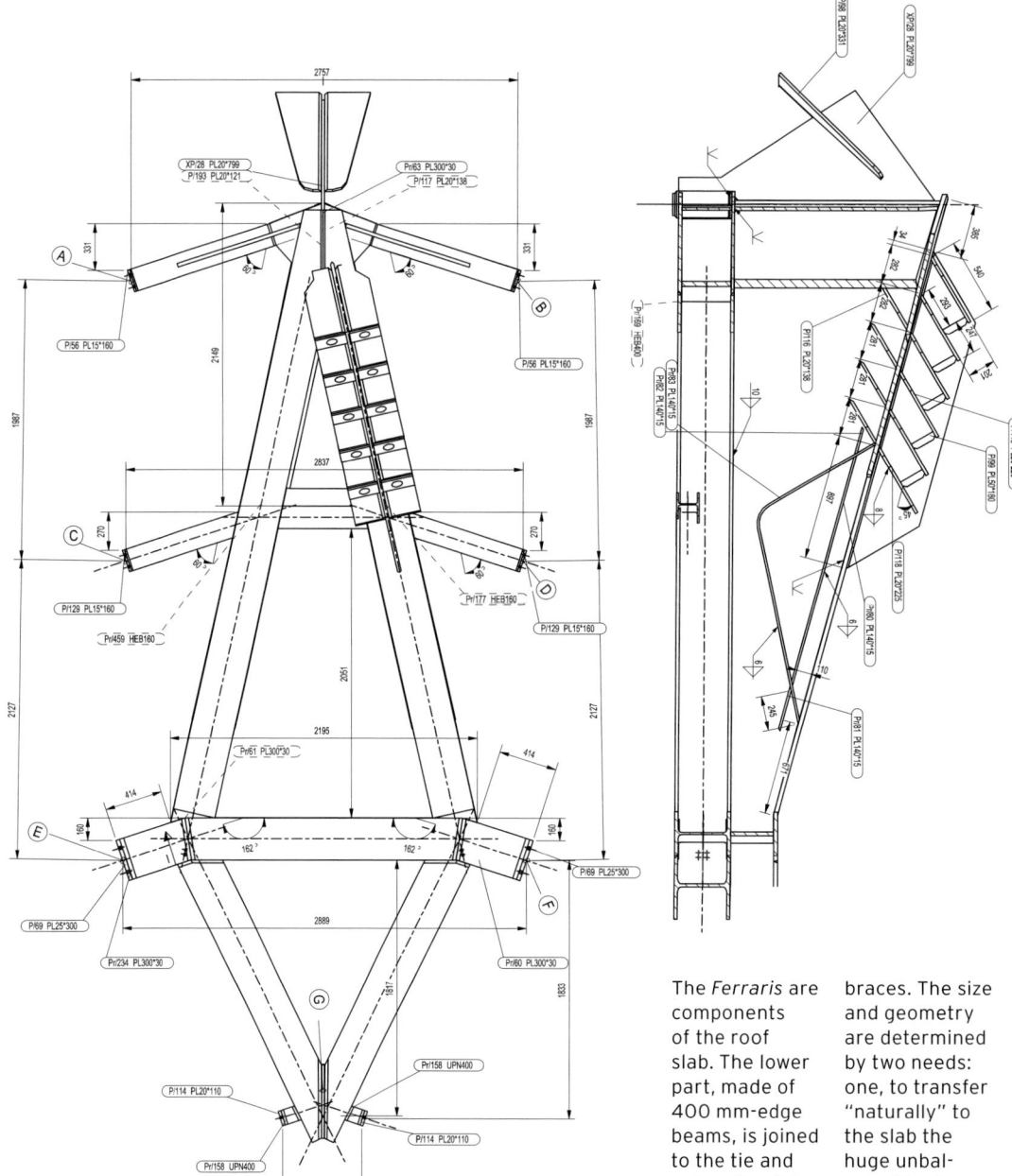

The *Ferraris* are components of the roof slab. The lower part, made of 400 mm-edge beams, is joined to the tie and outer rib, while the upper part, consisting of a truss, transfers the load to the top of the mast through ten post-tensioned braces. The size and geometry are determined by two needs: one, to transfer "naturally" to the slab the huge unbalanced horizontal load at the joint and, two, to avoid undue bending in any of the braces involved in the joint.

Each of the ten *Ferraris* contains 7,600 kg of S355JR steel, equal to the weight of the six real *Ferraris*. The plates range in thickness from 15 to 50 mm and were cut with a numerical control flame cutter.

The *Bananas*

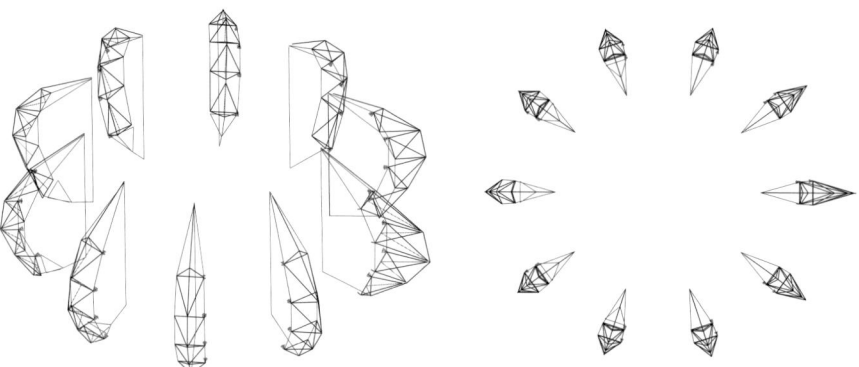

There are four different types of *Bananas*, with sizes depending on their location in the sphere and on the deformation of sunscreen.

The *Bananas* are the ten outer ribs which take the outermost load from the slabs and transfer it upwards to the upper gussets. Thus they work mainly in tension.

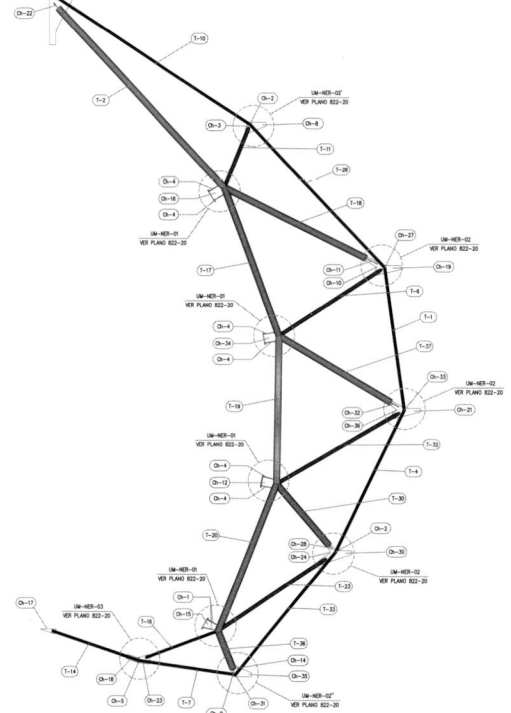

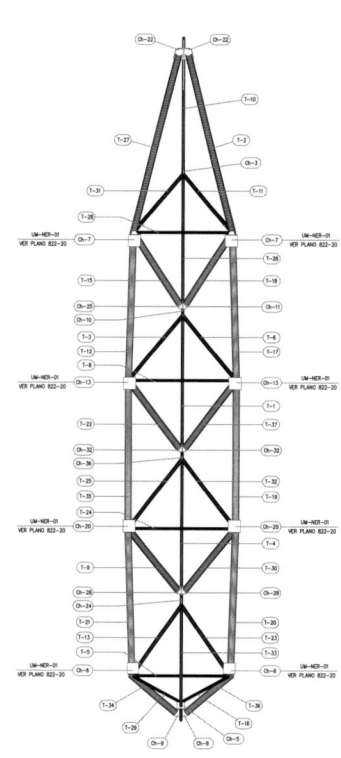

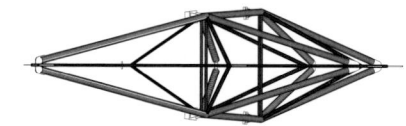

SUSPENDING A STRUCTURE

The *Bananas* were assembled in the workshop metal in one piece and are taken one-by-one to the worksite. It is only when these elements are in position that the structure reaches its final load state.

All together, the *Bananas* contain 1,178 m of S355JR steel tubing, weighing 41,120 kg.

SUSPENDING A STRUCTURE

Over 600 metric tons of steel went to making this building. Steel is highly sustainable, since it is the most recycled of all materials. Of the 1,327 million metric tons of steel produced worldwide in 2008, 34% was recycled from scrap, equivalent to the weight of two hundred Eiffel Towers or 1.6 million cars every day. Thus, we can say that it is the only building material that is always at least partially recycled. Steel is completely recyclable at the end of its useful life and can be recycled an unlimited number of times with no loss of qualities. No wonder then that more steel is recycled than aluminium, plastic and glass combined.

LOOKING THROUGH

RAL 9023, colour used for
painting the central pillar
from +18.12 m to +14.5 m

The invisible shell
Jaume Avellaneda

There's no doubt that the Crystal Palace in London, built in 1851, is a landmark in the history of architecture and technology, owing to the contributions which its designer, Joseph Paxton, made to the advancement of the use of glass in modern architecture. The technology used in this building represents a development on the English greenhouses of the time, although the type of glass Paxton used had been manufactured industrial for just four years. Paxton exploited contemporary technology, itself a product of the industrial revolution, to invent a new way of making façades.

For many years, glass, along with rolled steel and aluminium, has been considered the material most representative of modern architecture. Gropius's Bauhaus, Mies's first skyscraper projects and Le Corbusier's Cité du Refuge are good examples of buildings from the first half of the twentieth century that did much to establish this association between modernity and glass.

But the glass used in these buildings and was neither safe nor could it be considered, in some climates, a material favourable to comfort inside the building. Apart from its obvious virtues of enabling occupants to see out and light and solar radiation to come in, a welcome feature in the northern climes of Europe, this type of glass was unable to shield the interior environment from anything but wind and precipitation.

In the glass manufacturing process, as the melted mass of the primary components cools, a well-known phenomenon can occur: the appearance of superficial microcracks, thus significantly weakening the material and rendering it unsafe in more extreme conditions of wind and heat. Likewise, glass is known for its high thermal conductivity (1 W/m°C) and the fact that only certain wavelengths of energy radiations can pass through it. Specifically, it lets in ultraviolet solar radiation but is opaque to the infrared radiation emitted by pre-heated materials. The result is the well-known greenhouse effect: radiation penetrates through the glass into the building but scarcely dissipates back out. We could say that for modern architecture glass

Bauhaus School in Dessau, Germany by Walter Gropius built in 1926.

began as a necessary but inefficient material.

The glass industry, however, has long been aware of the limitations inherent in the material and, through research and technological development, has succeeded in improving its performance. Certainly one of the buildings that best demonstrate the advances in overcoming the material's safety limitations is the Willis Faber & Dumas Headquarters in Ipswich, UK, built between 1972 and 1975 and designed by the architect Norman Foster. The façade of this building is a curtain wall hung from the roof slab and is made of solid smoked-glass panels measuring 2 m by 2.5 m by 12 mm thick. These panes are bolted together by means of steel patches at the corners and joined along the edges with structural silicone. The construction of the façade was made possible by a number of innovations in glassmaking over the period between 1950 and 1970.

Firstly, in 1952, the Pilkington company patented the float glass process, which made it possible to manufacture larger glass panels with extremely flat surfaces and thus free from visual distortion. Secondly, the invention of tempered glass meant a considerable increase in tensile and flexural strength over conventional glass: the flexural strength of conventional glass is 200 Kp/cm^2 while that of tempered glass is 500 Kp/cm^2.

Later, in the 1960s, technologies were developed to bolt tempered glass panels together by means of metal plates, technology which has further evolved to the point where in today's façades the panels are joined to the supporting structure with virtually immaterial patch fittings. Also in the 1960s, structural silicone technology was developed in the US. Finally, metal-oxide tinted glass, also used in the Willis building, shields the interior from solar radiation and thus reduces air-conditioning costs, though at the expense of natural lighting.

However, despite the undisputed architectural and technological value of the Willis façade, today it can be considered obsolete for several reasons. The heat transmission of the glass, a parameter which measures heat losses, is around 4.10 W/m^2°C, a very high value compared to mod-

View of the entrance of the Crystal Palace, built in 1851 and designed by Joseph Paxton.

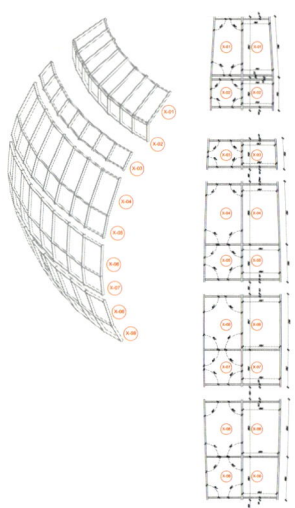

Geometric study of the outer façade. On site, we eventually managed to reduce even further the vertical structural elements with respect to the initial hypothesis and thus the glazing spans are larger, maximising transparency. Due to the particular geometry of the façade, no sheet of glazing is rectangular in form, nor are any two are on the same plane.

ern double-glazing, in which the two panes, one of which is low-e treated, are separated by an air chamber filled with argon gas. These new glazing units can attain heat transfers of just 1 W/m^{2}ºC, ie, four times lower than those used in the Willis Building.

Moreover, the new surface treatments applied to glass make it a highly selective material; transparent to wavelengths of visible radiation (390 to 760 nm), which means that, while having a high light transmission rate, it remains opaque to radiation of other wavelengths, thus preventing the transmission of energy inward.

Today, modern glass façades must meet a variety of needs, some of which—appearance, views, protection from the elements, strength under static and dynamic loads, acoustic insulation, fire safety—have pretty much always existed; but also other, much more recent needs, ie, contributing to the energy efficiency of the building, which means that the façade must provide optimal performance in terms of thermal losses and gains and natural lighting. Lately, we have seen the emergence of even newer demands which would have been unthinkable just a few years ago, such as façades that act as a micro-scale energy plants or, exploiting LED technology, as giant dynamic monitors capable of transmitting corporate images. Meanwhile, terms such as chromogenic, photochromic, thermochromic and holographic are now becoming part of the language of glass.

It is interesting to look at the specialised literature on glass from the past, for example *El Vidrio en la Construcción* by Félix Álvarez Martínez, published in 1958 by CEAC. Although it is an excellent book for its time, it barely touches on the subjects of solar protection, much less thermal or acoustic insulation. At the time, double-glazing with air chamber had not yet been introduced in Spain.

The iGuzzini Building in Sant Cugat del Vallès, by the architect Josep Miàs, is a fine example of modern glass façade design wisely adopting the technology offered by the industry.

The glass sheathing of the building, enclosing virtually the entire exterior and courtyard, overcomes three major challenges: how to control heat losses; how to limit solar radiation through glazing with a toroidal form and thus subject to a variable incidence of solar radiation; how to let in the maximum amount of visible solar radiation in order to optimise natural lighting in the office spaces; and how to achieve adequate interior acoustic comfort, especially considering the building's proximity to a highway.

In meeting these challenges, four types of glazing were used, corresponding to an equal number of areas of the façades. These areas were obtained by calculating, with the appropriate software, the incident energy on the different orientations of the façades and angles of incidence of sunlight on the surface at different times of year.

The south façade is clad in a hi-tech material—Stamisol®—which boosts solar protection without adverse impact on the quality of natural lighting or views from the inside.

From the standpoint of acoustic insulation, the composition of the glass used performs outstandingly thanks to the different thicknesses, 6 mm and 8 mm, and the butyral resin found in laminated glass.

In the 150 years of its modern history, glass has come a long way. While a single type of glass was used in the vast façades and roofs of the Crystal Palace, the Bauhaus or the Cité du Refuge, today we can design and manufacture glazed components with specific properties depending on the needs for strength, natural lighting, thermal insulation, acoustic insulation or appearance of the envelope, and we can safely say that glass is a material that not only is still associated with architectural modernity but now with technological modernity as well.

Jaume Avellaneda,
Ph.D. in Architecture, Professor of Architectural
Constructions ETSAV Vallès, UPC Barcelona Tech

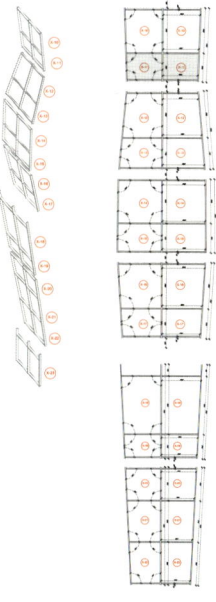

Geometric study of the inner façade. The courtyard is a wholly outdoor space, and thus the glazing as a proper façade.

Studying the south façade

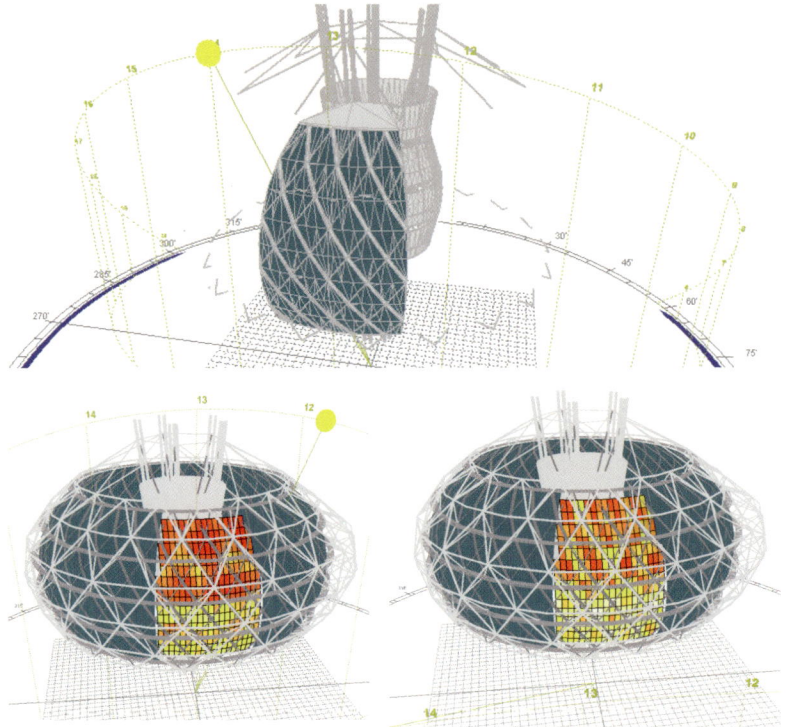

Due to its geometry, a spherical building receives an exceptional amount of solar radiation. In order to minimise the building's overall energy demands, we used ECOTECT simulation software for the solar load study. After feeding in all the parameters, the software calculated all the solar incidences and all the shade created by the structure, for each foreseen working hour and for each day of the year.

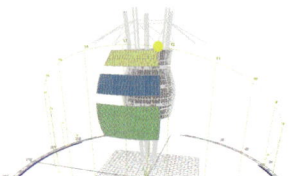

Areas of insolation distribution, assessed separately.

Effective Shading Coefficients
Latitude: 41.3°
Longitude: 2.1°
TimeZone: 15.0° [+1.0hrs]
Orientation: -3.4°

Month	Avg.SC	Max.SC	Min.SC
January	8.6%	46.0%	0.0%
February	14.7%	68.0%	0.0%
March	22.7%	100.0%	0.0%
April	27.5%	92.0%	0.0%
May	33.7%	98.0%	0.0%
June	32.5%	96.0%	1.0%
July	35.0%	98.0%	0.0%
August	29.4%	100.0%	0.0%
September	17.9%	62.0%	0.0%
October	13.5%	61.0%	0.0%
November	8.7%	46.0%	0.0%
December	5.8%	51.0%	0.0%
Winter	9.7%	55.0%	0.0%
Summer	33.9%	97.3%	0.3%
Annual	20.8%	76.5%	0.1%

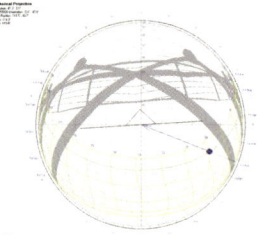

Effective Shading Coefficients
Latitude: 41.3°
Longitude: 2.1°
TimeZone: 15.0° [+1.0hrs]
Orientation: -10.0°

Month	Avg.SC	Max.SC	Min.SC
January	24.4%	76.0%	5.0%
February	23.9%	75.0%	2.5%
March	26.7%	100.0%	0.0%
April	31.9%	100.0%	0.0%
May	43.3%	100.0%	0.0%
June	42.5%	100.0%	0.0%
July	44.0%	100.0%	0.0%
August	31.3%	100.0%	0.0%
September	26.6%	100.0%	0.0%
October	22.5%	76.2%	2.5%
November	24.3%	63.7%	5.0%
December	25.6%	81.2%	2.5%
Winter	24.7%	77.1%	3.3%
Summer	43.4%	100.0%	0.0%
Annual	30.6%	90.9%	1.5%

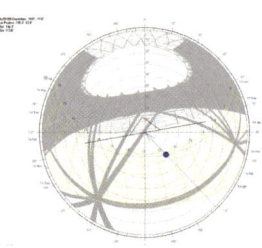

Effective Shading Coefficients
Latitude: 41.3°
Longitude: 2.1°
TimeZone: 15.0° [+1.0hrs]
Orientation: -9.4°

Month	Avg.SC	Max.SC	Min.SC
January	33.5%	75.0%	8.8%
February	23.5%	56.2%	11.2%
March	46.0%	100.0%	6.2%
April	81.2%	100.0%	27.5%
May	100.0%	100.0%	98.7%
June	100.0%	100.0%	100.0%
July	100.0%	100.0%	100.0%
August	72.5%	100.0%	21.3%
September	38.6%	100.0%	6.2%
October	23.1%	56.2%	8.8%
November	34.1%	81.2%	8.8%
December	37.0%	70.0%	12.5%
Winter	31.3%	67.1%	10.8%
Summer	100.0%	100.0%	99.6%
Annual	57.5%	86.6%	34.2%

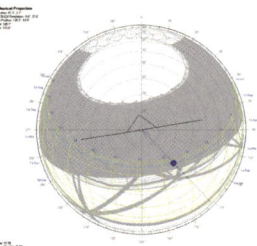

Studying the southwest façade

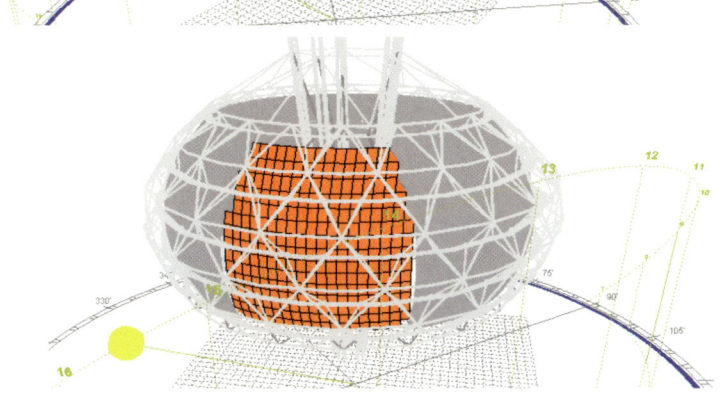

Computation came up with the following data:

· Stereographic diagrams showing the insolation on each pane in the façade, given its orientation and the season, at one-hour intervals.

· Stereographic diagrams of the shade factors, at each point and with the results from the insolation study.

· Calculation of the adjusted solar factor to find, based on the above data, not just a glazing that would do the job, but the one with the best thermal and radiation performance as an aide in designing the supplementary sunshade and maximising energy efficiency in climate control.

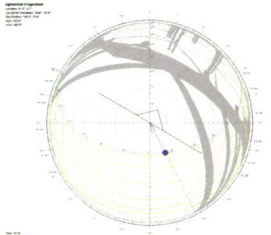

Effective Shading Coefficients

Latitude: 41.3°
Longitude: 2.1°
TimeZone: 15.0° [+1.0hrs]
Orientation: 30.6°

Month	Avg SC	Max SC	Min SC
January	16.1%	95.0%	0.0%
February	17.5%	100.0%	0.0%
March	23.8%	100.0%	0.0%
April	21.1%	100.0%	0.0%
May	18.8%	100.0%	0.0%
June	19.5%	100.0%	0.0%
July	16.7%	100.0%	0.0%
August	23.9%	100.0%	0.0%
September	22.5%	100.0%	0.0%
October	21.2%	100.0%	0.0%
November	11.3%	70.0%	0.0%
December	14.2%	95.0%	0.0%
Winter	15.9%	93.3%	0.0%
Summer	18.4%	100.0%	0.0%
Annual	18.9%	95.8%	0.0%

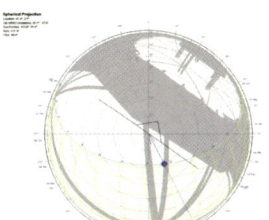

Effective Shading Coefficients

Latitude: 41.3°
Longitude: 2.1°
TimeZone: 15.0° [+1.0hrs]
Orientation: 35.1°

Month	Avg SC	Max SC	Min SC
January	24.7%	100.0%	0.0%
February	30.0%	100.0%	0.0%
March	32.8%	100.0%	0.0%
April	41.9%	100.0%	0.0%
May	42.0%	100.0%	0.0%
June	41.7%	100.0%	0.0%
July	46.8%	100.0%	0.0%
August	39.6%	100.0%	0.0%
September	37.1%	100.0%	0.0%
October	27.6%	100.0%	0.0%
November	26.3%	100.0%	0.0%
December	25.6%	80.0%	0.0%
Winter	26.8%	93.3%	0.0%
Summer	43.1%	100.0%	0.0%
Annual	34.5%	98.3%	0.0%

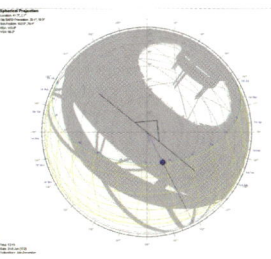

Effective Shading Coefficients

Latitude: 41.3°
Longitude: 2.1°
TimeZone: 15.0° [+1.0hrs]
Orientation: 39.1°

Month	Avg SC	Max SC	Min SC
January	45.1%	100.0%	16.0%
February	54.9%	100.0%	20.0%
March	66.6%	100.0%	20.0%
April	79.1%	100.0%	20.0%
May	78.7%	100.0%	20.0%
June	82.5%	100.0%	20.0%
July	81.2%	100.0%	20.0%
August	73.6%	100.0%	20.0%
September	65.5%	100.0%	20.0%
October	53.7%	100.0%	20.0%
November	43.4%	100.0%	16.0%
December	37.3%	100.0%	20.0%
Winter	45.9%	100.0%	18.7%
Summer	80.8%	100.0%	20.0%
Annual	63.5%	100.0%	19.3%

Solar glass definition

Type-B

Type-A

Type-D

Type-C

The 904 panes that make up the façade—no two of which are on the same plane and thus not subject to the same level of solar radiation—were divided into four groups of different solar specifications.

Type-A glazing, for the lower part of the courtyard façade, provides no special solar protection. It is made of 16 mm tempered glass, a 14 mm air chamber and 4+4 mm laminated glass. TL=77%; FS=70%; U=1.4 W/m² ºC.

Type-B glazing, for the north side of the outer façade, is composed of high-performance treated double glazing offering low solar protection: 6 mm tempered glass, 20 mm air chamber and 4+4 mm laminated glass (TL=76%; FS=55%; U=1.5 W/m² ºC).

Type-C glazing, for the east and west sides of the outer façade, is composed of high-performance treated double glazing offering high solar protection: 6 mm tempered glass, 20 mm air chamber and 4+4 mm laminated glass (TL=68%; FS=41%; U=1.4 W/m² ºC).

Type-D glazing, for the south side of the outer façade, is composed of high-performance treated double glazing offering very high solar protection: 6 mm tempered glass, 20 mm air chamber and 4+4 mm laminated glass (TL=65%; FS=40%; U=1.4 W/m² ºC).

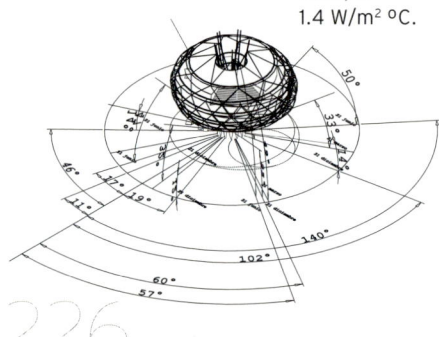

Based on these studies, the building achieves excellent energy ratings. By optimising glazing performance and adding a high-performance sunscreen, a 62% savings in energy use associated with climate control is attained.

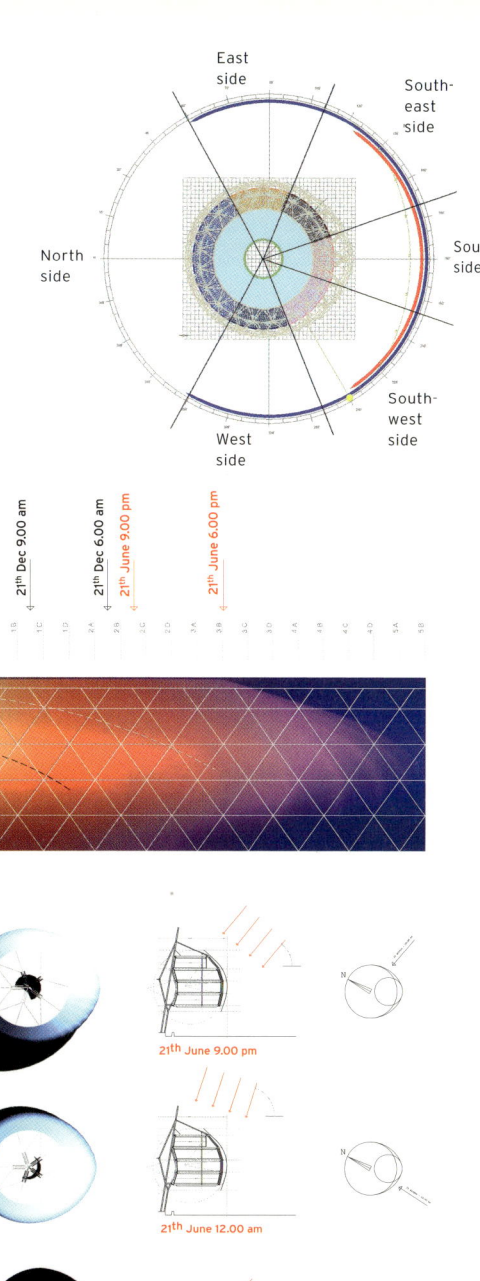

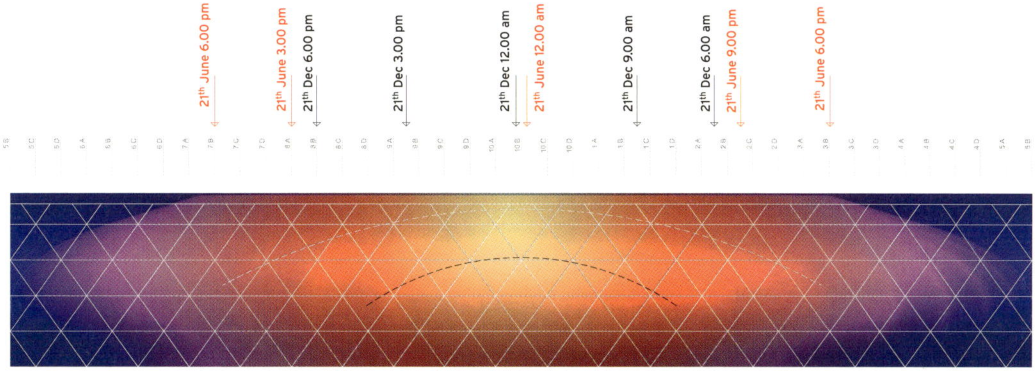

East side

South-east side

North side

South side

West side

South-west side

21th June 6.00 pm

21th June 3.00 pm

21th Dec 6.00 pm

21th Dec 3.00 pm

21th Dec 12.00 am

21th June 12.00 am

21th Dec 9.00 am

21th Dec 6.00 am

21th June 9.00 pm

21th June 6.00 pm

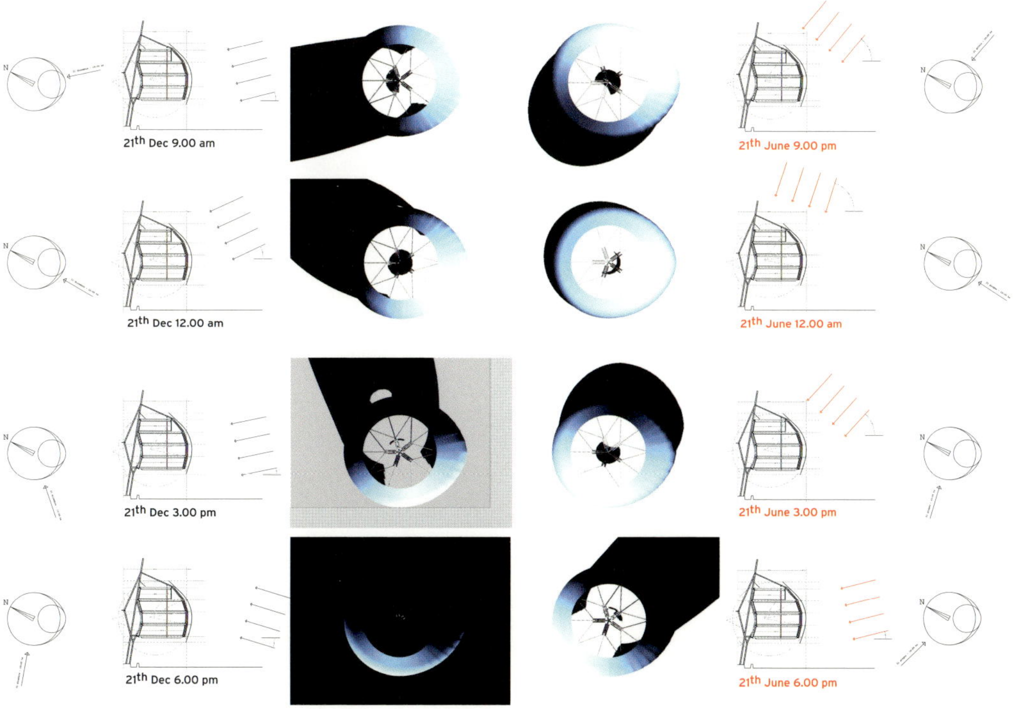

21th Dec 9.00 am

21th Dec 12.00 am

21th Dec 3.00 pm

21th Dec 6.00 pm

21th June 9.00 pm

21th June 12.00 am

21th June 3.00 pm

21th June 6.00 pm

227

Steel profile façade

The Jansen VISS TVS curtain wall system ensures complete thermal break. It is made of S235JRG2 steel complying with European standard EN 10025:1993, with 50 x 95 load-bearing mullions and transoms with glazing rebate. The cold-rolled sheet metal is coated with 50 to 150 micron Sendzimir (hot-zinc dipped) galvanising, complying with the standard UNE 37508. Weather-proofing is ensured with EPDM gaskets on the mullions and transoms, the latter also equipped with sealing gasket.

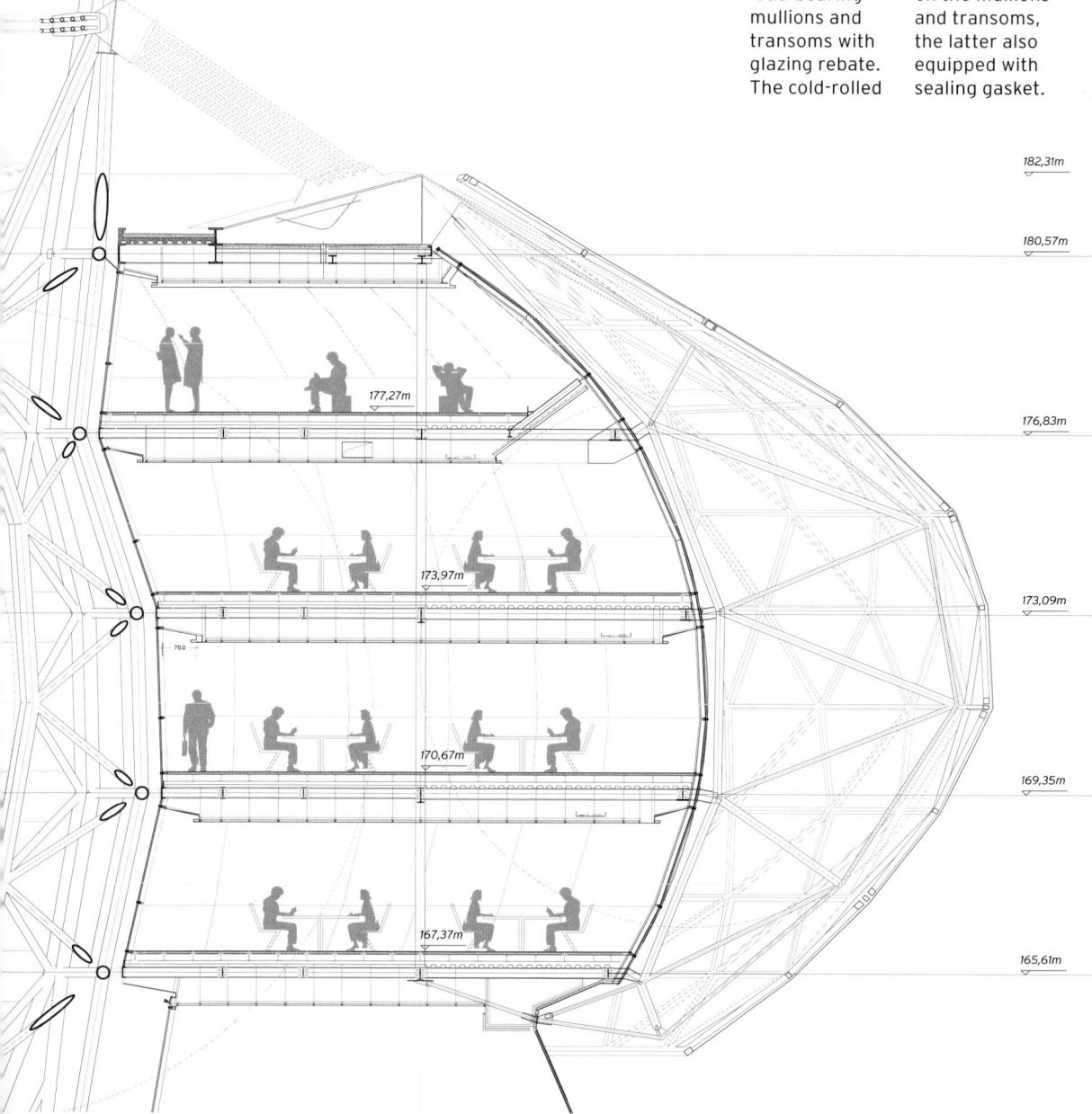

182,31m

180,57m

177,27m

176,83m

173,97m

173,09m

170,67m

169,35m

167,37m

165,61m

The components of the curtain wall are made of cold-rolled sheet metal. This process is performed at room temperature, starting with a strip of steel or AISI316 stainless steel of width equal to the perimeter of the profile to be made. The profiling machines are equipped with two pairs of rollers, between which the steel is passed; the pressure of the rollers shapes the profile to the desired thickness, determined by the form of the grooves in the rollers. This process is carried out on continuous, fully-automated rolling lines over 100 metres long. The profiles are made according to the strictest standards and the traceability of the steel is controlled throughout all the processes, from mill to site. The main quality certifications are:
-EN 10204-2.2
-ISO9001:2008 -ISO14001:2004
-OHSAS 18001:2007
-CE
When the profile rods are finished they are sent to the façade maker. Here the rods are cut according the angles indicated by the designer, the joints are machined, and the pieces prepared, protected and transported to the worksite. Over 15 km of Jansen VISS profiling and over 20,000 working hours in machining, welding, in-factory preparation and on-site assembly went into the spherical glazed enclosure of the building.

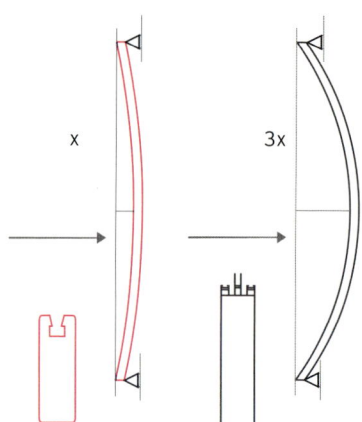

The elasticity modulus of steel is 3 times that of aluminium. This means that given equal spans and loads, and with the same section, the deformation of a steel profile is 3 times less than an aluminium one. By using steel rather than aluminium profiles, we are able to reduce the section of 30%, thus saving material and achieving greater transparency.

233

Due to the peculiar spherical-elliptical geometry of the building, there are no two continuous flat faces on the façade, so all profiles meet at angles on all three axes. A façade system with mechanical joints between the components, apart from the inevitable negative impact on aesthetics, is unworkable. On the other hand, steel enables complex joints with the same simplicity and neatness associated with 90° angles. Moreover, to avoid duplicating profiles in the mullions where angles are very acute, EPDM gaskets are used in fitting the panes, with a single profile, at the angles required by the geometry of the building.

All the mullions are welded according to the geometry of the sphere, which, in addition to creating joints embedded in the nodes and the consequent ease of calculation, allows us to reduce the section of the profiles, giving the façade an overall appearance of slenderness.

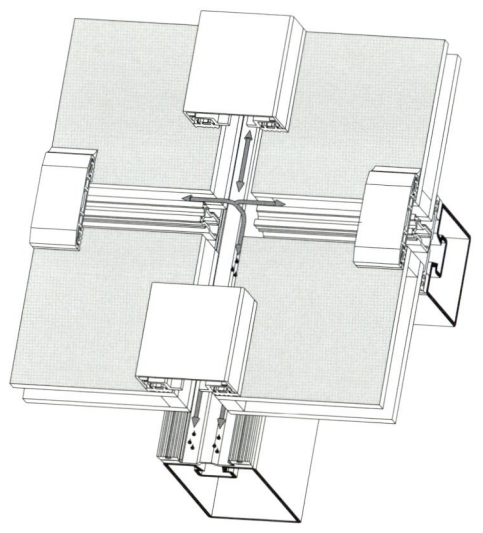

Water drainage
and thermal
break system
and rain test on
the façade.

235

Given the particular geometry of the ground floor and the sphere, the joining of the two faces, with completely different structural behaviours, could not be resolved with another joint in the façade system. For this enclosure, we used the same profiles as in upper floors (50 x 95) reinforced with a plate with perpendicularly welded edge on the inside. This profile is fixed to the ground and, rather than covering the entire height of the enclosure, it stops three quarters of the way up, leaving the glazing free. The top of the glazing is fitted into a longitudinal groove which follows the curve of the sphere, and in which sliding glazing gaskets are fitted to allow full movement of the upper building, independently of the more rigid ground floor.

The geometry of the building and its design with double, interior and exterior façade, with 2,840 m² of glazed surface, maximises transparency and the exterior-interior-exterior visual flow in the office building. Each point in the space is like a panopticon, visible from all other points.

239

CASTING A SHADOW

Selective membrane
José María González

Mediterranean architecture abounds in examples of façades shaded by lightweight materials in order to protect openings from excessive sunlight.

Contemporary architecture likewise values solar protection as an efficient means of improving thermal comfort, reducing energy consumption and controlling natural lighting inside the building; in short, façade protection to improve comfort and reduce environmental impact.

The leading figures of the Modern Movement had a certain passion for façades with large expanses of glazing. But the simplicity of the abstract form required a construction system that was indifferent to climate.

The design of the exterior envelope of the iGuzzini Illuminazione Ibérica building proposes modern abstraction by means of a complex constructive solution. The building resorts to solar protection on the large glazed surfaces of the façade as a means of adapting to its environmental conditions. Thus it overcomes the equation "transparency = exposure" that we find in the first curtain walls, as well as in some recent designs.

Solar protection improves thermal comfort in a building by shading the façade. Recent standards in Spain take a positive view of this traditional form of protection. Since the publication, in 2006, of the Technical Building Code Core Document on Energy Savings and the Decree governing the adoption of eco-efficient environmental criteria in buildings, shade factor parameters have been formulated and quantified in such a way that the effectiveness of a proposed solution can be forecast.

Energy savings are achieved primarily by controlling the thermal transmittance of the envelope and the adjusted solar factor. Thermal transmittance is determined by the characteristics of the glazing and its support system, both of which are discussed in an earlier chapter. The adjusted solar factor, on the other hand, depends essentially on two factors: the shade factor of the opening and the solar factor of the glazing. (For our purposes, the other factors involved matter less.) Therefore, the goal is to attain shade values which provide adequate levels of thermal comfort,

Image study of the outer mesh in the competition phase.

in order to reduce energy consumption. The effect of the solar protection is key to calculating the adjusted solar factor. Where the aim is to avoid diminishing transparency to light radiation, the shade factor of the opening is a more effective means for reducing the solar factor of the glazing.

In a building of this nature, it was not easy to find a shading solution that can adapt to the geometry of the façade, exploit solar heat input in cold weather, allow clear views of the beautiful landscape outside and optimise natural lighting inside. After extensive research into the latest technical solutions on the global market, the choice was high-performance tensioned membranes, which are adaptable to the geometry of the building's envelope than blinds or louvers.

Returning to the Mediterranean tradition, we note that the membrane is separated from the façade—and on the outside, of course—to achieve adequate shading and create a well-ventilated chamber through which air flows, thus cooling the surface of the façade. To enhance this effect, the membrane must be made of reflective material. Solar protection covering the façade, however, presents two problems: the action of wind on the membrane—both suction and pressure—and maintenance. Removable, modular solutions facilitate both maintenance and replacement when tearing or wear occur.

The sunshade on the iGuzzini Building is a one-piece membrane made up of a triangular textile patterns borne on a steel substructure with aluminium fasteners. The fabric, Stamisol® FT 381, is a composite of a cross-woven polyester yarn core with PVC coating on both sides.

The information provided by the manufacturer includes experimental data on the fabric's mechanical, thermal, acoustic and durability specifications and performance, as well as a life cycle analysis (being 100% recyclabe by means of using Texyloop® technology developed by Serge Ferrari S.A.S.). Here we will limit discussion to the characteristics that determine architectural image and mechanical and energy performance.

Study model of the sunscreen. Scale: 1:75. Material: laser-cut acrylic, welded and painted wire, soldered copper tubes. Model shown at the La Arquería de los Nuevos Ministerios, Madrid, for the exhibition "35+ Construyendo en Democracia, 35 años de Arquitectura Española". With this model we assessed the possibility of a smaller sunscreen that would rotate around the façade following the path of the sun.

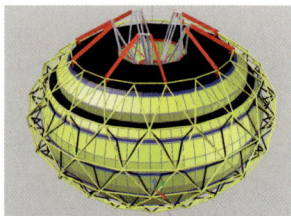

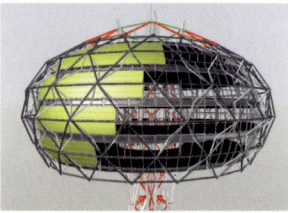

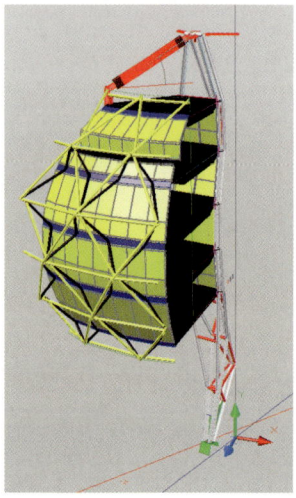

Study image
of the mobile
sunscreen.

Stamisol® FT 381 lends the building a different appearance during the day and at night. By day it is opaque and defines the texture, colour, and form of the building. At night, the lighting inside the building is visible from outside such that the interior defines the image of the façade. In daytime the fabric prevents glare from the sun on the glazed façade surface while offering almost complete outward transparency. Being highly flexible, it adapts extremely well to the curved façade.

The membrane and its bearing substructure are lightweight: less than 5 Kg/m². Due to its location, the building is subject to significant wind action. Under such conditions, to prevent tearing, in addition to the strength of the material, the whole—membrane and support—must be deformable, and its deformability must be compatible with the dimensional stability of the textile over its useful life. In order to meet the above requirements, during the manufacturing process the fabric is pre-stressed lengthwise and breadthwise while the coating is applied. This mechanical treatment improves its strength and dimensional stability. The design stage of the building included a graphical and numerical analysis of solar radiation on the façades, creating a radiation map which showed a non-uniform distribution on the façade of both radiation and sunlight hours. Accordingly, four areas in the vertical section of the façade were defined: the upper fourth is the most critical because it is subject to the highest radiation; the fourth below is subject to average radiation, and the bottom two fourths to less than average.

Based on this analysis, it was determined precisely where solar protection was—and was not—needed in order to manage the effects of solar action on the glazed façade. Factors of reflection, transmission, shade, absorption and sunlight transmission are determined by the performance of the textile, and it protects the façade from overheating in summer, reducing heat transmission into the building by 77%, thus reducing energy consumption and CO_2 emissions associated with air-conditioning by 47%. The ventilated façade further improves the energy efficiency of the building's envelope. Finally, while the combined effect of solar protection, ventilated façade and high-performance glazing succeeds in improving the building's environmental sustainability, the challenge of finding a balanced solution between thermal protection and efficient transmission of natural light is met by the considerable transparency of the fabric.

In sum, based on operational and technical rationale, but with a highly architectural final result, the solution for the building's façade is an interesting synthesis of modernity and "Mediterraneanity".

José María González,
Ph.D. in Architecture, Deputy Director of ETSAB
UPC Barcelona Tech

Digital study drawing of the continuous outer structural skin and geometric study of the modulation of this structure in relation to the partition of the glazed surface of the building.

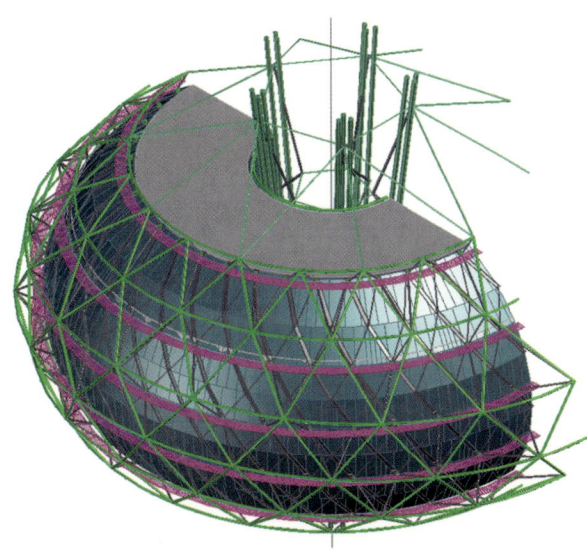

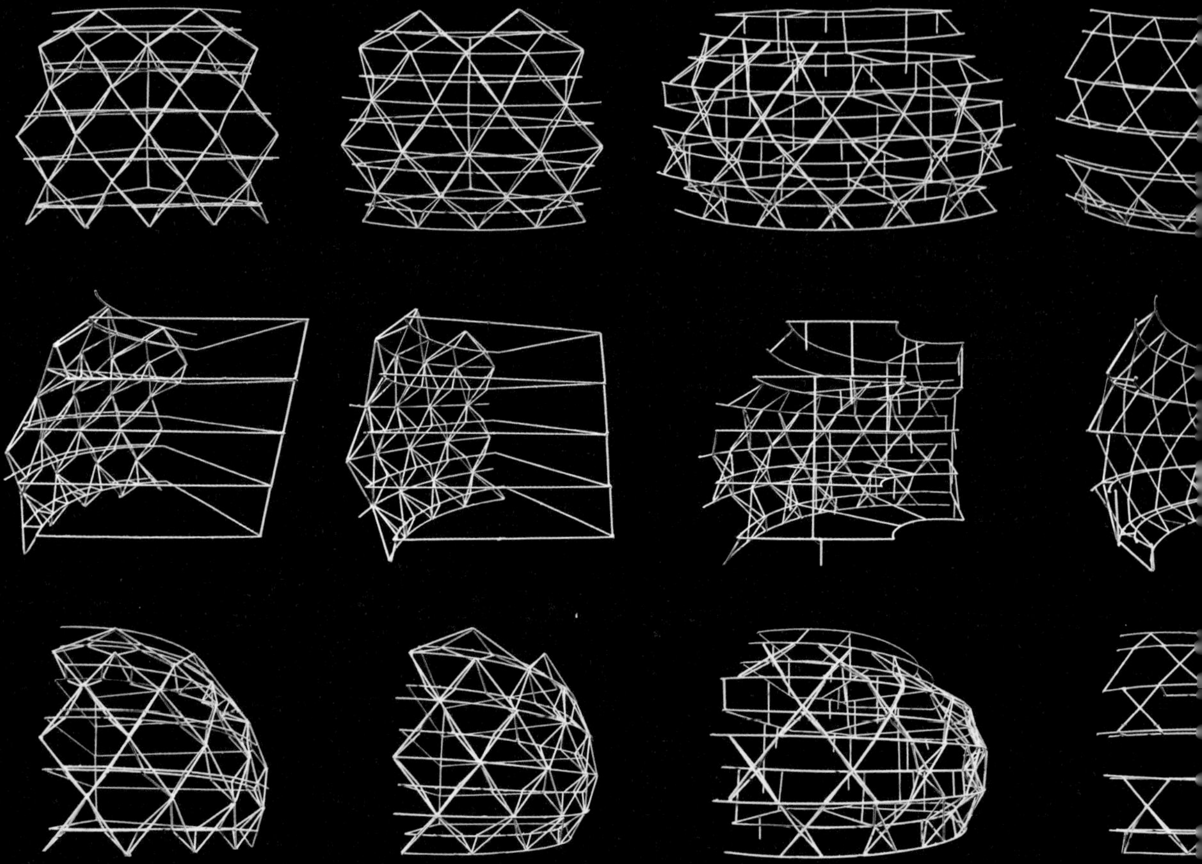

Series of models for the study of the outer mesh involved in the transmission of the slab loads. The first models show the non-specialisation of this area, which is conceived as a three-dimensional structure. This solution entails enormous complexity in the nodes, and an excessive amount of material. Emphasis is placed on identifying potential forms capable of bearing the outer part of the slab and providing a geometry for the sunscreen. The further specialisation of this outer surface, separating the two functions—structure and solar-shield—would result in the "outer ribs" and monolayer skin.

The final so-
lution gathers
the outermost
loads, focusing
the structural
function in the
ten ribs in the
surface, which
work with inner
tensioners and
at the same
time bear the
lighter-weight
sunscreen
structure.

Façade grid nodes

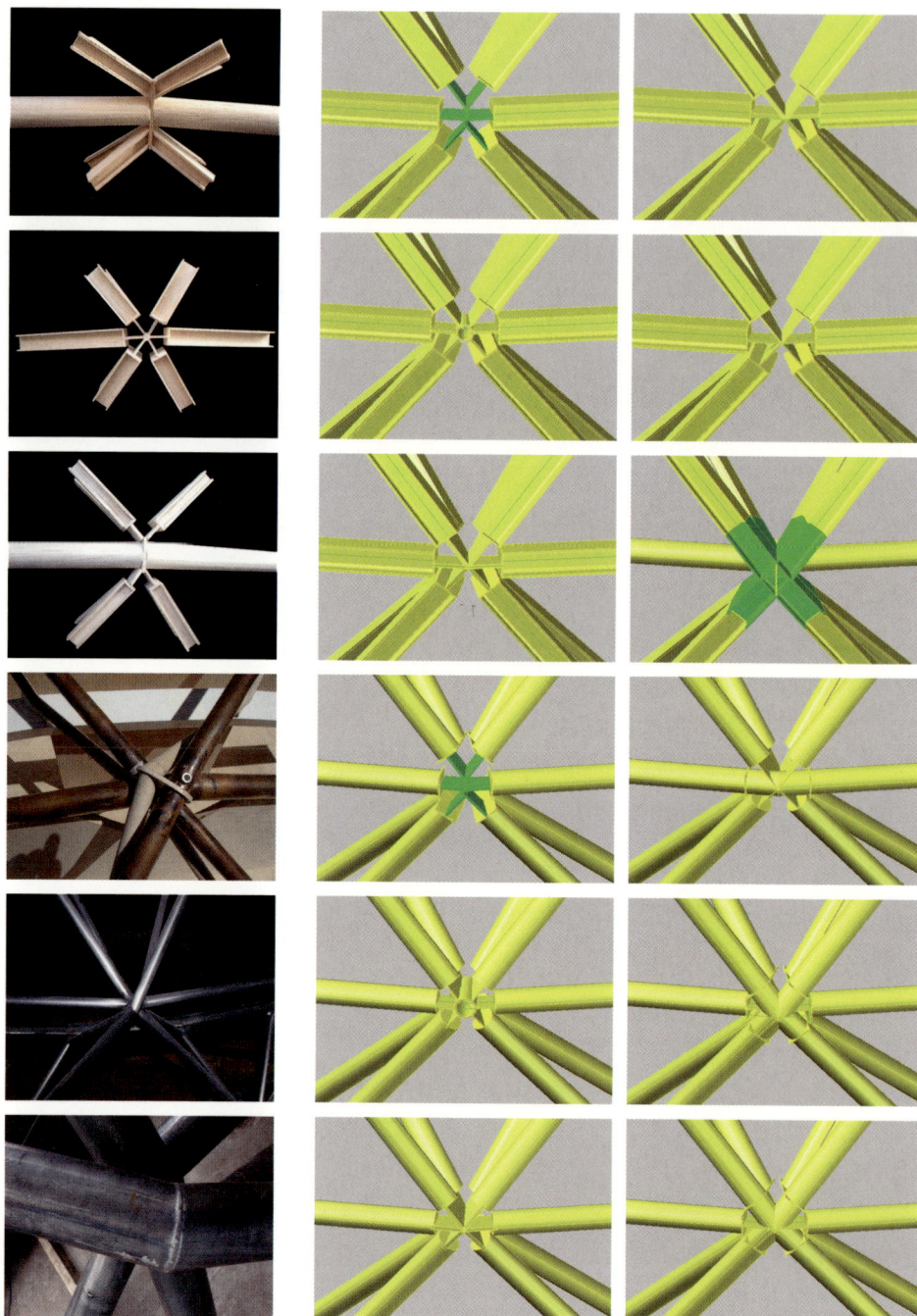

In the definition of the outer structural surface, several prototypes were made.
These joints also had to be able to incorporate the outer surfacial sunscreen support mesh. For this purpose, the different three-dimensional scale fastening models were built and tested.

The outer structural surface was tested with a 1:10 scale model. This prototype crowned the Catalan Architects Association (COAC) Building in Plaça de la Catedral, Barcelona, during the project exhibition.

249

Study models of the outer skin. Scale: 1:50. Materials: soldered wire and cotton string. Once we assumed the differentiation between the outer structure of the outer ribs and the sunscreen, we tried the possibility of using cables (strings in the model) rather than rigid profiles for the definition of the sunscreen. In this way, the entire skin is tensioned and will perform better under wind loads. In some cases, to achieve the convex form of the sunscreen, auxiliary bearing elements, such as bracing beams fixed to the structure of the outer ribs, were generated.

Auxiliary model
for the cons-
truction of the
outer mesh and
sunscreen
support.
Scale: 1:75.
Materials:
soldered wire
and balsa wood
rods. We tried to
come up with a
two-dimensional
mesh without
three-dimen-
sional bracing
elements, with
minimal fas-
tening to the
outer ribs.

In the final draft of the project, the two-dimensional sunscreen skin is fixed to the ten outer ribs, which are linked structurally to the ten roof brackets joined to the five masts of the central pillar. From a geometric point of view, the outer ribs are integrated into the regular modulation of the glazed façade and the triangulation of the sunscreen.

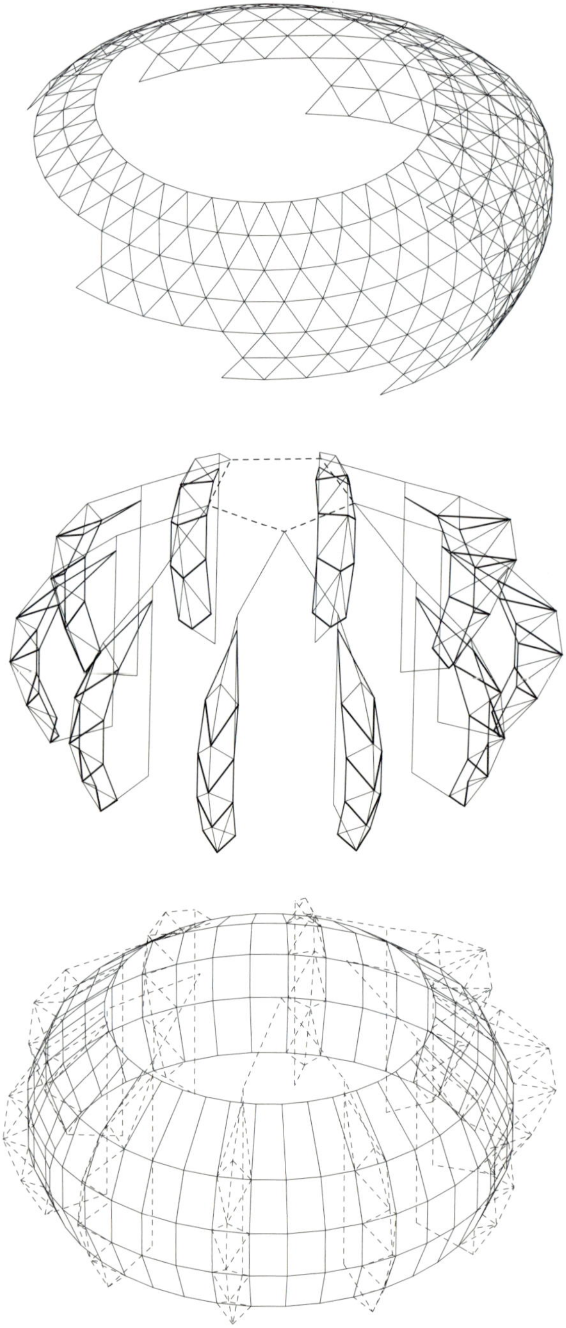

Building the spatial structure

In the structure for the outer skin, the SLO Single-Layer Ortz system was used. The fundamental characteristic of a monolayer structure is that, due to its form, and even when extremely thin, it can cover broad spans, rendering unnecessary a large number of structural elements, and giving the shield a lightweight appearance and maximum transparency. The sunscreen is developed as a spherical generating surface approximately 40 m in diameter and approximately 18 m high, which gives a working surface of 1,574 m². This single-layer structure does not appear on the north façade, where it is not needed, while its placement over the rest of the façade accords with needs for solar protection.

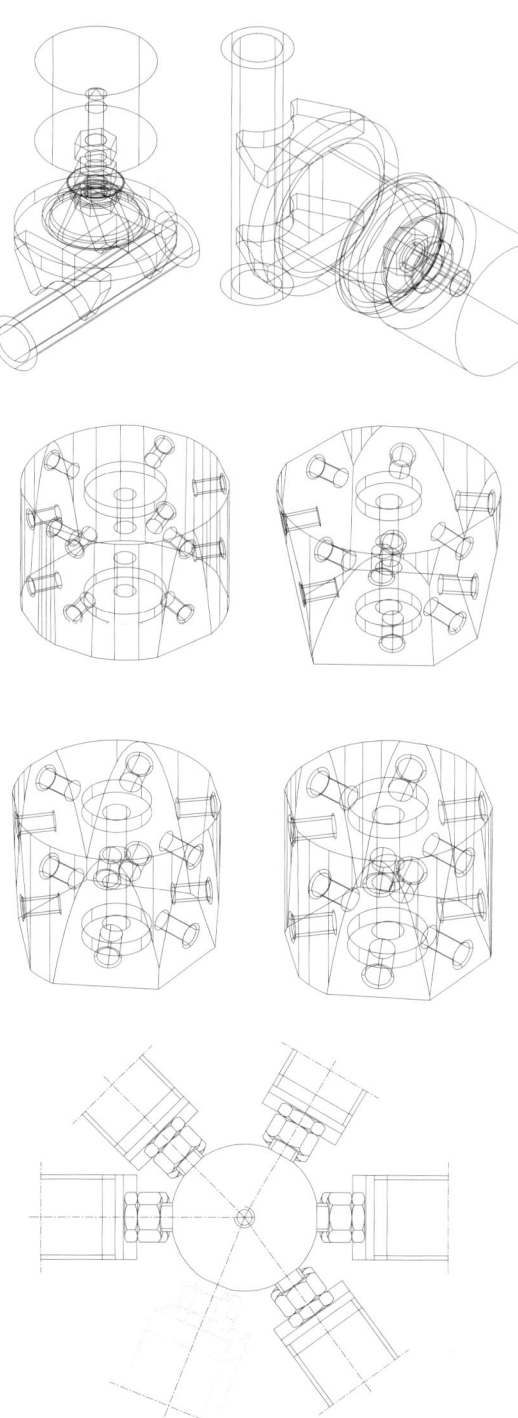

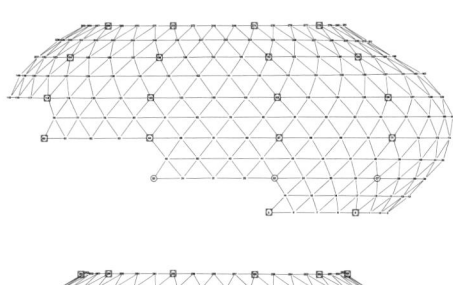

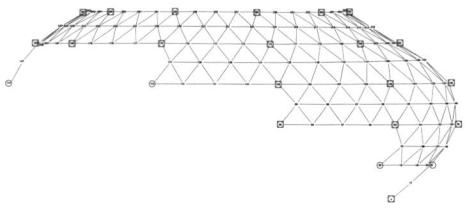

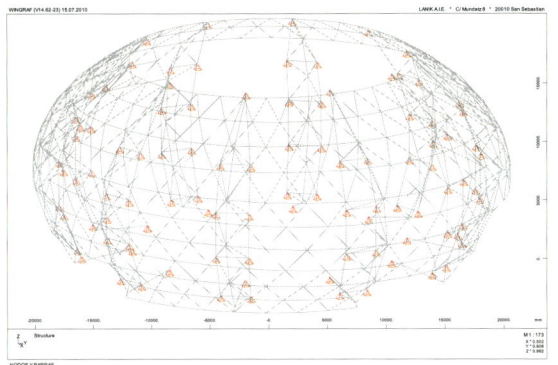

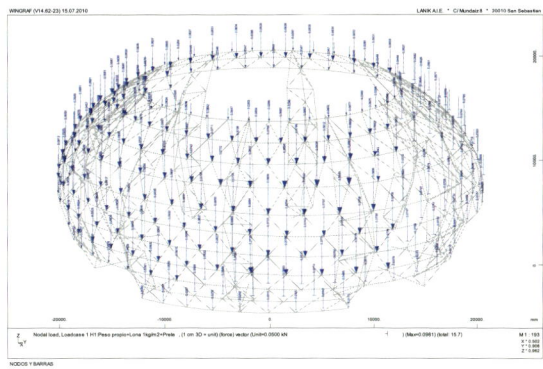

Using a Lanik computing system developed specifically for this purpose, we studied the loads affecting the skin and sized the tubes, bolts and nodes. We used a model of finite one-dimensional beam-like elements that simulate the tubes and beams. In this calculation assumption, the rib-slab nodes are considered fixed and articulated. The joining of the monolayer and the ribs was modelled with a tube which gave a lateral support stiffness of 4000 kg/cm. Once we had identified the theoretical sizing values of each element, we computed the interferences of the tubes, adjusting upwards the diameter of the base cylinder to avoid collision between adjacent pairs of tubes. The resulting diversity of elements meant that they could only be made with CAM systems.

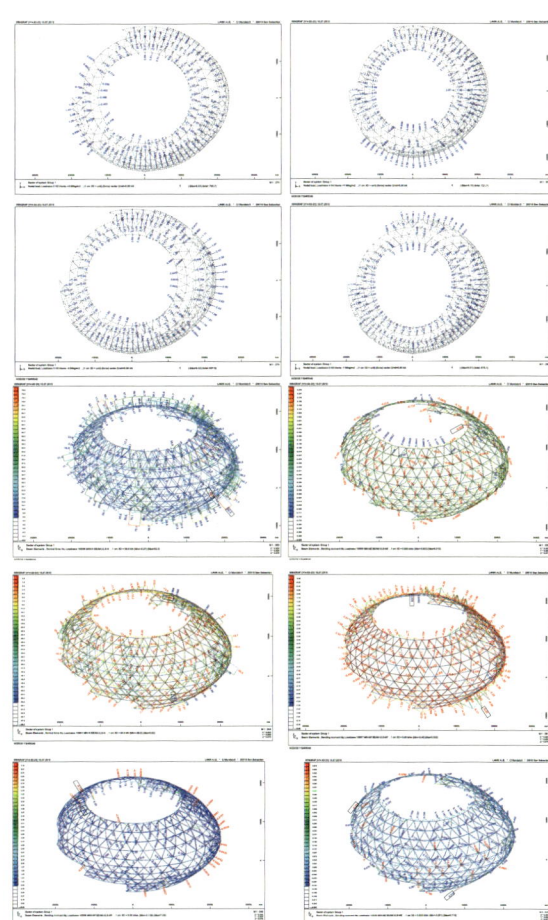

Due to their high stackability, the elements which come from the shop finished—including all the required coats of paint and marking to identify each node and tube—are delivered to the worksite in containers, thus achieving high space efficiency. Assembly is exclusively with bolts, meaning greater speed and safety in this stage of the construction process. Due to its dual-thread, with a high capacity to withstand bending, the SLO system enabled on-site pre-assembly of the parts of the cap between each of the outer ribs, which were then hoisted one-by-one with cranes and fixed in place. The nodes of the monolayer structure in turn ensure constant tensioning of the fabric, due to a mechanical system that allows for adjustment in case of changes in environmental conditions such as temperature or wind loads.

The 756 tubes that make up the cap are cold-formed tubular profiles welded lengthwise, measuring 120 x 80 x 4 mm, quality S275J0H and standard UNE-EN 10219-1:2007. The discs are solid cylinders with diameters ranging from 130 to 290 mm and made of C55E carbon steel, standard UNE-EN 10083-1. The two connectors between the tubes and discs are standard Ortz elements, M16/20 and M22/27 left-right dual-threaded bolts. The bolts are high-tempered to ensure increased endurance of the material without affecting its capacity. These elements are produced in very flexible and highly automated industrial facilities. Their prefabrication enables levels of diversification, precision and finishing far superior to those ordinarily found in steel manufacturing.

Skin tests

Based a triangular geometry we studied solutions using textile modules separated from each other, which was ruled out due to complex installation. Also ruled out were solutions using: metal mesh, due to excessive weight; woven-yarn fabrics, due to the long manufacturing time; and ETFE technology, due to imperfection and maintenance costs.

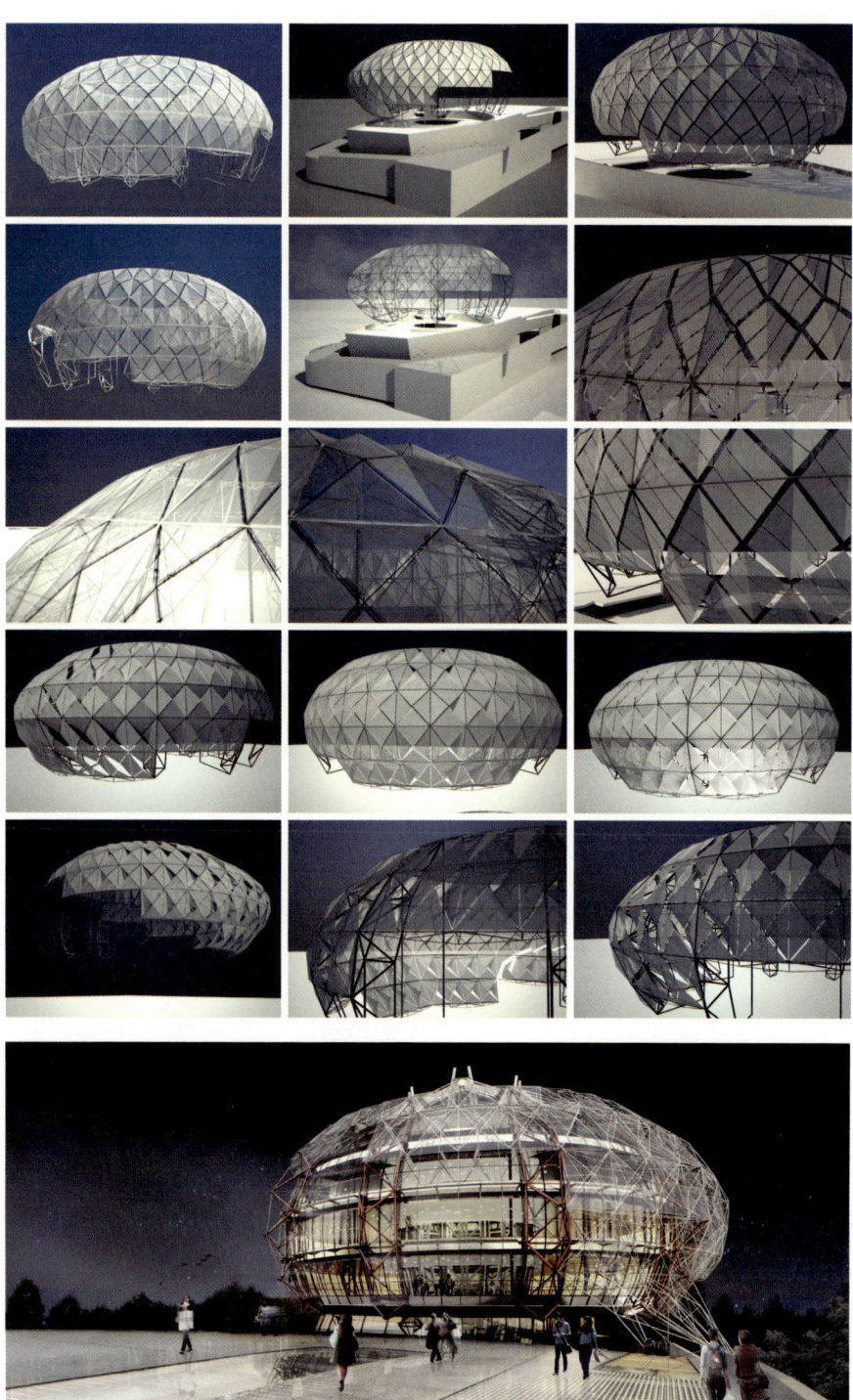

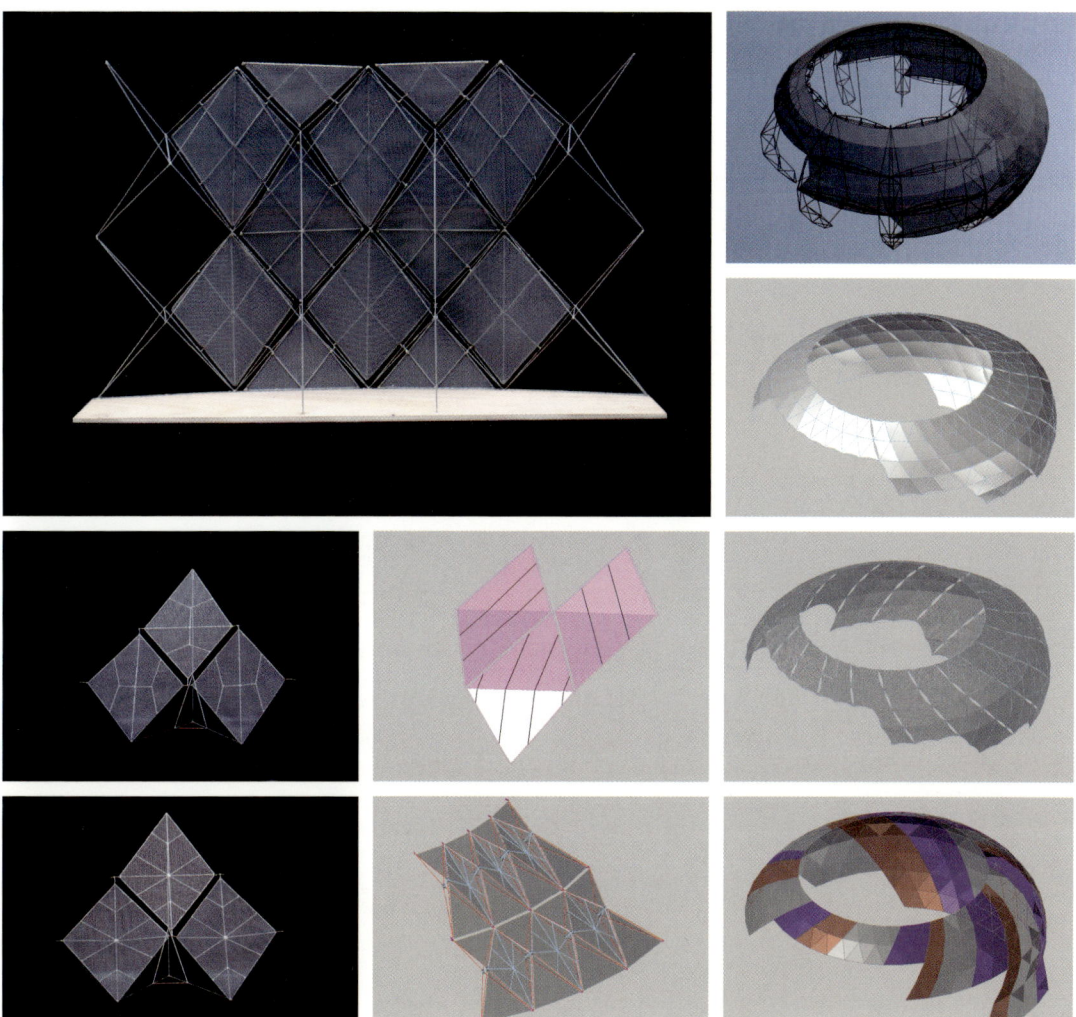

Several materials and configurations for the sunscreen were studied and tested. The project required a material that, in addition to its primary function as protection from solar radiation, offered high outward transparency. Moreover it needed to be extra-lightweight, to avoid overloading the structure, and flexible, to adapt to the spherical form and withstand wind stresses.

The fabric finally used on the façade for sun protection is STAMISOL® FT 381 mesh. The worldwide patented Précontraint® SERGE FERRARI technology pretensions the fabric for all coating operations, subjecting both warp and weft to regular, evenly distributed tension, thereby ensuring equal stretching in both directions.

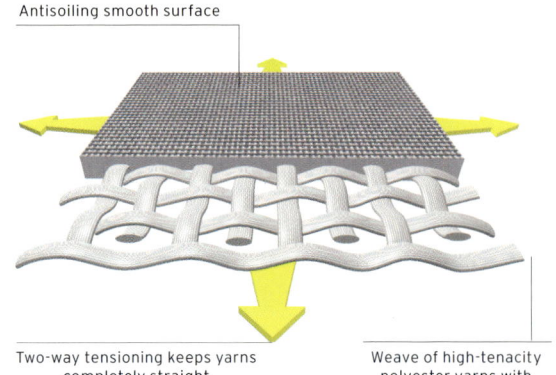

Antisoiling smooth surface

Two-way tensioning keeps yarns completely straight

Weave of high-tenacity polyester yarns with UV-protection

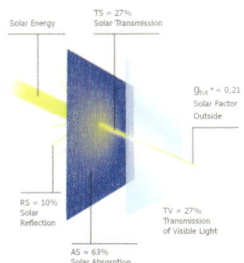

Solar Energy	TS ≈ 27% Solar Transmission

$g_{tot}^* \approx 0,21$
Solar Factor
Outside

RS ≈ 10% Solar Reflection

TV ≈ 27% Transmission of Visible Light

AS ≈ 63% Solar Absorption

381-3108

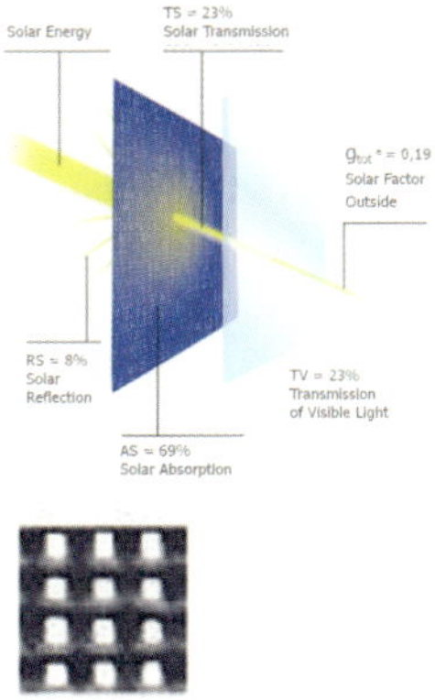

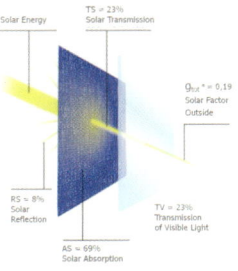

Solar Energy	TS ≈ 23% Solar Transmission

$g_{tot}^* \approx 0,19$
Solar Factor
Outside

RS ≈ 8% Solar Reflection

TV ≈ 23% Transmission of Visible Light

AS ≈ 69% Solar Absorption

381-3113

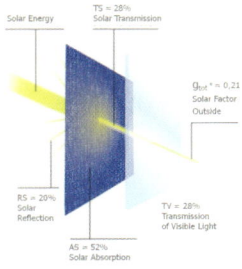

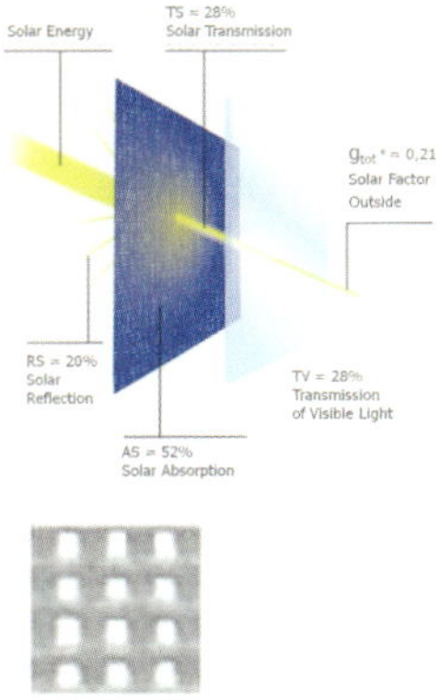

Solar Energy	TS ≈ 28% Solar Transmission

$g_{tot}^* \approx 0,21$
Solar Factor
Outside

RS ≈ 20% Solar Reflection

TV ≈ 28% Transmission of Visible Light

AS ≈ 52% Solar Absorption

381-3125

The fabric is a composite of a cross-woven polyester yarn core, PVC-coated on both sides. This solution offers transparency for outward visibility and cuts thermal energy incidence on the façade by 77%.

Three colours of STAMISOL® FT 381 high-performance fabric are used: hammered-metal 381-3125, chocolate brown 381-3108, and slate black 381-3113. On the façade, the three colours are arranged in diagonal stripes to accentuate the motion effect of the sphere. The membrane is made in one piece, using 1,574 m² of fabric, based on triangular modules made with numerical control equipment and joined together along nearly 2 km of high-frequency welded seam done in a specialised workshop.

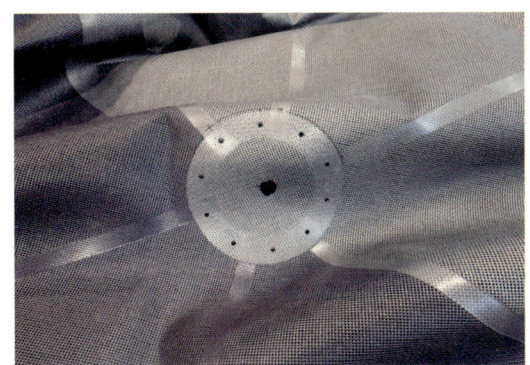

265

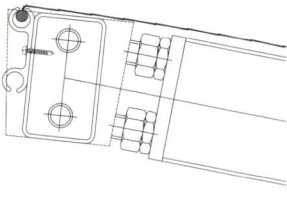

After the mono-layer structure is in place, the protective fabric is fitted to the upper to lower perimeters.
The fabric is fixed to the monolayer structure and then pretensioned at the nodes to adapt it to the outer geometry of the façade. The upper (01) and lower (02) parts of the fabric are fixed to the monolayer structure by means of aluminium profiling. In conjunction with the 295 nodes of the monolayer structure, a system of circular steel fabric-tensioning plates tailor-made for this project (03) was added. These plates, which also secure the fabric under wind pressure and suction, are equipped with threaded rods which pass through the node (02) and, by expanding, tension the fabric at the apex of each triangle, thus keeping it in a constant state of tension. IASO has developed, tailored and produced the membrane suit.

01.

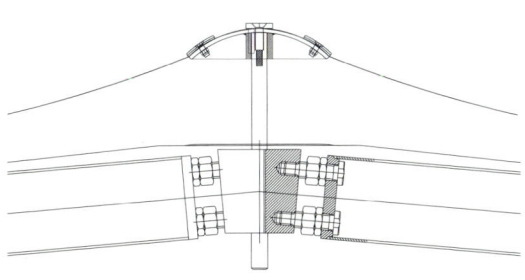

02

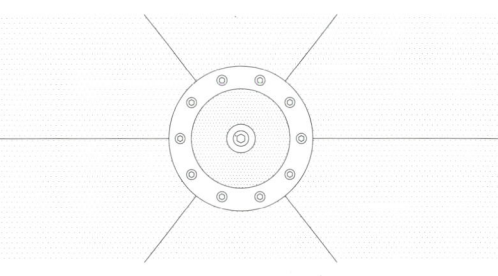

03

BUILDING IN
SUSTAINABILITY

Systems & mechanics
Josep Juliol

The sheer uniqueness of the building is evident. The systematisation, from a perspective of sustainability and energy efficiency, of the building's resources proved to be a challenge leading to success, given that it entailed the discovery of the most innovative and efficient solutions for the thermal, lighting and ventilation comfort of the interior spaces with the minimum energy demands possible. This has been the main objective throughout the architectural design process and, at the same time, the shaping of the building.

The starting points of the project were, on the one hand, its focus on passive systems, maximising sunlight, wind and water in order to achieve the greatest possible energy independence, and, on the other hand, its use of next-generation active technologies in complementing these passive systems, optimising resources through the use of management technologies and systems as a tool to further rationalise consumption.

The passive design achieves thermal and lighting comfort conditions through strategies that take advantage of specific natural physical phenomena. Firstly, the floating office volume is designed to control natural light from the courtyard and outer façades throughout the day. Secondly, it uses the earth's natural thermal inertia wherever the programme could be located underground (logistics depot, showrooms and artificial light testing labs, in fact the largest surface area in the programme). Thirdly, in the summer a flue effect is created by connecting the terrace around the building platform (at a lower elevation) to the courtyard of the office space (with opening at a higher elevation). This effect creates a natural airflow that lowers the temperature of the courtyard façade. Thus, in thermal terms, the courtyard acts as an extension of the offices, reducing energy losses by maintaining a similar temperature. In winter, a similar phenomenon occurs, albeit in reverse: the still-warm stale air from the offices is injected into the courtyard, thus lessening heat escape. Finally, between the glazed outer façade and the fabric membrane a natural convective air flow is created, which refreshes and lowers the surface temperature of the fa-çade in summer. Thus, despite the large glazed surface of the office volume, energy losses are avoided by protecting it with "air", both in the courtyard and, by means of the fabric membrane.

The use of intelligent active systems complements the building's natural functioning in meeting its needs with regard to climate, electricity, informatics and communica-tions, access control, fire detection and extinguishment, and water management. Before we go any further, it is worth noting that this is a highly automated building: in-side, we find no switches or keyholes.

Here we will provide an overview of the following aspects of the building: the central water collection grid, the use of LED technology for energy efficient lighting at night, the independent medium voltage and emergency electric power supply measurement plant backed up with UPS for the safety, security and computing systems, and the over-all security and management network monitored, as are other overseas branches, from the iGuzzini headquarters in Italy. The building's uniqueness is coupled, then, with the most advanced, environmentally-friendly systems and implemented with the latest technologies.

Starting with the climate systems, two 433 kW McQuay high-performance water-cooling units with HFC 134 refrig-erant and low sound emissions, are installed outside the building, facing north to obtain cooler outside air. By hav-ing two units in operation, we achieve redundancy while reducing power consumption, since consumption is lower with two units running in parallel at 60% than a single one at 95%. The cooled air from the units is sent to the end outlets through a primary flow circuit by means of double fixed-flow pumps and two variable-flow secondary circuits (level -2 to level 2 and level 3 to level 4), according to the occupation of the building. The end outlets are high-per-formance, three-speed fan coil units to handle peak loads with power ratings to match localised needs will minimis-

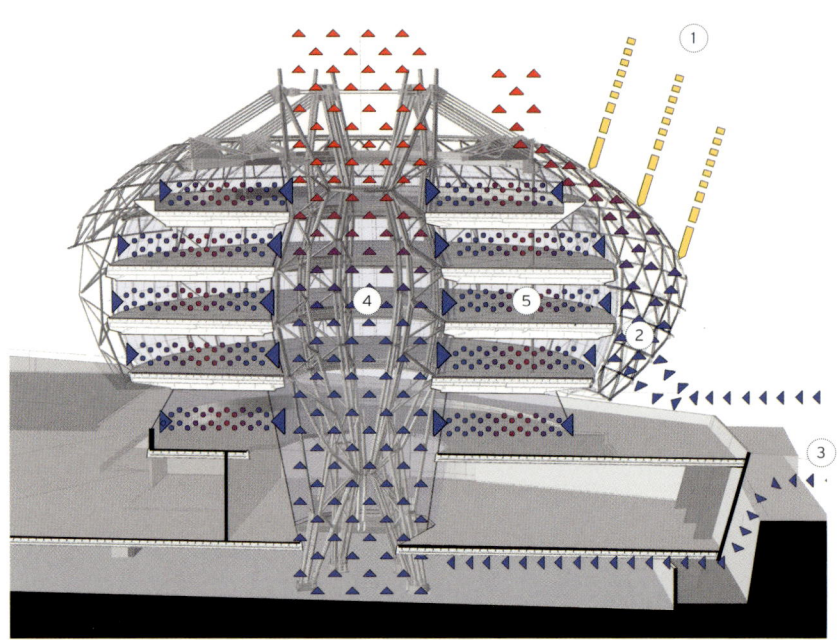

Summer
ventilation
system.
1. The sun rays
are filtered
by the textile
membrane.
2. Natural
ventilation +
convection
creates a fresh
thermal barrier.
3. An airflow
enters the
building through
the trough and
arrives to the
central space.
4. Chimney
effect in the
central space.
5. The offices
are refreshed
naturally by the
fresh flows (4
and 2).

ing noise, equipped with two-way control valves and ambience thermostats incorporated into a single control unit
for each zone or office space. The entire system is managed through a central control unit with an open-mode
main computer bus and partial regulators distributed with
computerised control.

Following the same redundancy criteria as the cooling
plants, heating is produced by two Adisa model 350-B95
high-performance 294 kW natural gas condensing boilers
with heat exchangers, primary and secondary circuit sep-
arators, and a Carel model VG180 natural gas humidifier
system to maintain the necessary level of humidity and
avoid hypotrophy among the building's users. The heating
circuits and components are similar to those of the cooling
system. The anticipated hot water needs for the building
are covered by a boiler circuit with exchanger and storage
tank, coupled with a solar panel hot water system which
feeds into the main hot water circuit.

The electrical supply systems are based around a 25 kV
medium-voltage controller located at the periphery of
the building, and thus accessible to the utility company.

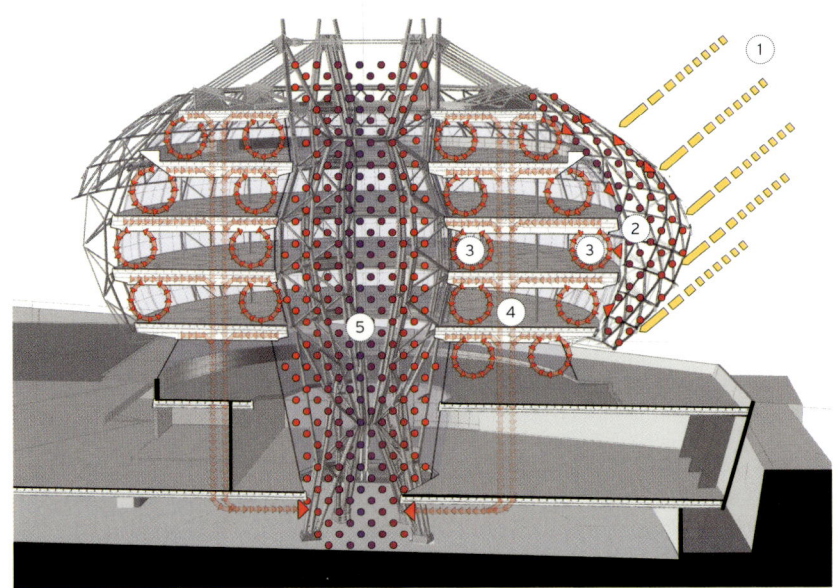

This secure connection is connected to a 1250 kVA TMC dry-type transformer at 25 kV with additional protectors in the basement. Located next to the transformer are a main distribution frame, a Gesan 358 kVA standby generator (covering all systems and circuits) and the UPS (Uninterruptible Power Supply) units to ensure power to the security alarm and computer networks. At each floor, the electrical architecture includes distribution frames for both the emergency and regular circuits. Electricity is distributed both through the hi-tech raised floor (in which the electrical and computer outlets can be located wherever needed) and through the drop ceiling (fire and low-voltage detection systems, lighting control, special and emergency lighting). The lighting control system and its configuration were of course designed to incorporate iGuzzini's next-generation systems, based on protocols of centralised control and management, and capable of adapting, at any given moment, the composition of both interior and exterior lighting, as well as the intensity of lighting on each floor, to changing natural light conditions, thus contributing to overall sustainability.

Winter climatic system.
1. The sun warms up the air behind the membrane increasing the temperature of the inner façade.
2. The thermal bridge is reduced.
3. The hot air helps to warm up the offices.
4. The stale air is injected to the central patio from the bottom.
5. The stale air helps to reduce the termal bridge from the inside.

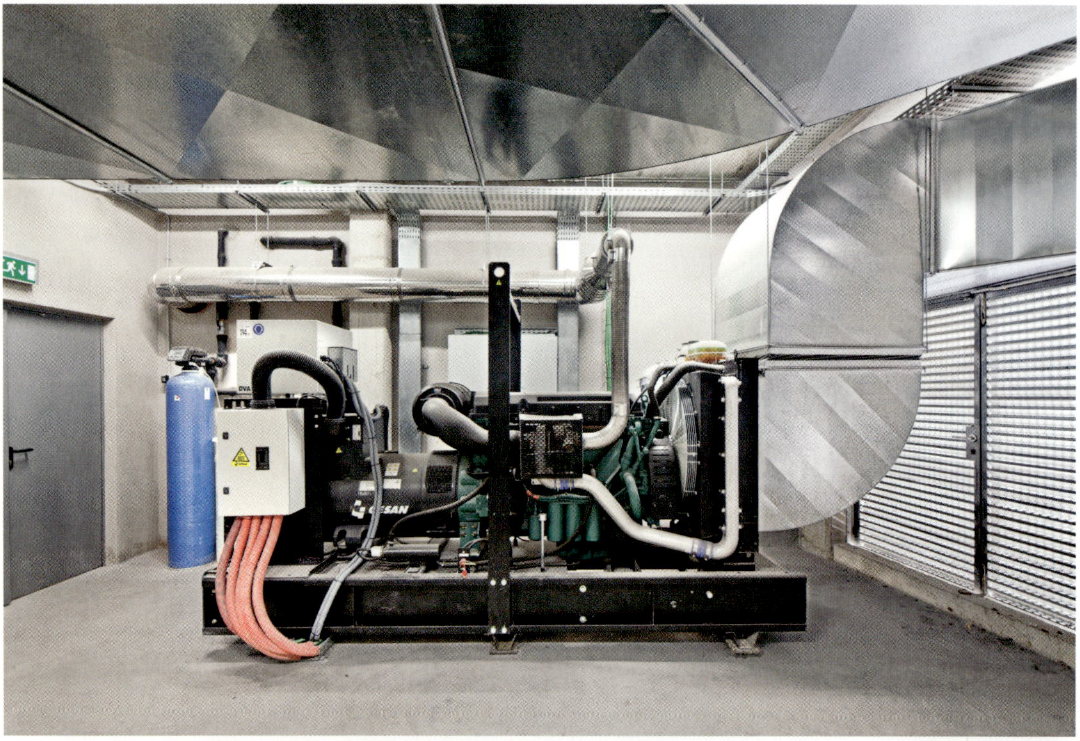

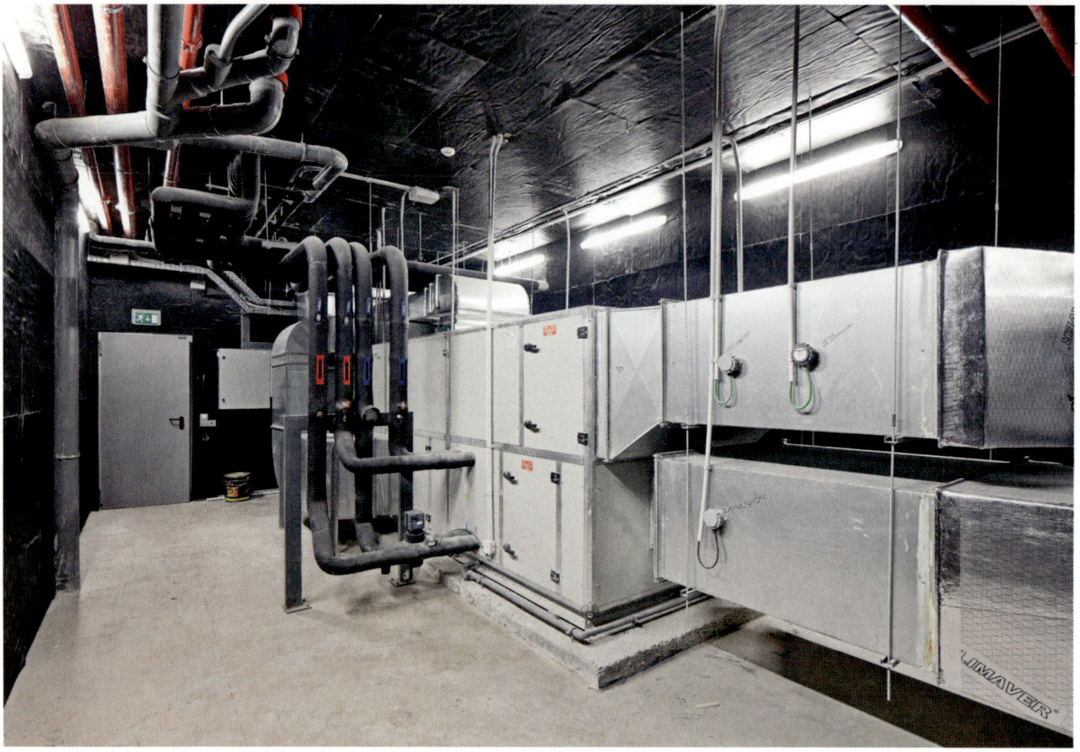

The project sought to leave the roof clear, as if it were another façade. Accordingly, all major technical installations are located in the second basement, enclosed in the concrete box, and occupying nearly 1000 m². Outside the box, running around it is the lower terrace. This terrace provides natural ventilation for the machinery, as indicated by code. The terrace also provides space for all maintenance and replacement work.

As for the computer and communication systems, all the main services—telephony racks, hubs and fibre optic links to the rest of the floors—are located in the basement. As a back up, all of these systems are connected to the UPS, which, in turn, is fed by the standby generator in the event of an emergency. Each floor has its own accessible and controlled server location rack, as well as a security rack which houses the company security systems and is accessible only to qualified iGuzzini staff. In addition to these systems, the foyer, auditorium and each floor are equipped with next-generation audiovisual media to keep users abreast of such things as new company products and technology.

Another outstanding feature, equally based on innovative technologies, is the access control system. The entire building is equipped with security systems in accordance with iGuzzini standard protocol for CCTV and access control centralised at the company's main headquarters in order to facilitate integrated management of the company's branch facilities. Accordingly, access is controlled by card readers at the entrances, and supplemented by other communication and security devices such as intercoms, magnetic contacts for opening, retainers, motorised doors, automatic barriers and special security checks. As we pointed out above, the building operates without any keys.

As for the fire detection and extinguishing systems, apart from the network of smoke and fire detectors, we should point out that the building is equipped with a 110 m³ rainwater collection tank and standard pumping units consisting of electric pumps, connected to the main power grid and to the standby generator, to feed the building-wide sprinkler system. The building is also up to code in terms of having on each floor a fire hydrant equipped with hose and fire extinguisher and the proper emergency signage throughout. Finally, we should note the rainwater and sewage pumping system. Because it is located at the basement level, lower than exterior rainwater collector, it was necessary to ensure correct drainage and avoid problems in the event of heavy rainfall. Thus, as a first means of protection in extreme weather conditions, a storage tank with a capacity of 20 m³ was installed and equipped with ABS submersible pumps with a capacity of 3 x 60 m³/h (2+1), also fed by the main and standby electrical supply. In addition, rainwater (from roofs and terraces) is collected in another storage tank and recycled to water the landscaped areas.

We would like to conclude this technical description by pointing out that the design of this building in each of its component parts was the product of an ongoing dialogue between architectural ambitions and the requirements of the technical systems, in which efficiency in thermal, light and noise management, and, ultimately, energy saving, defined the final form of the building, a form which, in a perfectly natural manner, the building thus assumed, openly manifesting itself as a result of this encounter, which from the outset prioritised accompanying the wise use of resources through proper design strategies with the latest technologies and the most innovative energy management systems.

Josep Juliol,
Engineer and founder of PGI Grup

The trough and courtyard play a very important role from the standpoint of climate.
In summer, cool air from the terrace is channelled through ducts to the courtyard, where a convective flow of cool air is created that helps lower the temperature inside the offices. The opposite happens in winter: stale air from offices is injected into the courtyard, providing 2-3º C temperature gains in offices without using extra energy.

The office floors are equipped with drop ceilings made of open-core slats, through which run all the climate, fire detection and lighting connections. The occupancy and lighting sensors (there are no light switches in the building) are also located in the ceilings. Each office floor functions as an open space in terms of climate, but climate control is designed such that each floor can be compartmentalised into twenty-one climatically-independent spaces. This approach ensures optimum levels of comfort with any configuration of the space.

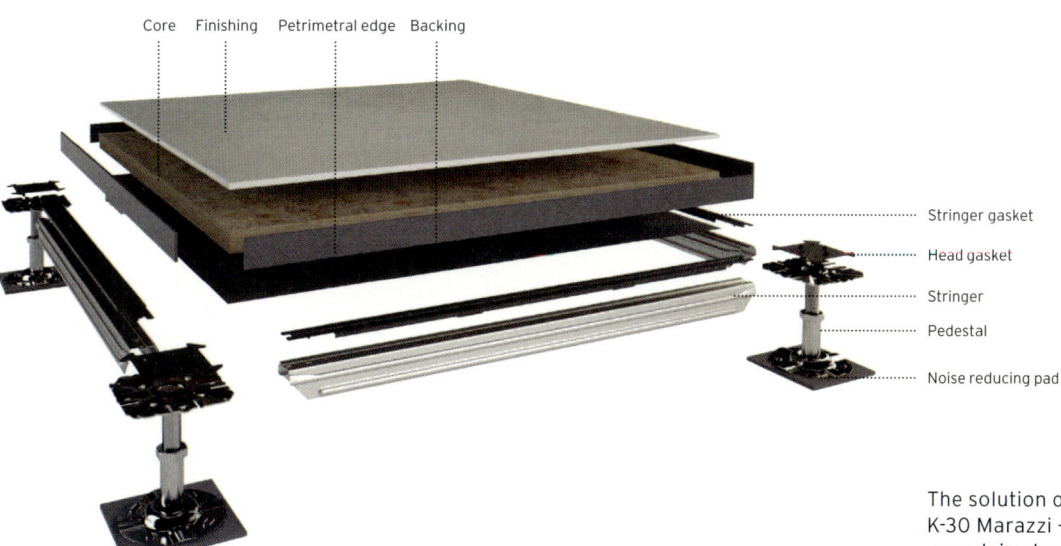

Core   Finishing   Petrimetral edge   Backing

Stringer gasket

Head gasket

Stringer

Pedestal

Noise reducing pad

The solution of K-30 Marazzi + porcelain stoneware withstands a concentrated load of up to 900 kg and reduces footfall noise by 28 dB.

BUILDING IN SUSTAINABILITY

The outdoor showroom pavement is in fact a hi-tech raised floor for exhibiting the company's entire outdoor product range.

MANAGING
THE PROJECT

Work in progress
Carles Bou

Painstaking planning of the project enabled prefabrication of the parts of the metal structure, subsequently assembled on site. The underground building, on the other hand, was built with precast concrete systems.

The design of a building means working documents endlessly shuttling back and forth from one desk to another, and the same goes for the execution phase. And throughout this process, the aim is to attain the greatest possible precision in order to arrive at the best possible outcome. Obviously the design work and its step-by-step progress towards an end begins with the first drawing, first hunches and first models, but it is through the collaboration among the different experts that the final terms of the building are defined, and not only in regard to its form. Decisions regarding structure, technology, construction and energy, scheduling and costs also depend on their input. Teamwork is thus essential both at the earliest stages and in the management of the actual execution.

The first designs must be incorporated immediately into software design systems. At the same time, work starts on the building of models and prototypes to facilitate ongoing spatial assessment of the results. Obviously, from the outset the project includes the assessments of different experts—architectural technicians, planners, and engineers—focused on their specific fields but with an understanding of the project and its goals. Such moments require the involvement of the client who understands and is able to take an active role in key decisions here and throughout the process, not only in terms of form but also scheduling and costs. In the case of iGuzzini, a company strong not only in design culture but also in technical capabilities, they were able to stay with us through the entire process and their contributions were crucial to the result.

The complexity and innovation inherent in the building required a sophisticated 3D drawing system that would facilitate the integration of each of the specialists involved, using software capable of easily calculating a range of elements—structure, solar radiation or thermal performance—for fast, efficient interaction among the different experts. The building's extremely innovative nature necessitated the use of a 3D structural calculation system. Accordingly, to ensure optimum thermal control in a building of unique geometry and high exposure to the sun, several computing programs were used to calculate its interior climate. We should emphasise the unique geometry arrived at in designing the two-dimensional structural-mesh support for the sunscreen which boasts virtually perfect outward transparency while reducing drastically inward heat transmission. A system developed specifically for the building keeps the fabric in constant tension under changing ambient temperature and wind conditions. Of course, the most sophisticated software available was used in the glazing study, which resulted in the choice of 4 types of glazing with different heat transmission coefficients in accordance with their exposure to sunlight.

Using PERT planning with automatic adjustment mechanisms built into the critical paths to manage time and costs throughout the process, execution of the project was scheduled to take 38 months. Clearly, the complexity and uniqueness of the works were going to require continuous adjustments to the initial plan. In the end, the objectives in terms of time and costs were met successfully. We should also emphasise that owing to the nature of the design, the works could be divided into two distinct units. While on-site work started with the execution of the foundation and the perimeter retaining walls, at the same time, at different factories, work was underway on the precast reinforced-concrete pillars and hollow-core slabs for the entire underground building, as well as the building's hanging structure, in particular the first part of the pentagonal central pillar. Finally, work on the casing of the underground building, the main foundation and its containment walls was carried out simultaneously with the in-factory manufacturing of the corresponding part of the precast reinforced concrete structure and the main structure of the central pillar. This sort of overlapping of jobs is essential in works with tight scheduling, since it has a clear positive impact on the builder's indirect costs, and thus on the final cost.

The completion of the underground building coincided with the execution of the slabs of the hanging building. Indeed, the fact that a large part of the building could pre-

Uruguayan barbecue at the worksite with the project team and clients. Arnau Miàs with a chocolate-made iGuzzini building.

287

Weekly meetings at the metalworking shops where the structure is being made are necessary to ensure the work goes according to design. In these workshops the project is redrawn, sometimes even on the materials themselves.

fabricated greatly shortened total execution time.

At the same time, in order to advance decision-making, a workshop was set up for building to-scale prototypes, not only of specific elements but also of the most complex spaces, in order to test and assess the building materials to be used in them. An entire office unit, complete with façade, expedited the final decisions regarding the characteristics of these spaces. The actual metal floor and ceiling structures were built, to which eventually would be fixed the glazed sheathing with steel joinery, the inter-office envelope, the false ceiling and raised floor. This exacting level of definition facilitated the choice of materials and elements as well as the on-site verification of their characteristics and behaviour and decision-making thereon. Thus problems could be anticipated and resolved with the utmost speed and efficiency, without having to interrupt the works, which would have had a huge negative impact on scheduling and costs.

Obviously, certain elements would have to be resolved during the works, but as planned in order to meet objectives they accounted for a small proportion of the total. Meanwhile, specialised labs were testing each construction element to certify compliance with the applicable regulations. The latter process led to the building certification guidelines being amended to include the technical specifications of some of the most innovative elements.

In sum, the building is an example of time and costs management in a project where the anticipation of problems, based on a detailed planning and feasibility studies and close monitoring of the entire works process by the developer, project team and the works management, proved crucial.

Carles Bou,
Civil Engineer,
Technical Advisor and Project Manager of iGuzzini BCN HQ

The design process starts on a drawing board or computer screen, and continues on the worktables of the shops, or on walls at the worksite as the building goes up. We are particularly interested in the continuity in the change in scale of these drawings.

PROJECT DEFINITION

| MONTH 1 | MONTH 2 | MONTH 3 | MONTH 4 | MONTH 5 | MONTH 6 | MONTH 7 | MONTH 8 | MONTH 9 | MONTH 10 | MONTH 11 | MONTH 12 | MONTH 13 | MONTH 14 | MONTH 15 | MONTH 16 |

COMPETITION

PROJECT

TENDER

FIRST
STONE

Scheduling
and budget-
ing enabled
close control of
the execution
process and the
ongoing costs
of the build-
ing through-
out. A control
system of this
sort enables
constant adapt-
ability to the
normal course
of the works in
order to meet
time and cost
targets.

BUILDING SERVICES

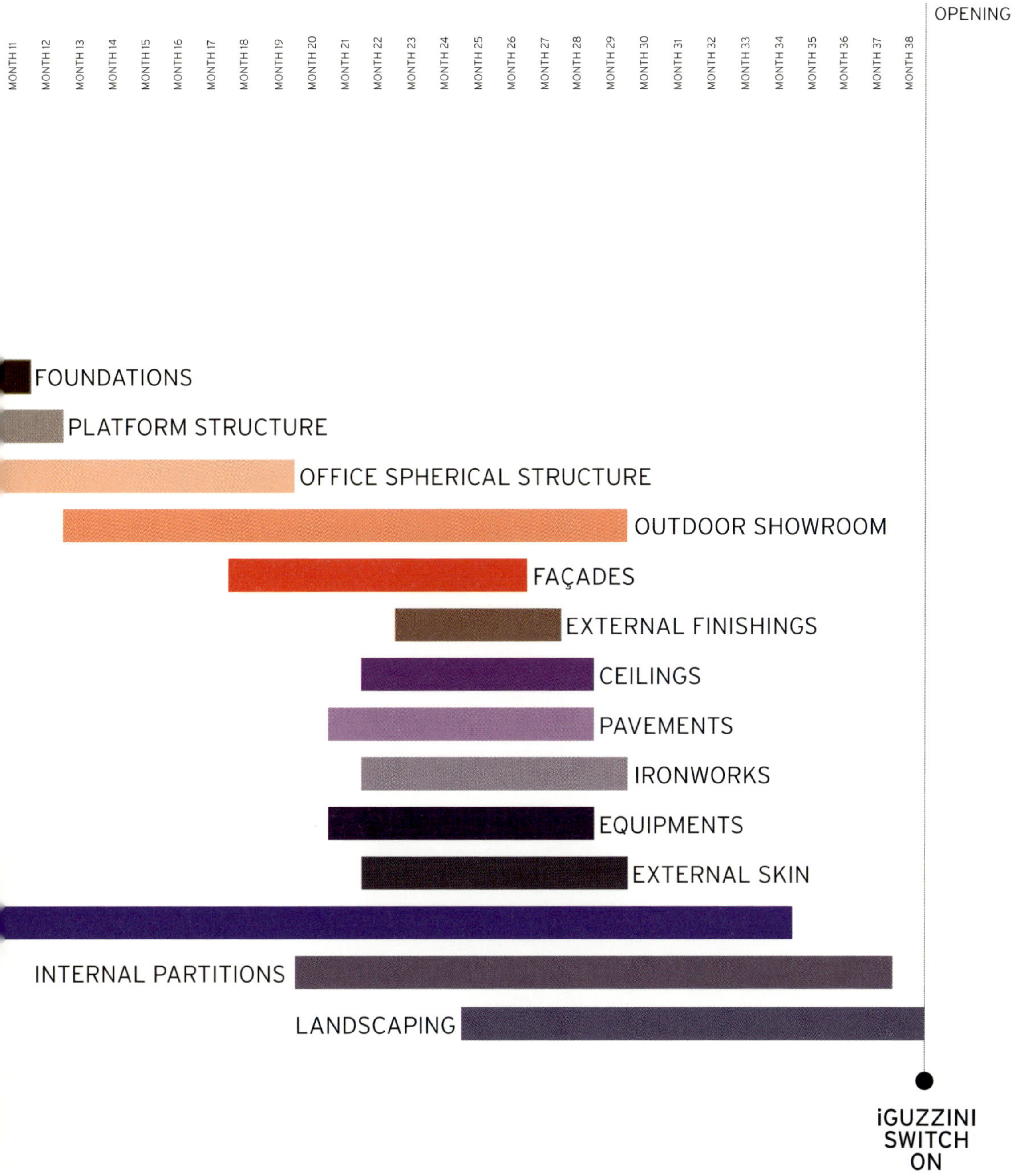

MONTH 11 MONTH 12 MONTH 13 MONTH 14 MONTH 15 MONTH 16 MONTH 17 MONTH 18 MONTH 19 MONTH 20 MONTH 21 MONTH 22 MONTH 23 MONTH 24 MONTH 25 MONTH 26 MONTH 27 MONTH 28 MONTH 29 MONTH 30 MONTH 31 MONTH 32 MONTH 33 MONTH 34 MONTH 35 MONTH 36 MONTH 37 MONTH 38

FOUNDATIONS

PLATFORM STRUCTURE

OFFICE SPHERICAL STRUCTURE

OUTDOOR SHOWROOM

FAÇADES

EXTERNAL FINISHINGS

CEILINGS

PAVEMENTS

IRONWORKS

EQUIPMENTS

EXTERNAL SKIN

INTERNAL PARTITIONS

LANDSCAPING

iGUZZINI
SWITCH
ON

291

MANAGING THE PROJECT

Cost control of the works is periodic and adaptable to circumstances in order to meet objectives without margin for error.
The works team continually monitors the ongoing work, not only to ensure optimum execution but also to anticipate any problems that might arise. Indeed, this amounts to a conversation with the building in which the whole team is involved.

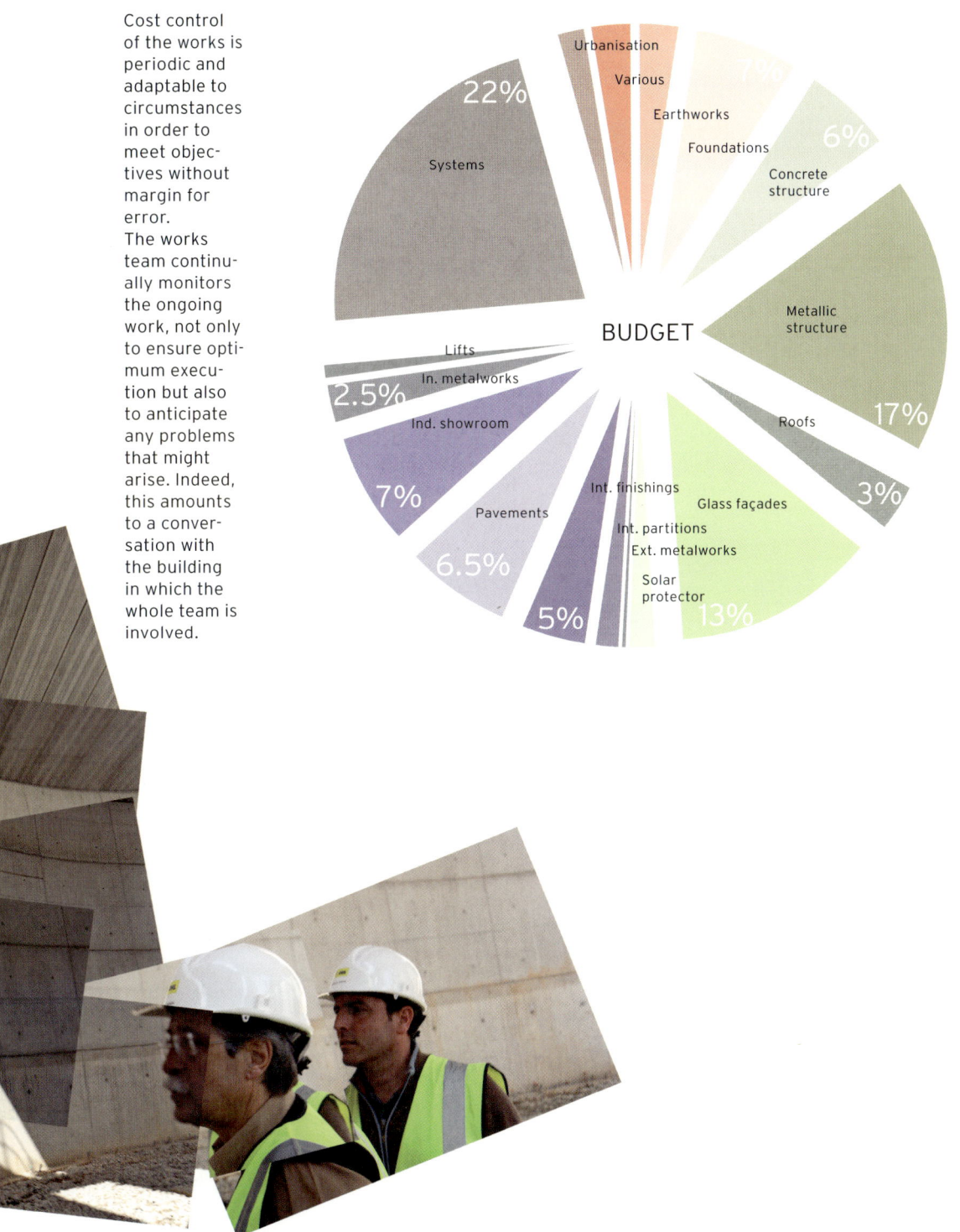

BUDGET

- Urbanisation
- Various
- Earthworks
- Foundations
- Concrete structure
- Metallic structure — 17%
- Roofs — 3%
- Glass façades
- Int. finishings
- Int. partitions
- Ext. metalworks
- Solar protector — 13%
- Pavements — 5%
- Ind. showroom — 6.5%
- In. metalworks — 7%
- Lifts — 2.5%
- Systems — 22%
- 7% (Foundations area)
- 6% (Concrete structure area)

Sequence of the central pillar and the lowering of the radial slab structure. There are moments in building that take us back to the origin of the project or that transport us to another, possible project. We like to think of these moments of great intensity during the process as the source of other possibilities yet to be discovered.

Some images of the construction process turned out to be surprising. Once the waterproof layer was laid on the platform, was tested with water.

1:1 scale mock-up of an entire office module. An office was built to scale in order to check all the materials used and assess their efficiency.

Since the be-
ginning of its
construction,
the building
has been
periodically
visited.

The construction process describes literally how the building was conceived. In mental terms, the central pillar contains the rest of the project. As if we were dealing with a Meccano set, the slabs are lowered, their perimeters braced by the three-dimensional outer girders. And the building is covered layer by layer.

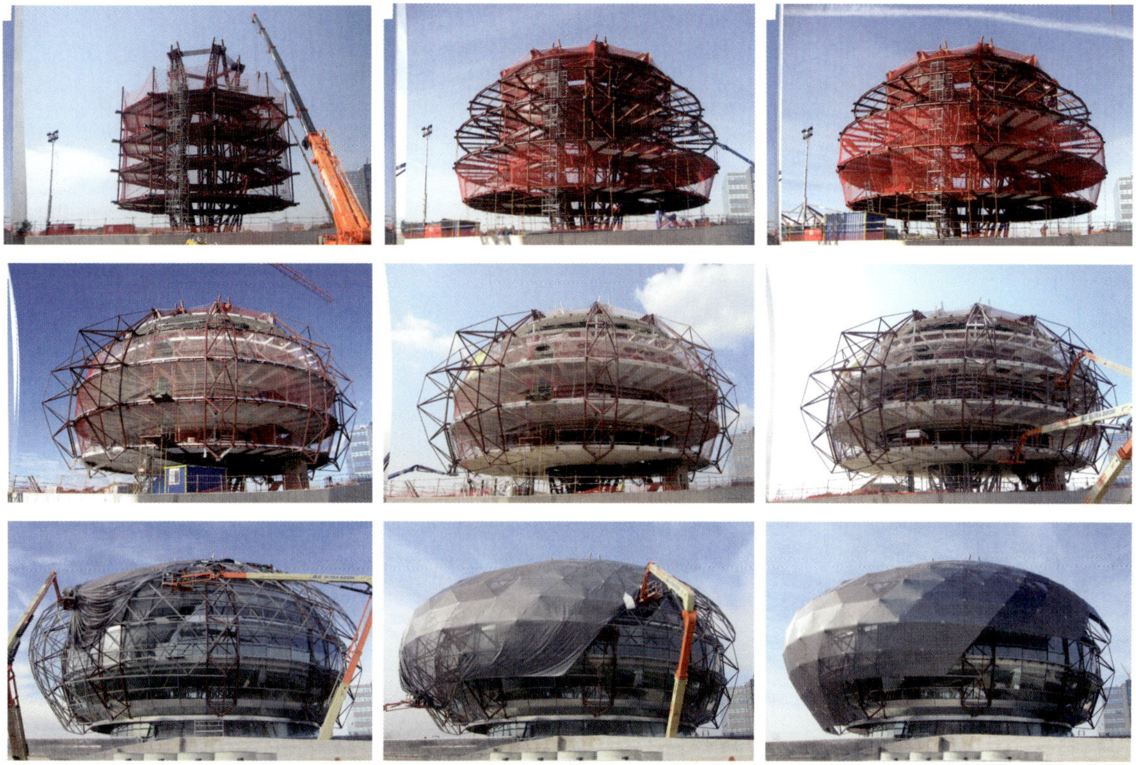

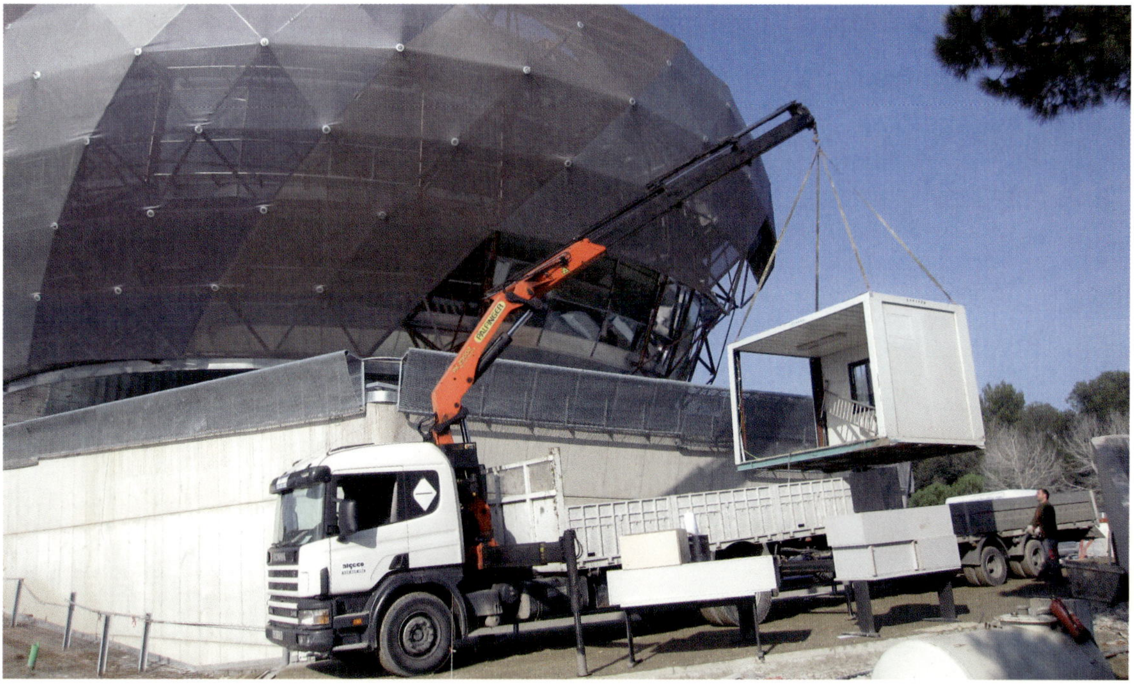

LIGHTING
LIGHTNESS

iGuzzini lighting iGuzzini

Josep Masbernat

iGuzzini approached the challenge of designing the lighting system for its new Spanish headquarters from the perspective of a manufacturer of lighting systems and reaffirming the message of its mission: to study, understand and make understandable light, furthering its integration in architecture and its function through industrial design.

In its conception, the overall lighting design is divided into three main categories. First, architecture, as means of lending at night the building and its grounds a certain "text" as a means of communication. Second, function, seeking the most suitable solutions for the different the work environments, logistics and warehousing spaces, offices, reception areas, and traffic zones. And finally, exhibition, with the goal of creating spaces for the display of lighting systems in different conditions and requirements specific to its spheres of application.

These architectural and functional requirements are met with high-performance solutions in keeping with the building's energy sustainability. On the one hand, this is achieved through the application of LED technology, and, on the other, through optical systems suited to each environment, always operating in conjunction with natural light. In this sense, lighting is wholly managed by the Master Pro control system, developed and marketed by iGuzzini, which uses presence and luminance sensors to adapt the luminance values and their periods to the actual needs of each space, according to both the presence of people and natural light conditions.

Let's begin with a description of the architectural approach, founded on the environmental concerns and the main formal characteristics of the building.

The company building stands on top of a large open esplanade, a sort of forecourt or outdoor showroom, which covers the warehousing and logistics spaces and which in turn is delimited by a large lower terrace.

A combination of horizontal and perimeter lighting was chosen for this esplanade. The former illuminates the

Top: First stone event. Miquel Chiva and Josep Masbernat offering a present to Sant Cugat Mayor, Lluís Recoder.
Bottom: Josep Miàs welcoming Sant Cugat Council, Lluís Recoder and Mercè Conesa.

horizontal planes of the skylights over the warehousing space and the pedestrian route from the outdoor car park at one end of the esplanade to the main entrance beneath the office building. The perimeter system frames the esplanade in order to provide subtly integrated ambience lighting, and is complemented by the lighting of the lower terrace, which seeks a differentiating, stage-like effect by flooding it with variable light using both RGB linear and LED systems.

The building, with its slightly imperfect spherical form, is read differently depending on the configuration of the lighting, which can be combined to produce the desired image. The building's structure is highlighted in different manners: the ribs by following the three-dimensional nodes with powerful spots; the crown by lighting up the ties connecting the ribs to the central pillar; the latter—which supports the entire building—by means of strong lighting upward from its base. Likewise, the sloped perimeter planes of the drop ceilings are lit up, thus stressing the horizontal aspect of the building and its division into several floors. In the latter case outer perimeter lines of RGB lighting have been added to enhance the changeability the exterior image of the building.

The exterior system is rounded out by lighting integrated into the expanded metal fencing along the access road, highlighting its modulation and the unique reflective effects of it material, the pergola over the car park and the corporate logos.

The functional approach underscores the offices as open spaces with natural lighting from the outer and courtyard façades. This area is equipped with a specifically designed recessed LED system with high visual comfort optics, providing pleasant and uniform lighting, and is intelligently managed by means of presence and luminance sensors in accordance with the geometry of each floor. There is not a single light switch or standard lamp in the entire building.

In the warehousing area, the architecture of the space and

From top to bottom: Josep Miàs talking about the project with Mercè Conesa, Josep Masbernat, Miquel Chiva. Press conference during the opening of the building. Miquel Chiva, Paolo Guzzini, Adolfo Guzzini and Josep Miàs. Opening ceremony. Opening speech. Federico Ciattaglia (Italian Consul in Barcelona), Paolo Guzzini, Adolfo Guzzini, Mercè Conesa, Miquel Espinet, Miquel Chiva and Josep Masbernat.

305

Historical lamps
manufactured
by iGuzzini
01. Medusa - L.
Massoni, 1966.
02. Disco - C.
Casati, 1968.
03. Piccola - G.
Ponti, 1968
04. Alicante - C.
E. Ponzio, 1967.
05. Cespuglio -
E. Lucini, 1969.
06. Nitia - R.
Bonetto, 1971

layout with rows of shelving is enhanced by a linear fluorescent system combined with accenting of the pillars.

In consideration of the layout of vehicle slots, the indoor
parking garage is lit with iSign fluorescent luminaires.

The lighting of the truck ramp and warehouse roundabout is achieved with LED spots combined with accent
lighting of the central pillars, lending them prominence
and a sculptural nature.

On the ground floor, we find different lighting systems in
the reception and dining areas. The former is equipped
with LED spot lighting; the latter with fluorescent luminaires for ambient lighting.

In both areas, the system also includes localised LED elements, and is designed to be fully adjustable and to facilitate the addition of more spotlighting in order to create
different types of environments, wherever and whenever
the need should arise.

Finally, the building includes three large showroom and
work areas for the display of the different lighting systems and their applications:

−The outdoor showroom, the double-curved esplanade
covering the logistics area, which designed to serve as
a theatre for all sorts of outdoor lighting configurations,
with hi-tech raised flooring with interchangeable pieces
of various finishes;

−The indoor showroom, located on level -1, in the part of the building enclosed in a concrete box with no natural light, which adapts the standard iGuzzini corporate image to a complex, curvilinear environment, and includes an events and conference hall;

−The light theatre, located on level -2, a large, triple-height hi-tech space for experimentation and testing of all types of lighting and effects.

Each of these areas offers the ideal environment in terms of darkness and light control, for displaying with the utmost rigour and precision the different ranges and qualities of iGuzzini lighting.

Josep Masbernat,
Technical Director of iGuzzini Illuminazione Ibérica S.A.

07. Lucciola - F. Lenci, 1972.
08. Poliedra - F. Ragazzo, 1970.
09. Laser - Ufficio progetti, 1985.
10. Cestello - G. Aulenti and P. Castiglioni, 1993.
11. Lingotto - R. Piano, 1990.
12. Greenwich - Foster & Partners, 2000.

The platform

A. The main path is lit with a raking light–iWay LED (16 x 1.2 W LED neutral white)–avoiding perforations in the prefabricated pavement.

B. The warehouse skylights–Linealuce LED are (21 W, 3100 ºK colour temperature)–are seen from above as light boxes.

C. In order to highlight the steel fencing, it is lined with LED strips (24 W, 3000 ºK colour temperature).

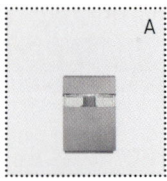

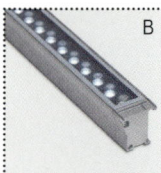

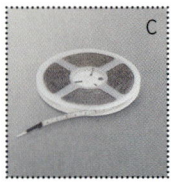

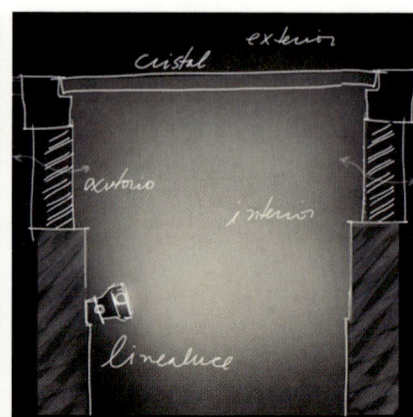

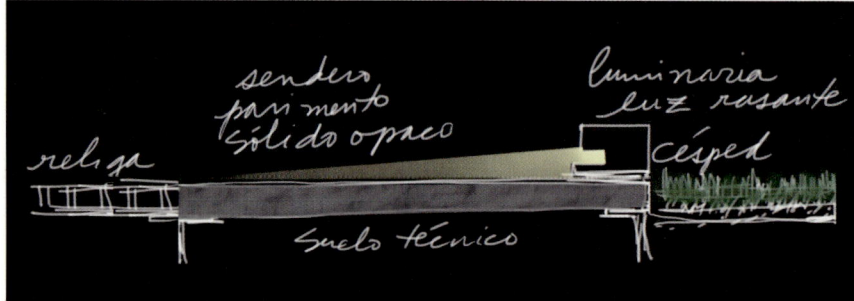

D. The outdoor car park lighting is integrated in the pergola structure. A pair of lights is placed on each side of the beam. iPro LEDs are fixed to the structure with a specially designed arm (9x1 W, 3100 ºK colour temperature).

E. Instead of painted markings, the parking spaces are indicated with LED Plus (1 W, 3100 ºK colour temperature).

D

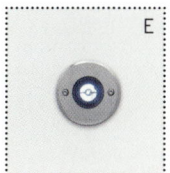

E

The trough

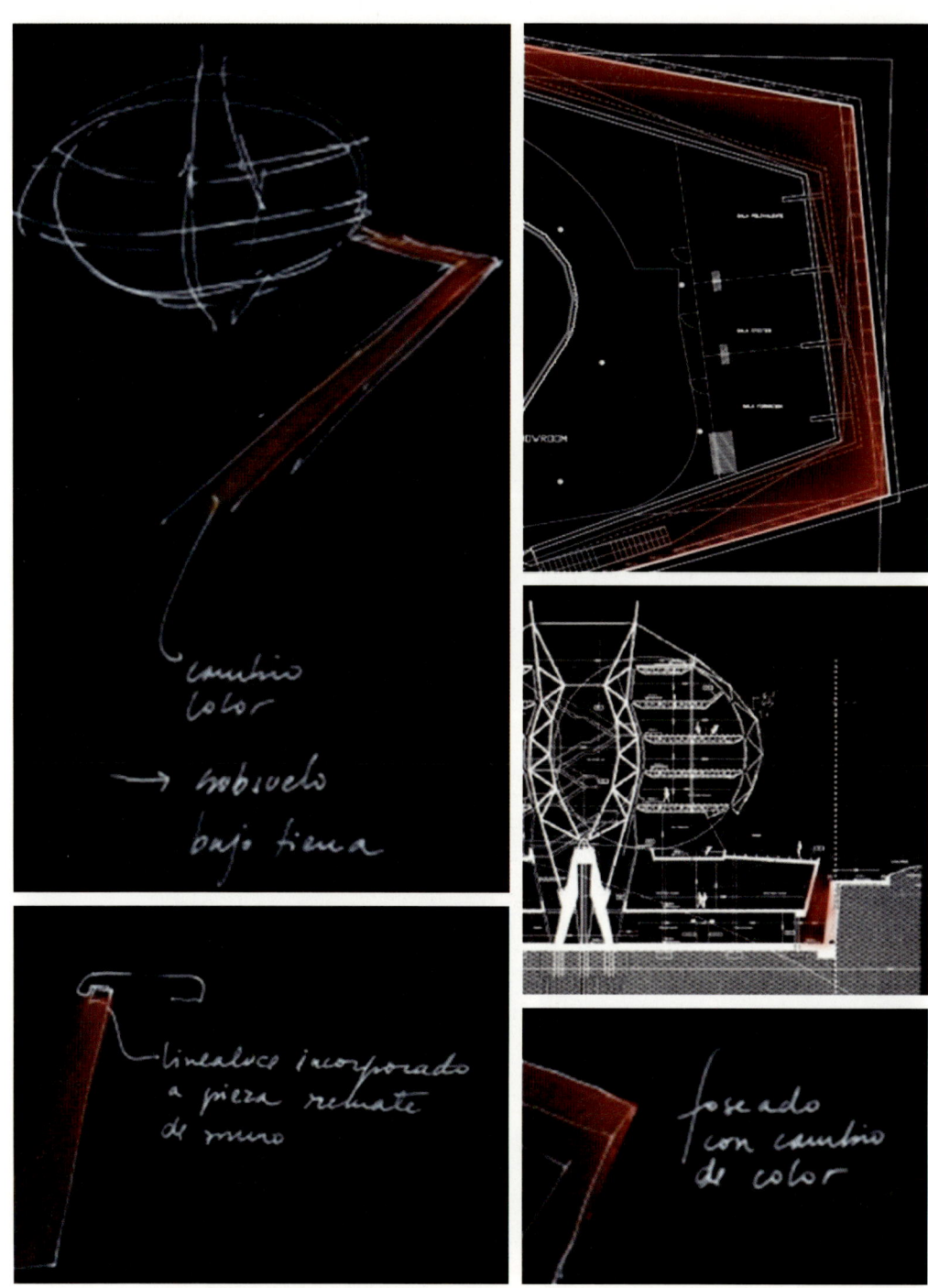

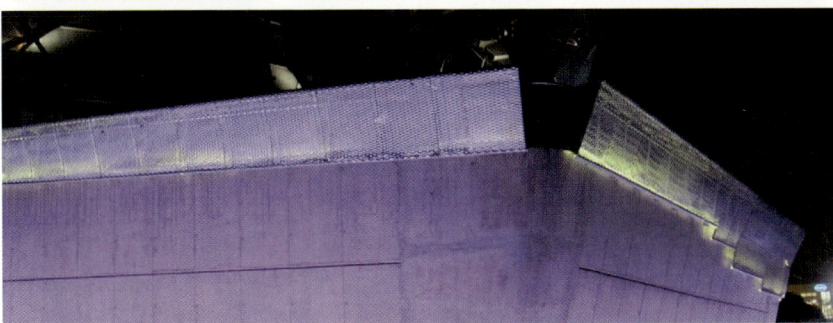

F. The platform trough changes from day to night with colour-changing lighting Linealuce LED RGB (adjustable 39 W DALI) with a custom remote light control system.

F

Sphere external structure

G. Slabs are lit round their edges, emphasising the spherical shape, with a white light, X26 High Flux (warm white).

H. The white light is combined with an RGB LED strip with computerised control.

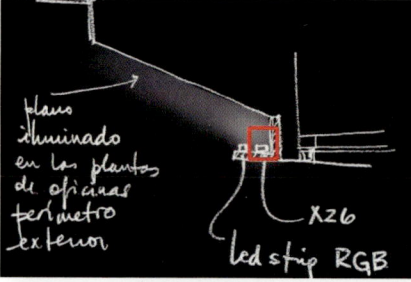

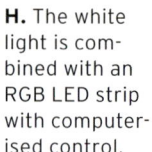

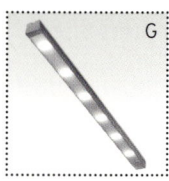

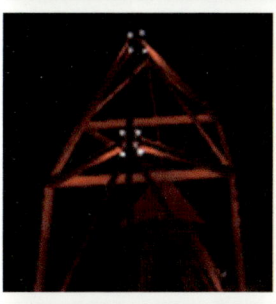

I. To highlight the space between the glazed shell and the fabric façade, spotlights are located on the structural nodes. The lights used are Miniwoody LEDs (warm white colour temperature).

I

Sphere internal structure

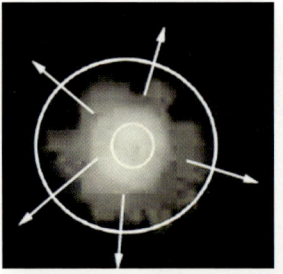

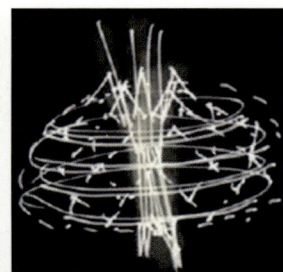

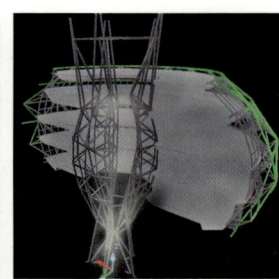

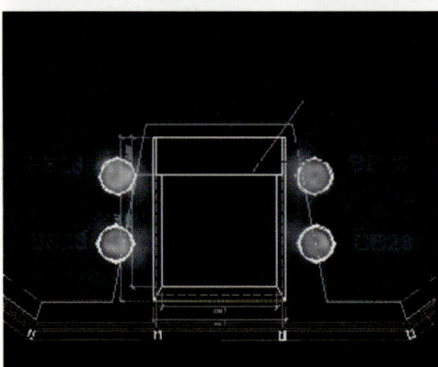

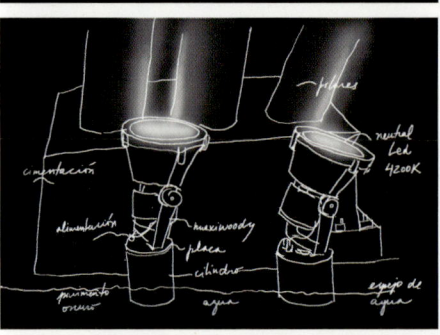

J. The entire spherical volume is borne on a vertical structure made of five masts. At night, lights accent the points of contact, the points of greatest tension in the structure. Maxiwoody LED are used for this (36 W, 4200 ºK neutral white colour temperature).

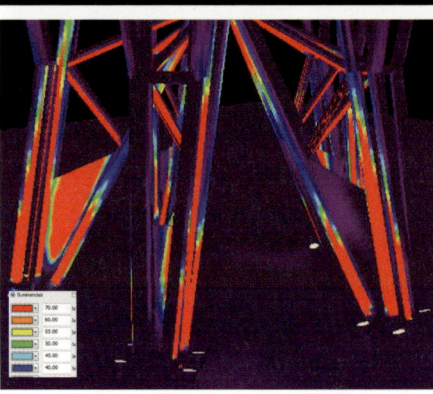

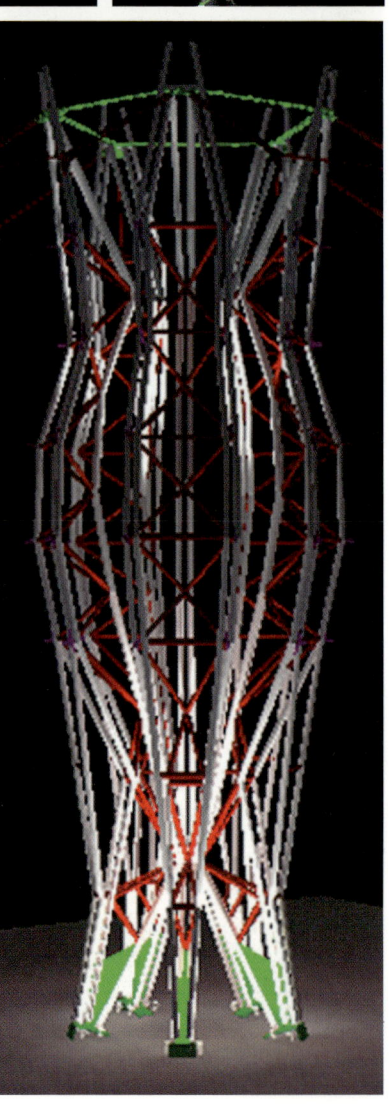

The sky underground

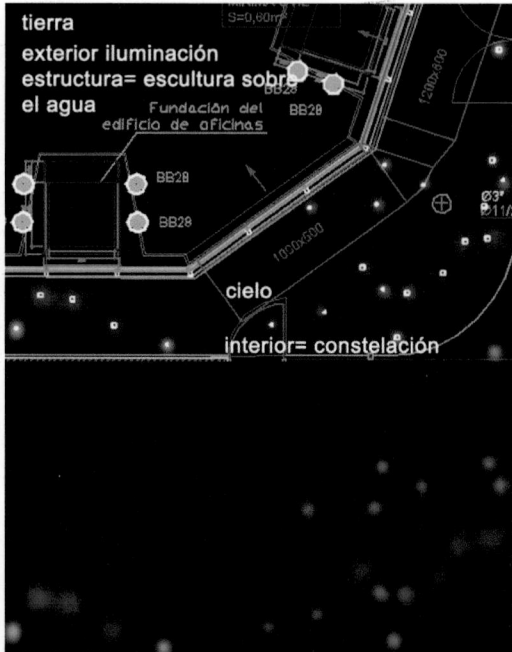

tierra
exterior iluminación
estructura= escultura sobre
el agua   Fundación del
           edificio de oficinas

cielo

interior= constelación

K. This circular, perimeter space around the courtyard is lit up like a night sky, symbol of the project. One of the lights used is Deep Laser LED Medium (6X1.5 W, 3200 °K colour temperature).

L. The other light used is Deep Laser LED Small (1X1.5 W 3100 °K warm white colour temperature).

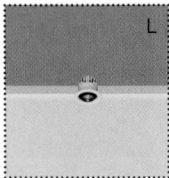

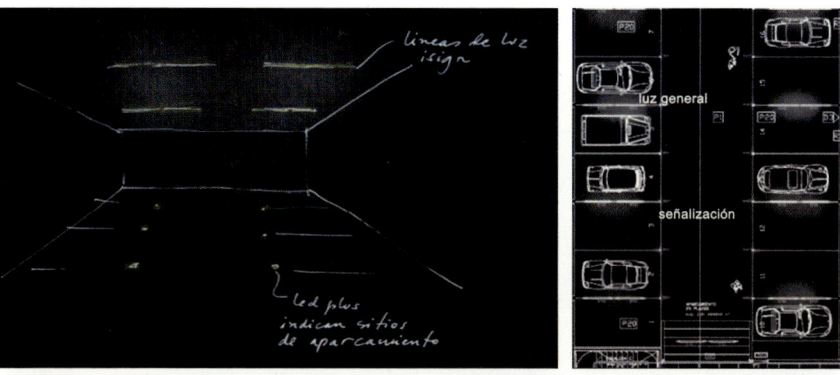

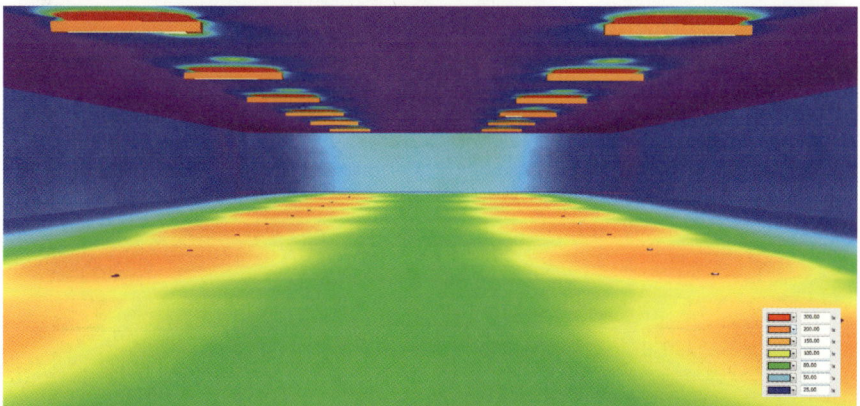

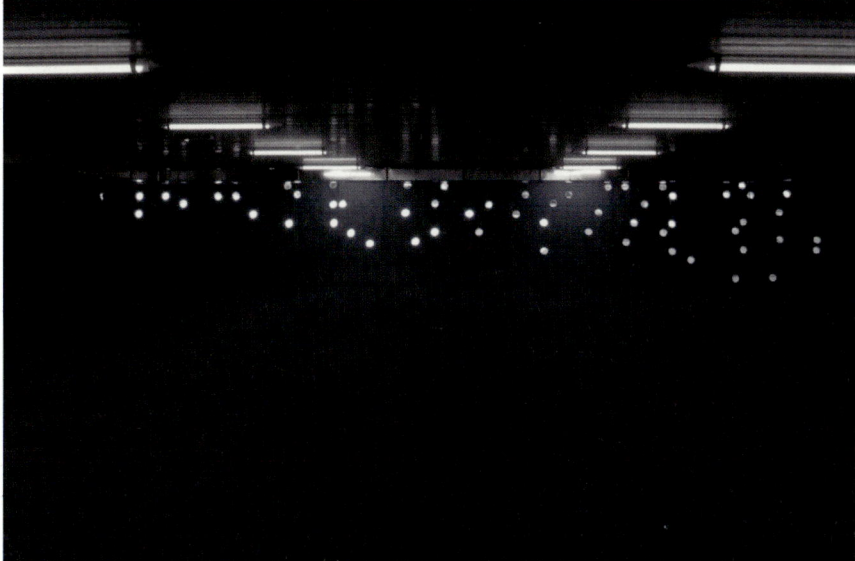

M. The underground parking garage is equipped with comprehensive lighting: iSign (54 W adjustable T16 DALI) combined with openings in the concrete wall.

N. Parking spaces are marked with Led Plus 0.4 W spotlights controlled by a light equalizer for a system capable of creating a range of light scenarios.

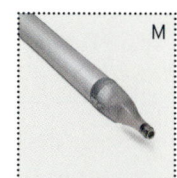

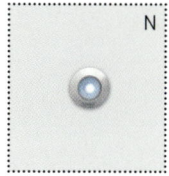

Warehouse
and logistic area

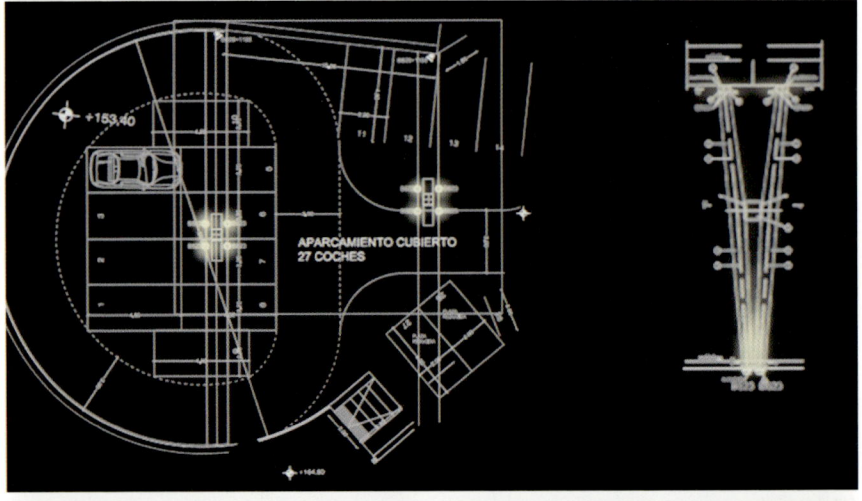

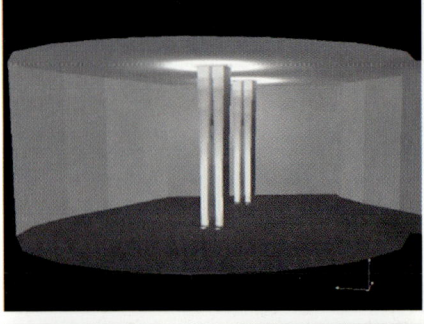

O. Due to the difference in material and their central position with respect to car and lorry flow, the pillars are lit like sculptures that seem to be separated from the ground and from the ceiling they bear, using Light up (spot optical, adjustable lamp, CDM T 70 W G12).

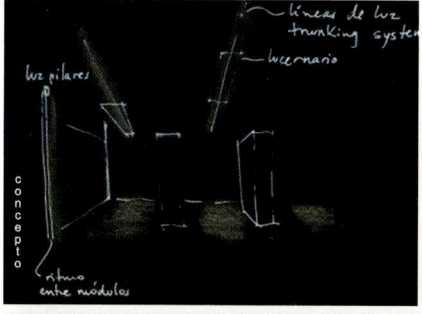

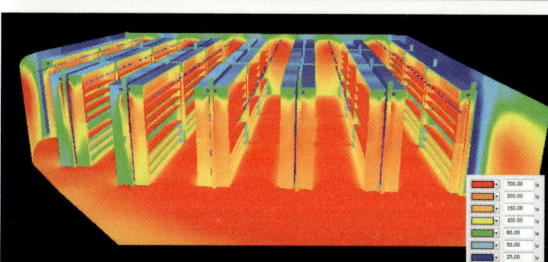

P. For the warehouse area, linear lights were chosen in order to emphasise the form of the space, using a trunking system with enough power to provide lighting from a height of seven metres (fluorescent lamp, T16 80 W).

D. The outstanding elements of the space, such as the pillars, are highlighted with spotlights, iPro LED (spot optical).

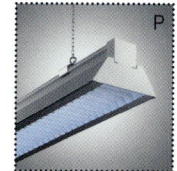

Hall & cafeteria

Q, L, R, S, T.
For the public areas, a grid of lights of different sizes is recessed in the ceiling and allows a great variety of scenarios and lighting levels: Pixel Plus LED, Deep Laser LED, iRound LED Exterior, and possible spotlights.

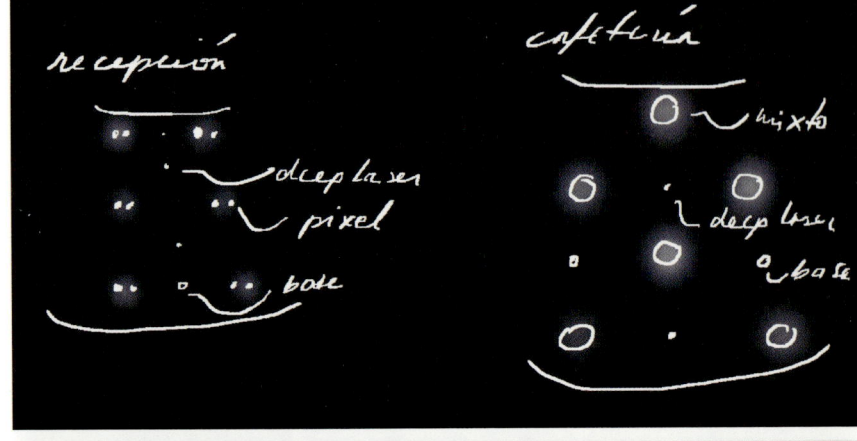

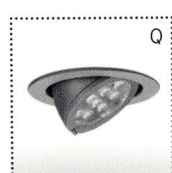

Q

L

R

S

T

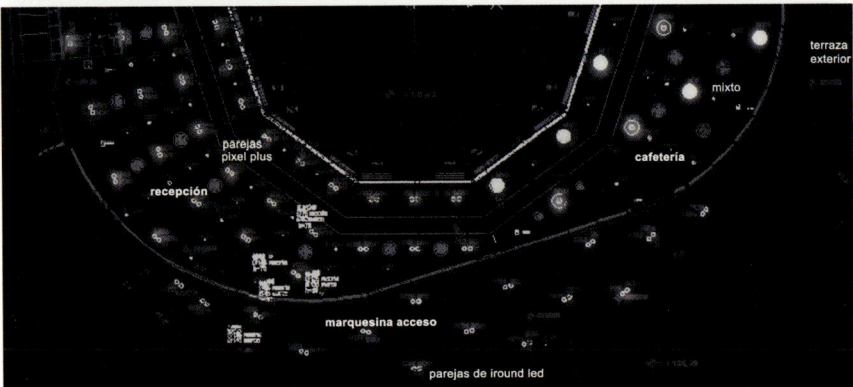

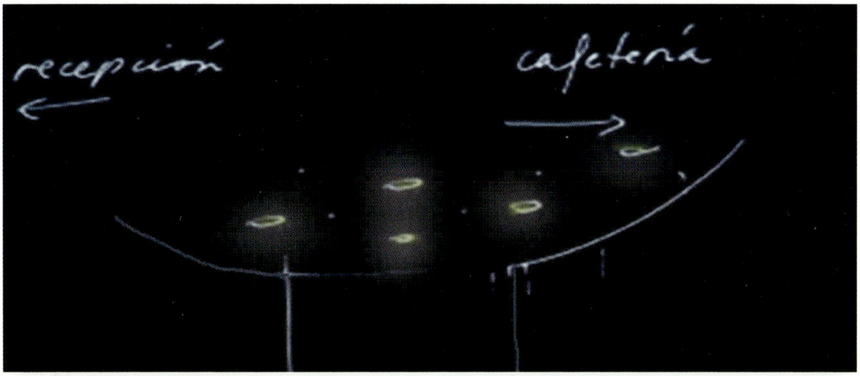

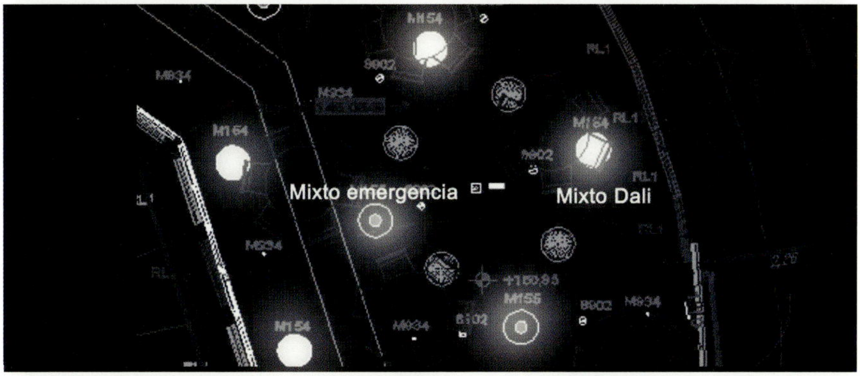

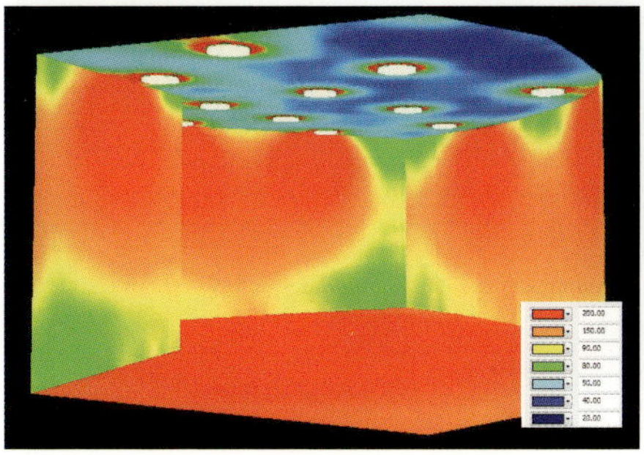

U, L, S, T. In the cafeteria, a similar grid is used, but with a more static main lighting system: Mixto light, Deep Laser LED, and possible spotlights.

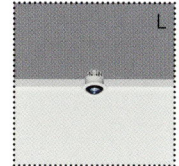

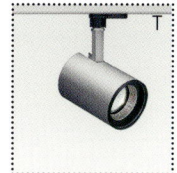

Offices

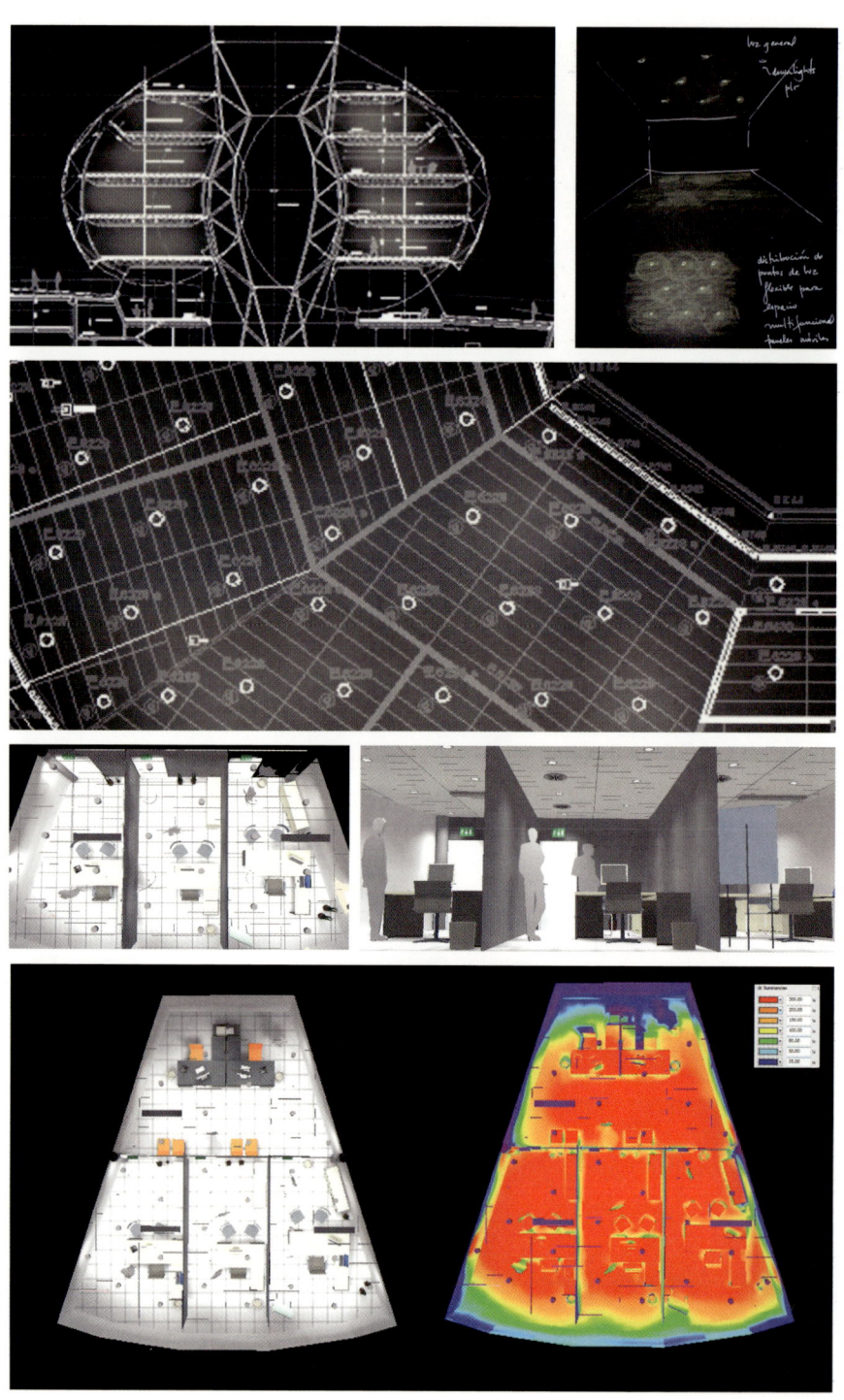

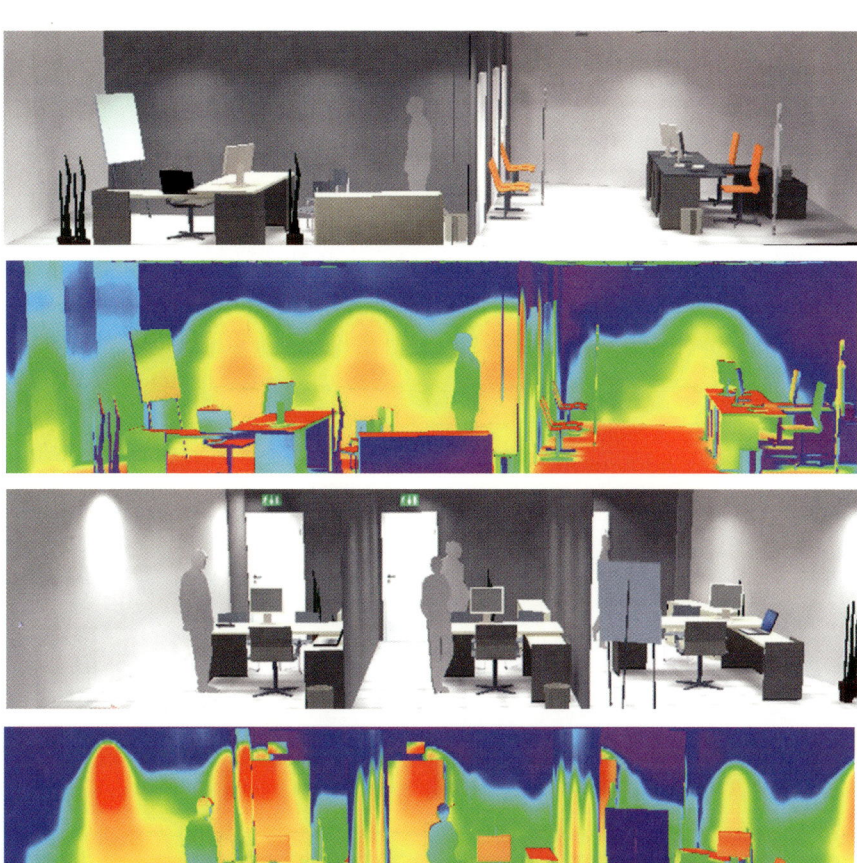

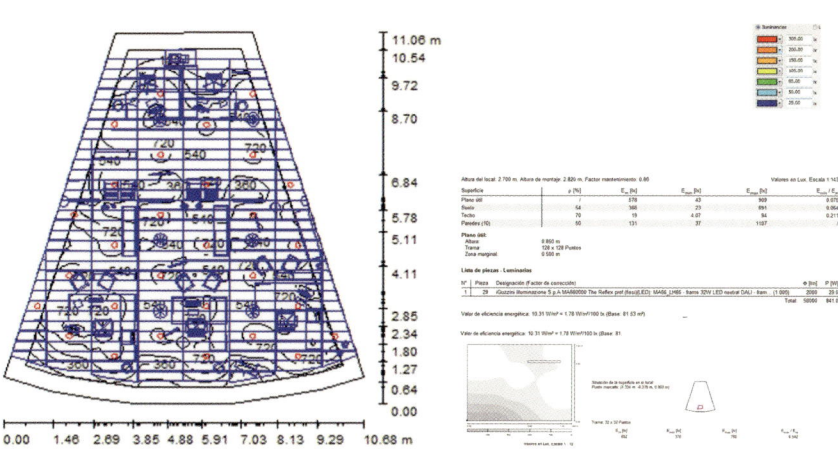

V. Due to the open plan of the offices, the lighting project is drawn as a grid of lamps, climate and sound systems. The light used in this case is the Reflex LED with high lighting performance (adjustable DALI lamp, 2000 Lm, 32 W, colour temperature 4200 ºK).

LIGHTING LIGHTNESS

The office building was conceived with the idea of ensuring natural light in all work spaces.

However, where artificial lighting is used, it becomes a demonstration of the capacity of artificial light to highlight architecture.

327

The artificial lighting enables new readings of the building, accenting one part or another, even changing its volumetry.

At this high-
way inter-
change, the
building
becomes part
of the play of
light from the
roads and of
the spectacle
of lights that
is produced.

Promoting
iGuzzini Illuminazione S.p.A
    Adolfo Guzzini, Chairman
    Paolo Guzzini, Antonio Santi, Franco Nibaldi, Sandro Rita, Danielle Cappelletti, Pier Giovanni Ceregioli
iGuzzini Illuminazione Ibérica S.A.
    Miquel Chiva, Managing Director
    Josep Masbernat, Technical Director
    Jesus Gómez, Paz Hugues, Gala Martinez, Silvia Carazo

Architect
Josep Miàs

Architecture project team:
    Silvia Brandi, Project Leader
    Carles Bou, Technical Advisor
    Architecture: Pablo Varesi, Adriana Porta,
    Fausto Raposo, Hélène Barbot, Andrés Dejanon,
    Mario Blanco, Horacio Arias, Anna Mañosa,
    Janine Woitoshek, Margherita Corbetta,
    Mannick Eigenheer, Isabelle Glenz, Diogo
    Henriques, Francisca Marzotto, Ines Reis,
    Diego Romero, María Tapias, Xavi Bas
    Models: Mario Blanco, Horacio Arias, Marika
    Leoni, Stefania Carboni, Margherita Corbetta,
    Mannick Eigenheer, Isabelle Glenz, Diogo
    Henriques, Silvia Lai, Pier Francesco Lisci,
    Roberta Luna, Francisca Marzotto, Ines Reis,
    Diego Romero, Emanuela Scano, María Tapias,
    François de Montgolfier, Dafna Servadio,
    Nina Dorici, Blanca Rieder, Patrick Hitzberger,
    Stefania Ballero, Antonello Ragnedda, Ugo
    D'Ascanio, Davide Balestrazzi, Pablo Martinez
    Díez, Federico Licini, Chiara Ricci, Pedro Nadal,
    Fabio Zampese
    3D: Lucas Cappelli, Janine Woitoshek,
    Sebastián Parra

Structure consulting team: BOMA, Brufau, Obiol,
Moya y Asociados
    Agustí Obiol, Advisor
    Josep Ramon Solé, Project Director
    Araceli Guaita & Raquel Martínez, Project Leaders
    José Manuel Balién, Analyst Engineer
    Mari Carmen Barquero, *Stagiaire*

Systems engineering team: PGI Engineering
    Josep Juliol, Founder and Director
    David Tuset, Engineer and Project Leader
    Jordi Llosa & Luis Lagomarsino, Project Engineers
    Guillem del Oso & Marc Camós, Engineers
      and Construction Managers

Constructive system advisors: UPC-Universitat
Politècnica de Catalunya,
Architectural Construction Department
    Josep Maria González, Jaume Avellaneda,
    Carles Diaz

General contractor
OHL, OBRASCÓN HUARTE LAIN, S.A.
    Joaquim Arnau, Construction Delegate
    Eva Burgués, Supervisor
    Josep Maria Argenté, Site Manager

Main partner companies
iGUZZINI ILLUMINAZIONE IBÉRICA S.A., lighting
    Josep Masbernat, Technical Director
    Paz Hugues, Lighting Designer
    Jacopo Messi, Technical Assistant
NG-TRUMSES, Metallic structure
    José Luís Jimenez, Director
MARAZZI ENGINEERING – MARAZZI, raised floor - floor
JANSEN A.G., curtain wall
SERGE FERRARI S.A.S., textile solar protection
IASO S.A., tensile membrane

EDITION

Josep Miàs
MiAS Architects
MiASMAIN Mateu 19 bxs
MiASROOM Sant Cristòfol 12 bxs
E-08012 Barcelona
T +34 932 388 208
F +34 932 388 209
www.miasarchitects.com

Managing
Silvia Brandi

Coordination
Xavi Bas

Texts
Adolfo Guzzini, Josep Masbernat,
Josep Miàs, Silvia Brandi, Agustí
Obiol, Vicente Guallart, Josep
Ramon Solé, Jorge García
de la Cámara, Marco Atzori,
Sebastiano d'Urso, Jaume
Avellaneda, Josep Juliol, Josep
Maria González, Carles Bou

Translations
Ted Krasny

Graphic design
& digital production
ActarBirkhäuserPro

Printing
Ingoprint

Every effort has been made to
contact copyright holders of
images published herein. The
publisher would appreciate
being informed of any omissions
in order to make due acknowl-
edgement in future editions of
this book.

Special thanks
To Adolfo Guzzini, Miquel Chiva
and Josep Masbernat, from
iGuzzini Illuminazione, and to
those who have made this building and book possible.

© of the edition, Actar &
MiAS Architects
© of the works, their authors
© of the photographs,
   their authors
© of the texts, their authors

ISBN: 978-84-15391-12-8
D.L.: B-13655-2012

Printed and bound
in the European Union

Distribution

ActarBirkhäuserD
Barcelona - Basel - New York
www.actarbirkhauser-d.com

Roca i Batlle 2
E-08023 Barcelona
T +34 934 174 993
F +34 934 186 707
salesbarcelona@actarbirkhauser.com

Viaduktstrasse 42
CH-4051 Basel
T +41 61 5689 800
F +41 61 5689 899
salesbasel@actarbirkhauser.com

151 Grand Street, 5th floor
New York, NY 10013, USA
T +1 212 966 2207
F +1 212 966 2214
salesnewyork@actarbirkhauser.com

PROMOTING

MAIN SPONSORS

SPONSORS

COLLABORATING INSTITUTIONS